Instructions Not Included

Instructions Not Included

PAULA HAMILTON

MICHAEL JOSEPH
LONDON

MICHAEL JOSEPH LTD
Published by the Penguin Group
27 Wrights Lane, London w8 5tz
Viking Penguin Inc., 375 Hudson Street, New York, New York 10014, USA
Penguin Books Australia Ltd, Ringwood, Victoria, Australia
Penguin Books Canada Ltd, 10 Alcorn Avenue, Toronto, Ontario, Canada m4v 3b2
Penguin Books (NZ) Ltd, 182–190 Wairau Road, Auckland 10, New Zealand

Penguin Books Ltd, Registered Offices: Harmondsworth, Middlesex, England

First published in Great Britain 1996
1 3 5 7 9 10 8 6 4 2

Copyright © Paula Hamilton, 1996

Set in 12/14pt Monotype Sabon
Typeset by Datix International Limited, Bungay, Suffolk
Printed in England by Clays Ltd, St Ives plc

ISBN 0 7181 4077 X

The names of some of the persons in the book have been
changed to protect their privacy

I dedicate this book
to my mother

Look to this day, for this is life
This is the very life of life
In its brief course lie all the verities of existence
There's the bliss of growth
The splendour of action
And the glory of power

For yesterday is but a dream
Tomorrow is only a vision
But today, well lived, makes every yesterday
A dream of happiness and every tomorrow
A vision of hope

Therefore look after your day.

Sanskrit prayer, Anon.

Contents

Acknowledgements

This book would never have been completed had it not been for the support of the following people:

Jacqui Wallace, who invented the pinboard format I worked from, who typed up the bulk of this book and consistently gave me encouragement and support.

Bryony Evens at Christopher Little, who tirelessly helped me through my editing process; who cajoled and bullied, and when that didn't work, made me coffee, sat me down again and held my hand to the end.

Christopher Little, my agent, who believed in the book when it was just a twinkle in my eye, and who, after 16 months of my dithering, shouted at me, 'Just write the damn thing, will you!'

I also wish to extend my thanks on behalf of Titch, my dog, to Patrick Walsh, who may have stumbled in and out of her drinking bowl in the agency office, but who generously took her out for walks and widdles.

Ian Wilson, my manager, who had to cancel or move just about every engagement in my diary, to give me the time and the space I needed to write this book.

Susan Watt, my editor, who had insight and belief in *Instructions Not Included*, understood what I was aiming to achieve and brought what could have remained just a dream to fruition.

My mother, for her courage to allow me to write of our history.

My brothers and sisters, for standing by me and trusting me.

My friends, and they know who they are, for their patience and understanding.

From my heart – thanks.

Prologue

Bang, bang, bang. The house, even though it was a solid old Edwardian building, felt as if it was being shaken to its foundations. I was terrified. I heard them calling.

'Miss Hamilton, *Daily Mail*, we need to talk to you.'

I went up the stairs and peeked out of the window, feeling like an intruder in my own home. The lawn was swarming with press, some in suits, some in Colombo-type grubby beige rain-coats. Some faces I recognized; I could see a woman with a notepad stepping back as my neighbour slammed the door in her face. It intrigued me that she went straight back for more.

'Miss Hamilton!' The shouts echoed through the house. 'Miss Hamilton, we know what happened, we need a statement for the press.'

I sank to the floor, sobbing. Kenneth had said it would be dis-astrous if our friendship ever came out. But the pressure had been too great; I'd let everyone down, myself, the charity, my friends, my family. I felt lower than the spider that was crawling across my foot. I looked at my hands — I always looked at my hands when great upset occurred, as if to say, 'Get me out of this, make this nightmare stop.'

The phone pierced the brief silence. I crawled on my hands and knees out of the room, cursing the fact that the boxroom had remained curtainless for two years. It was Kenneth.

'Stay where you are. Have you spoken to anyone? Your family? Katie?'

'No.'

'Don't talk to *anyone*. Jeremy knows of a treatment centre in

Florida. We can get you out. Security will take you over the back fence into a car, and will drop you off at Heathrow. Brenda will fly with you, to protect you. Do not tell anyone where you are going – no one. Do you understand?'

'I understand.' It came out in a strangled squeak.

Was this really happening? Just three weeks before I had been in Aruba enjoying the wonderful lifestyle. Now here I was in London, stinking of booze and fear.

Katie, in the meantime, had pushed her way through the press and into the house. Her face was white, dark circles under her eyes. She had been in the cab – she was bringing me home from a business meeting in a restaurant where I had got drunk – and had witnessed everything. I had an alcoholic blackout and needed to be filled in with the details of what had taken place.

'You climbed into the front seat with a bottle of champagne, then you dropped it on the floor and went crazy.'

'I did what?'

'You cracked the windscreen with your left hand. I think it was the signet ring that did it. You kicked the dashboard, then tried to rip out the radio.'

'Why, Katie, why?'

'I don't know, Polly, you just lost it. One minute you were okay, the next you'd gone mad. The taxi driver drove you to Brixton police station. You were pleased and said, "Good". Then the police arrested you. That's when you started to shout about Kenneth, and that's why all the press are outside now.' She began to cry.

'It's okay, Katie, we'll figure something out. I've rung Kenneth.'

Horror filled her eyes. She knew what this would do to Kenneth and me, and to the charity. She knew that somehow we had to get through it, but at that moment neither of us could possibly imagine how.

I packed a bag, then dressed in a white shirt, cowboy boots and a long coat. I'd had a bath that morning but nothing, no amount of scrubbing, could take away the filth I felt was in me –

all over me. I couldn't look in the mirror – the shame was horrendous. I toyed with the idea of ending my life. I sat on the edge of my bath with a razor blade in my hand, wondering what was going to happen if I got blood on the mat. Would Madeline, my housekeeper, be able to remove the stains? My body jolted back to reality. The press were now screaming for my attention through the letterbox as I walked down the stairs.

Security called. 'In five minutes be in the back garden. Be prepared to climb a seven-foot gate, a brick wall and a five-foot spiked railing at the end of the alley, leading away from the house.'

I hugged Katie, crying and telling her it would be okay. The dogs were in the sitting-room, and the cats sat in the kitchen, looking at me as if to say, 'sister, you've really sunk yourself this time.' I took a last look around my home – my beloved home. I had nearly lost it to my ex-husband, nearly lost it so many times: struggling to start the charity, paying salaries by modelling and working for the BBC. So many conflicting jobs always crashing into each other. God, had life always been so difficult? Had it always been like this?

I put on a hat and picked up a small leather backpack. I ran out of the door, tore through the back garden and over the gate. No problem. There they were, feet away from the press who were preoccupied with each other on the front lawn. Over the gate, over the wall. One of the security officer's mouths gaped as I tossed him my backpack. I guess they thought I'd be too shaken up to function. It was show time, folks, I had to be brave in front of these men, and keep my mouth shut.

There were two cars, one of which was a decoy. I could actually see the press and I almost wanted to laugh. How long would they wait: hours, days? I closed my eyes and prayed: 'God, just get me through this and I promise I'll never drink again.'

CHAPTER ONE

Up and Running

I always knew I would be famous.

I first told my mother this at the age of three, when we were living in South Africa. My family went out there when I was very young. My sisters and I travelled out with my mother and stepfather Johnny. My half-brothers were born there. I was happy there, with plenty of freedom to run around barefoot, discovering all the animals around our big white house. My school was an unusual one, teaching alternative education. We were encouraged to develop as people before starting to learn conventional subjects such as maths and English. If I had been allowed to stay there and get to know myself at an early age, my life could have been different.

Instead, we were moved back to England and put into a series of private schools. Our family was always different, partly because of our South African ways and accents, and partly because we behaved differently to other children. Our home was not a happy one; my mother always seemed to be running away from her problems, and Johnny had brought his own problems with him. I was also dyslexic, which caused problems with my schoolwork, and so, in a series of desperate attempts to fit in with the other children, I found myself hanging out with the rebellious crowd in every school I attended. I got a bad reputation, making me more miserable, and even an exchange programme to the States couldn't help me. By then I believed what everyone said about me, in the playground and on my report cards, and I was convinced I was no good to anyone, let alone myself.

When I left school at fifteen, I had no idea of what I was going to do with my life. With no qualifications, I settled for a string of local jobs, none of which lasted very long because of my attitude. The only one which sticks out in my mind is the first, working at a cement factory. I was actually working alongside the men there, heaving sacks of cement around and doing hard physical work. At first no one thought I was able to do it, but after five weeks I had proved myself and earned the respect of my male colleagues. I had also proved to myself that I could do anything I put my mind to, if I wanted it badly enough. Amazingly, the cement factory seems to be the single most impressive job on my résumé; it still wins me work, even today.

After working for about six months, I had exhausted the local area and started to scan the newspapers. Always in the back of my mind was the thought that I would somehow make my mark, and I was always on the lookout for anything that could help me realize my ambition to be famous. One day, scanning the national papers, I spotted an advertisement:

DO YOU DREAM OF BEING A MODEL?
ARE YOU OVER 5 FT 8 INS? HAVE A GOOD FIGURE AND
GOOD LOOKS?
THEN CALL US FOR AN APPOINTMENT

Being a model was certainly one way of becoming famous. Although I had no personal confidence in my looks, I had by then been told that I was pretty enough to try modelling.

'Mum,' I yelled. 'I need some money. I have to go to London for an interview.'
  'What for?'
  'A modelling job.'
  She definitely wasn't into this. She told me if I wanted it, I had to do it myself – so I did. I called and made an appointment, stole into my sister's room, and raided her wardrobe. Death by bongo-bongo if she found out. I caught the bus to the M4, got out and started to hitch a ride to London.

It was seven-thirty in the morning, the traffic was thick. I soon got a lift from a man who spent the next forty minutes telling me how dangerous it was for young girls to hitch, while patting my knee the whole time.

'Yep,' I agreed. 'Yep, and do you know how dangerous an angry, fucked-up sixteen-year-old can be? Keep your hands on the wheel!'

He looked at me. Something in my eyes showed him I wasn't spoofing. Yes, anger has power in it – a tool I knew well by now, and my protector. Although I didn't have a very high opinion of myself, I didn't want strangers to see that, so I put on a determined face in public. Of course, this caused problems, especially at work, but it also got me what I wanted.

Arriving in London was a blur. I made my way by Tube, and the noise and the smells thrilled me. I had no doubt the agency would take me on, not because I was beautiful, but because I wanted it so much. I arrived at the address. A gold plate with the agency logo shone brightly, dazzling my eyes. I missed the step, tripped and went down, hitting both knees painfully on the pavement; to make matters worse, the heel came off one of my boots.

Well, I'm here, I thought. I'm going in anyway.

All my original composure gone, I hobbled up the steps. I must have looked a sight as I walked in. A beautiful blonde woman asked my name. She told me to sit and wait. I looked around; the walls were lined from top to bottom with stunning faces from the covers of *Vogue* and other magazines. What was I doing there? What the hell did I think I was playing at? After what seemed hours, a woman called me into her office.

'Yes?'

'I want to be a model.'

'Any experience?'

'No.'

'Any professional photographs?'

'No.'

'Sorry,' she apologized. 'You need a portfolio. How tall are you?'

'Five foot nine.'

'Do you have good hands? Let me see. Large, aren't they?'

'Are they?' I replied, looking at my hands as if seeing them for the first time.

'You bite your nails.'

'I can stop.' I was now desperate.

She explained what would be expected from any girl who was accepted as a model. Being able to model meant that you had to realize that you had a look that would sell, not that you were beautiful. Many a beautiful girl's look was lost to a camera's lens. I hung on to that bit of information. I could have a look even with big hands. I eventually learned how to hide them well in my photos.

'You need to convince a photographer to do portfolio photos for nothing because he likes your looks. Or you pay him.'

'How much?'

'Oh, that depends. Between three and five hundred pounds.'

Three and five hundred pounds! I was dumbstruck. That was a fortune. I'd never seen that amount of money in my life, let alone spent it.

'Well, that's how it works, the rest is up to you. If you ask Janice at reception, she'll give you a list of photographers who will test you. As I said, the rest is up to you.'

She dismissed me by picking up the phone and waving me out of the room. My face must have looked crestfallen, because the receptionist said, 'Cheer up, could be worse.'

I looked at her and she smiled. 'Why don't you get a job? Any job. Save up. You've got to fight for it. Those girls did.' She pointed to the sea of faces mocking me from their covers.

I'd made up my mind. I was going to be a model.

I hobbled out of there with a list of photographers, some contact names for the future and a bucketload of determination. On the way home I bought a newspaper, and looked at the classified section. Something caught my eye. 'ESCORTS NEEDED to show businessmen and families around London.'

Now, that was something I could do. I knew where Madame Tussaud's was, Harrods, the Tower of London, etcetera. Feeling a little better, I let the train carry me home. I sneaked back into the house, up the stairs, and returned my sister's clothes. Just as I was closing her door, she came up the stairs.

'What are you doing in my room?'

'Oh, there you are,' I replied innocently, 'I thought I'd pop in and say hi.'

'Hello.' She looked at me suspiciously. Close call!

The next morning I thought about nothing else but calling the escort agency. I talked it over with my mother.

'But, darling, you don't know London. They will want tour guides who know where to go, and well, much, much more.'

'Mummy, I'll learn on the way. I'm not asking you, I'm just letting you know.'

I called the number. A male voice answered. I gave my name and told him I was answering the advertisement. I lied about my age, saying I was eighteen. I also lied about my experience, having learned the hard way that I wasn't going to get anywhere with my real record.

'When can you start?'

'Tomorrow if you want.'

'Are you presentable? Do you know how to dress? No jeans.'

'Of course not.' Bugger, I was going to have to risk life and limb to nick Susie's clothes again.

'There's an American businessman staying at the Hyde Park Hilton. Meet him at seven-thirty tomorrow morning. His name is Mr J.C. Brooks. Show him a good time. First trip by the sound of it.'

'Right.'

'You collect fifty pounds from him, you keep twenty-five for yourself, and bring the rest in when you're finished.'

'How long should I show him London?'

He laughed. 'Well, if he's still with you at two in the afternoon, then ask him if he wants you longer. If so, it's another fifty pounds. Same deal. Got it?'

'Fine,' I replied confidently.

'We'll meet tomorrow. Good luck.'

Well, that was simple enough. I sauntered into the kitchen, told Mummy I had got the job, and asked if she would lend me the Tube fare up to London.

Next day, I arrived at the Hilton, went to the reception and asked for Mr J.C. Brooks. They gave me his room number. I called up on the house phone. As soon as the phone was in my hand, my stomach deserted me, and started going off on its own.

A voice answered. 'Hello, Mr Brooks speaking.'

'Hi, I'm from Escort Tours.'

'Come up to room 228.'

'Okay.' I looked around for a lift. My palms now sweating, I reached his room and knocked on the door. A huge, chubby, balding man opened the door. I said hello and he asked me if I wanted a drink. I refused politely and told him that, as he was paying, we ought to get going.

'Oh, good.' He wobbled over to the bed, pulled back the sheets and patted them, all the while looking at me.

I was shocked. 'What the hell are you doing? What do you mean? What are you doing?'

'You're from Escort Tours, aren't you?'

'Yes, I am, I'm here to show you around London. That's what we do.'

He looked so foolish as he fumbled with the bed, pulling the sheets back.

'You want to see London, don't you? We have a lovely city. We could go to Harrods or the Tower of London. It's very old. I hear Americans love old things. The dungeons are really spooky.'

He sat down on the bed, resting his hands on his knees. His big bulk shook and I felt very uncomfortable. I thought he was crying. He looked up at me and bellowed. He laughed so hard that even I began to giggle. 'I thought you were a call girl,' he spluttered eventually.

Now I was doubled over, laughing my head off. 'You thought I was a call girl,' I said, trying not to laugh, and to stop the pain in my side. 'Do you mind that I'm not?'

'Oh no, not at all.' He was really good about it.

We left the room, arm in arm, good friends already. We shared a secret, and I felt very grown up as we left the hotel. I did show him Harrods, and we ended up having a huge cream tea at the Ritz. He told me about himself. It was quite sad really. He had a good job, he had money, he had all the things he wanted when he set out as a young man, but he wasn't happy. His marriage was on the rocks because he travelled so much. He hardly knew his sons because he was never at home. When I asked if he had shared this with his wife, he replied, 'No.'

So we sat there, and I held his hand, feeling so bad for him. 'Hey,' I said, 'when was the last time you and your wife went on holiday?'

He looked at me. 'About four to five years ago.'

'Well, no wonder. Why don't you take her somewhere?'

He said she had always wanted to go to Hawaii.

'Well, take her there, slow off work for a bit. Tell them you're sick, that you need a rest. Buy her some clothes while you're here.'

So that's exactly how we spent the rest of the afternoon. We sat on the floor of a travel agency in Piccadilly, with brochures strewn around us, planning his second honeymoon. We decided on a five-star hotel. I haggled with him to go from business to first-class flights. He bought the tickets. Then we shopped till we dropped. He bought me a scarf which I still have today. At the end of the day he paid me. He took my hand. 'You're a very special person, you really are. I've had a great day. Thank you.'

'Go on that holiday. Call your wife, tell her you love her.'

'She'll think I'm drunk,' he laughed. He kissed me on the cheek and said goodbye.

After the first misunderstanding, everything had gone really well. I felt I'd done something really special. On the way home I looked at all the middle-aged men, thinking, Do you love your wife, or have you lost it all to your work?

When I got home, I called the escort agency back.

'How was it?'

'Great,' I replied and told him the story.

'You did what?' he said, laughing. 'You didn't pull any tricks?'

'No, I was dead honest. He was really sweet. Anyway, he's gone back home, and he's going to take his wife on holiday. I've got the money. When's the next job?'

Kindly, he told me there wouldn't be a next job.

I was shocked. 'I thought I'd done well, that you'd be pleased.'

'You were supposed to sleep with him.'

'*Supposed to sleep with him!*' I shouted back.

'This is an escort agency for call girls,' he eventually said.

My mother, who had heard the conversation, dragged the phone out of my hand and shouted down the line. Esther Rantzen and the police were mentioned. She slammed down the phone. She looked at me. I didn't know if she was going to hit me. Instead she laughed, and hugged me to her. 'Oh, Pol, whatever are we going to do with you? Didn't you know?'

'Know what?'

'About all that before you went.'

'Of course not,' I replied indignantly.

Oh, bloody hell, what a day. Well, at least I had fifty pounds towards my portfolio.

Later on I answered another advertisement for a 'model'. At the time I answered it, I had no idea of the devastating effect, and the repercussions, it would have on me. I met with a so-called agent. He took photographs of me in swimsuits, saying he would get me assignments. I was sixteen, a virgin and as green as they come. Part of me appeared very grown up; that was a front and a good one. Underneath was a little girl who wanted love and approval, but was totally oblivious to these needs.

I waited for days at home for the telephone to ring. I hadn't yet told my family. My mother kept asking me if I'd met someone. I lied, and said I was waiting for my girlfriend to ring, that she thought she'd found us a couple of summer jobs. A few days later the call came. It was for a job in Spain; two hundred and fifty pounds a week. I was beside myself. I told my family that afternoon at tea. I showed them the portfolio of photographs I had done. My mother wasn't too pleased, but I didn't care. I was going to be a model!

But it wasn't to be – not this time, anyway.

I met with the photographer and his wife at the airport. I slept on the plane, and when we arrived at a villa the photographer showed me to my room. We had supper, and chatted about work for the next few days, talking about locations and so on. I felt so grown up and I could hardly sleep for excitement.

In the morning I bounced out of bed and had coffee and cigarettes. The photographer's wife, Alice, did my hair and make-up, then passed me a sarong, and I wrapped it around myself while she went to get the costume. The first shoot was at the villa. I was excited. I looked in the mirror; my eyes were huge and smudged, my lips red. I flirted with my image, fascinated with the woman whose reflection responded to me. For the first time, I felt beautiful.

I walked outside to watch the photographer set up.

'Sit over there, will you?' It felt like an order rather than a request. 'Good, now drop the sarong so that it just pools around you.'

'But I haven't got my swimsuit on yet,' I protested.

He looked at me. 'Well, we can put it on later. Just drop the sarong and put your legs up, no, just put one leg up.'

I didn't understand what this man wanted. His wife came out. Thank God. I looked at her hands, they were empty. Had she forgotten the swimsuit? Tears welled up in my eyes.

13

She came and sat next to me. 'Your agent didn't tell you, did he?'

'He told me it was a swimsuit job.'

'Oh, bloody hell, not another one. God, tell her, Alice, tell her, will you? I'll fix her a drink.' The photographer left Alice and me alone.

Alice told me the shoot was for nude photographs for Sweden, that every model started this way. No one would ever see the photos. She said I'd feel better after a drink. I told her I wanted to go home. She said that if I did I would owe the air ticket, plus my fee. I didn't have that kind of money.

'Well, come on then, be grown up. You want to be a model, don't you? Look, it's how I started and I've had a good run. Come on, now.'

All the while she held my hand, a gentle smile on her face, like that of a mother coaxing a child into the dentist's chair. My mind whirled – I could handle this, I could. I wanted so much to be accepted, I wanted so much for this to be it, for everything to be all right. I struggled with these thoughts. She said no one would see them. Come on, Poo, don't be a scaredy cat, I thought.

Just then the photographer came out, a drink in his hand. I focused on it. The ice clinked against the glass. It was decorated with a little, pink umbrella, and the colour of its contents was blue. 'Come on, drink this up.'

I took a gulp and the liquid burned my throat. It soon hit my stomach, and I began to relax. Alice passed me a rolled cigarette; it smelled sweet and sickly. I had never smoked marijuana before, although I knew that's what it was. My head began to feel light and I didn't remember much more about the shoot.

And that's how I lived for those seven days. In a world full of drugs and haze.

When I shot those photographs in Spain, I was sixteen years old. Yet, sixteen years later, I was unable to stop them being exploited again in the newspapers. I went to counsel to issue an injunction against use of the photographs but the law was not on my side. Instead, it seemed to be saying loud and clear that it was perfectly acceptable to exploit my youth. The photographs, which they'd promised would never be seen, were published in *Mayfair* and *Penthouse*. My stepfather hit the roof, my friends from the small village in which we lived looked at me as if they didn't know me – they didn't. No one knew me, I didn't know me. All I knew was the humiliation and the shame. It only enhanced my feelings of loathing towards myself. Self-loathing was a familiar feeling. I'd hidden it most of my life. Wishing I was someone else, wishing to belong to another family at times.

I could no longer live at home, or in the village. I needed to move myself away from the memories. This was the beginning of many geographical moves to try to escape from myself. And every time I moved on, I would arrive at the destination with me in tow. I took myself everywhere I went, and with myself came along all my baggage, too. There would be no escape from it until I could learn to face myself.

So, I moved to London and met Andrew. I lived with him and his parents for two years until I realized that they were sapping my independence and hard-won confidence. I had to get away again if I were ever to realize my modelling ambitions.

At the age of eighteen I cashed in my trust fund by imitating my mother's voice on the phone to her solicitor and flew to Spain, where I had a friend.

I landed in Marbella, hot, excited and nervous. The taxi ride was terrifying, the roads treacherous, and made more so by the erratic driver, taking each bend as if he were in a Grand Prix. Grand Prick, I thought, and chuckled.

I arrived at Angel's house, cool, white, Spanish architecture – to me, a palace. A pool led to a manicured lawn, palms shading yet smaller palms, delicate bougainvillaea draping itself like a colourful tart along the wall tops. A dog barked – relief, he was behind a fence, a mean, black and menacing presence. I walked to the veranda. White muslin curtains blew gently back and forth as I walked up the steps and put my bags down.

Suddenly the curtains swept aside and Angel backed out, ducking as a bottle flew over her head and smashed at my feet.

'Out, out, you little whore, and don't come back.'

Clothes, hairbrushes, shoes flew out one after the other. Angel turned, her face red and puffy, a hand print perfectly formed on the side of her face.

'Mother, please, please.'

But her mother was having none of it. 'Not another word – OUT.'

Angel's mother slammed and locked the door. I stood, not daring to move. The dog was silent.

Angel looked at me. 'Hi.'

'Hi back,' was all I could manage. She began to pick up her things, I stooped down to help. Suddenly the window above us was flung open, and a stereo sailed through it, smashing inches away from us. Records, tapes, books and a ridiculously large pink rabbit, all flew out. We ducked into the doorway and looked at each other. We began to giggle, and then we laughed, deep belly laughs. I suddenly felt warm pee.

'I've peed myself,' I cried. 'I've bloody well peed myself.'

Eventually we'd packed all of Angel's things as best we could. She'd gone down the hill to call a taxi. I sat at the gates of the house, nervously looking over my shoulder in case her mother had another fit. Angel had come home asking for money. She was sixteen and pregnant, yet she looked twenty-five. Her mother had flipped, she'd had enough. She had problems of her own: like living in Spain, but not able to go out in the sun due to too much Retin A leaving her skin as white as a vampire's, cold and beautiful. The whites of her eyes had a blue-yellow tinge, due to too much use of Eye Dew to take out the glaring red, the kind caused by drinking. Yes, she had troubles of her own. She couldn't keep age at bay. All her energy went into that. And now she was being confronted by Angel – stunning, volatile – who could floor a grown man, metaphorically speaking, with a swing of her hips, whose breasts had a life of their own and whose mane of hair shone black even in the shade. Angel had 'come to bed' eyes, and they did – often.

What to do now? Angel and I waited for a cab; what turned up was a brown Jeep with a gold eagle on the bonnet, driven by a silver-haired man with four German shepherd dogs leaping about all over the place.

'Hi, Angel.'

'Hi, Banana.'

'Going somewhere?' he asked tactfully.

'To the airport.'

'And your friend?'

On the spur of the moment I said, 'The Marbella Club.' I'd heard of it and decided at that moment I was going to stay around for a while. After all, I'd only just arrived and there was nothing back there for me.

We took Angel to the airport. She took a flight to Paris, to her father.

'Good luck,' I said. 'Call me and let me know what's happening.'

We hugged goodbye, I watched her, and then watched the men who watched her go. I wondered if she knew what she had. She had sexuality. Lucky cow!

I stayed with Banana for a while, until I met Diego in a bar. He was in a wheelchair because of a motorcycle accident, and I started a relationship with him. It was not a physical attraction; it was more of a friendship, and I felt safe. Here was a man who sought my company, not my body, and somehow that gave me a feeling of self-worth. But, while living with Diego and his mother, I had a brief fling with Banana's son, Carl.

Diego's mother heard about this and, to protect her son, she began her mission to have me move on.

'Paula, you are meant for bigger things.'

'But, Mama, I don't want to leave Diego.'

'Paula, sit down. Diego can never have children. What's

happened to him is tragic. You're nineteen years old. You need to move on. Model, become an actress.'

We sat with iced tea on the lawn. The late afternoon sun danced and shimmered off the sea. Magic hour. Humming birds were busy sucking up the last juices of the day.

'I love Spain.'

'Then don't leave it. Go to Madrid. Go to a modelling agency and get work.'

I sipped my tea. Mama got up abruptly from the swing seat and the glass clanked against my teeth. She hobbled across the lawn, her sarong clinging to her. Mine fell off me continually. Perhaps it was her large bosom that kept it in place.

She returned a few minutes later with a vodka bottle. She sat down, unscrewed the cap and gestured to me. I held out my glass. She dolloped a generous amount in and I watched the oily substance settle. Pouring the same amount for herself, she turned and looked me right in the eye. I watched her own fill with tears.

'You will leave at the end of this week. Three days from now.'

She reached between her breasts and withdrew a bundle of pesetas. 'Here is one hundred thousand pesetas, enough for you to catch the bus to Madrid and a few nights at a hotel.'

I began to protest. She covered my mouth with her hand. The tears now escaped, trickling down the crevices at the corner of her mouth.

'You will go. You will become something great. You will not stay here and rot in this fake little village on the edge of no-where.' I knew she was right.

'Not a word to Diego.'

The day before I was scheduled to leave, I had told Diego I wanted to see if I could model, that I was going to Madrid. He had sat quietly in his chair. 'You must go, but don't come back.' With that he'd spun on his wheels and had not returned by the time I left.

*

I took the bus on a mean, airless day. The temperature soared. No one came to see me off. No one knew I was going. As a parting gift, Diego had placed on my bed a white silk parachute suit that I had admired for a while. Little did I know, when I entered that bus and sat through the journey glimpsing olive orchards and arid hills, that it was the beginning of many a journey that would take me all over the world, making all my dreams and fantasies come true.

I arrived in Madrid in the early evening. I was hot, tired, crumpled, thirsty, apprehensive and cocksure, all at the same time. I waited patiently for my luggage which arrived on the platform with a none-too-gentle thud, raising dust. I looked at it. My worldly possessions lay at my feet, along with the sixty thousand pesetas I had left in my pocket. I took out the scrap of paper I had been carrying with me since I had visited that modelling agency in London and suffered my first disappointment.

STARS MODELLING AGENCY – JOSÉ – (TELEPHONE NUMBER)

I decided against ringing, picked up my luggage, crossed the road into a bar and asked for a vodka and tonic. The barman responded to my request with an admiring look. I had learned how to deflect interest, and so challenged any further conversation. I sipped my drink with a straw and ate peppered red sausage and slices of dry white bread, non-salted. Taking a napkin, I wiped the grease from my mouth, finished my drink, screwed up the napkin and threw it at my feet. I bid goodbye to the waiter and he wished me good luck. I turned around, smiled and thanked him. His generosity touched me. Yes, I was going to need a lot of luck.

I picked up a taxi and instructed the driver to take me to Martin Campus. There, I walked across the road in the semi-darkness. The heat slipped off the day, allowing me to breathe deeply. Climbing the stairs to the agency, I prayed silently: Dear God, please make this work. I walked in without an appointment.

'Yes, can I help you?'

I put my luggage down. 'Hi, hope so. Had a hell of a journey. I'm from Bobton's Modelling Agency in London. Did you get my telex?'

'No,' she replied.

'Oh,' I said in mock surprise. 'Jill, the owner, said she would call you.'

'May I see your portfolio?'

'Yes, of course you can, except I stupidly left it on the plane with my composites.' (Composites – cards with four photographs, vital statistics and name of agency.)

'I see.'

'Jill says I'm one of her best young hopefuls. Thought I'd pit-stop here before I go on to France and Italy.'

José, who'd been listening to the conversation patiently, asked, 'How long have you been modelling?'

'Oh, about a year and a half.'

'Have you done editorial?'

'Oh yes, catalogues and advertising.'

'Aha, I see.' The telephone rang and he took the call. After a minute or so, he put down the receiver. 'Do you have somewhere to stay?'

'Not yet.'

'Well, Karen Castle is looking for a room-mate. She lives two streets away. Can you start tomorrow?'

'Yes.'

'A job just came in and I think you fit the bill. Corte Inglese's a good client. They trust us without seeing you.'

'Great.'

'Just take a seat. I'll write down your details. The rest of the forms we can do later.'

My heart pounded. I couldn't believe my luck. Jesus, I hoped he wouldn't call Jill and find me out.

He gave me Karen's address and details for work. I practically floated down the stairs. My first real, proper modelling job. It hadn't entered my head how I was going to cope with tomorrow. I just felt so damned good.

I met Karen, liked her and she seemed to like me. I moved in there and then. The apartment was large and beautiful. Wooden floors complemented large rooms. I had my own bedroom and bathroom. The kitchen was bright and modern. Each room had a little balcony and blinds. The apartment block was well maintained. Down in the basement was a gym with excellent facilities, including a pool. I was very at home there.

Karen was about five years older than me and filled me in on the modelling world. I told her about the job. 'Billboard advertising for Corte Inglese.'

'Gosh, that's lucky.'

I hadn't told Karen I wasn't a professional model, so I could not really go on about how excited I was about the booking.

The next morning I woke early, showered, washed my hair, shaved my legs and pits. Nervously dried my hair, and dressed in jeans, T-shirt and sneakers. I packed my make-up, hairbrush and a tin of hairspray. I wrote my details in my diary, ordered a taxi and was off for my first real day's work as a model.

I arrived at Corte Inglese. There was a studio on the top floor. I met the photographer, the make-up artist and the hairdresser and introduced myself. They were all very friendly. I had arrived before the three other models. I was to be in a shot with the four of us wearing coats. We were each to model a different colour. I had a calf-length green coat, a green hat, green glasses and green matching shoes. I thought I looked like a tree.

The aim was to show how Corte Inglese could coordinate what they sold, and that you could buy it all under one roof. Thank goodness there was a make-up artist and a hairdresser. Neither spoke much English.

'What foundation do you like?'

I spied her bottles. 'Oh, Clinique.'

'Good.' She matched my skin colour and applied the foundation. 'You have beautiful skin, you should stay out of the sun.'

'Mmm,' I replied, thinking of all the long, hot, lazy days I'd spent on the beach in Marbella.

I watched, fascinated, as she transformed my face. After she finished she handed me over to the hairdresser, who had been given the brief that all the girls' hair should be up and under the hats. We chatted and laughed. I listened to the other models. No English, thank God, otherwise I would surely have been found out. One model was particularly well known; I recognized her face. I felt both excited and scared.

At last, all ready, we were dressed by the stylist and our hats put on, then we lined up in front of the camera. I was able to see us all in a mirror and noticed that I didn't stick out like a sore thumb. With all the moving during my childhood, I'd spent years adapting to different environments. Now I had done it yet again. I was going to be able to pull it off. Monkey do what monkey see! I just copied the other girls as we shot different angles for over an hour.

Twenty rolls of film and three changes of clothes later, I felt confident and beautiful. I felt accepted and I belonged. I got quite a high every time the photographer said, 'Paula, very good.' He even once told the others, 'Copy her move.' *Copy her move.* Wow, and they did.

One thing I had learned very young was that if I said I could do something, and was given the chance to prove it, I did it. The second lesson was that if you didn't want to get found out, you had just one chance to get it right.

The agency called and spoke to me after the job was finished.

'Well done, they really liked you and have booked you for a trip for five days next week.'

I felt like I'd been doing it all my life. That's how my professional modelling career started, in Madrid, in 1979. I built a little portfolio and stayed for five months. No major disasters. I was a little bit lonely because I didn't really know anyone. I didn't know how to make friends. I was working quite hard and would come home at night exhausted, and sleep. At weekends I'd go dancing like any other young teenager and drink. But somehow it was all right.

*

Karen wasn't working well and wanted me to pay more rent. I obliged. But two weeks later she wanted me to pay the lot. I told her I couldn't do that and she said I would have to leave. I was ready to go home. I hadn't seen my family for over a year. So I packed and left two days before Christmas, laden down with presents.

As soon as I arrived in London, I called Bobton's to make an appointment to go and see them, to see if they'd take me on. José gave me my chance; he'd had a hunch. A girl who was capable of bluffing her way into an agency, who had the gall to stand there and lie her head off without blinking an eye, could quite possibly pull it off. I hadn't let him down and he didn't let on that he knew. The day before I left he had called me into his office.

'You've done really well. You've built yourself a portfolio, you're a pro, you know how to handle clothes, look good. You can work with others, you're punctual. You have a classic face with aristocratic airs and graces. You have the makings of being a top international model. You have only one thing to watch out for. In fact, three things: DRUGS, ALCOHOL and LIES.'

That last word stopped me in my tracks.

'Yes, I knew you weren't a professional model. I called Jill at Bobton's the next day. She'd never heard of you.'

My face was red with shame and embarrassment.

'I figured you were pretty desperate and needed a break. The rest was up to you. You proved one hundred per cent that you could do it.'

Rarely had I ever been caught out, yet here, at the same time, I was receiving praise. José came over and hugged me.

'Come back and see us. If you get big in Europe, we can do some direct bookings, which means that the clients will pay air fares and expenses. Now, off you go and *succeed.*'

It wasn't until years later that I heard that José was in the fellowship of AA and had realized he was dealing with someone who was potentially an alcoholic. He recognized the behaviour before the addiction took over.

Returning to my family home was difficult. My younger brothers were still at school, my younger sister was at college and my older sister was setting up home with her husband. My mother was still with my stepfather; a tense silence existed between them that, at the best of times, meant polite indifference towards each other. I didn't know how to talk to my stepfather, so I didn't. I felt flat and uncomfortable. I was modelling and had no one at home to share that with: the life-style, the fast pace, the excitement. I couldn't relate to their quiet days and routines. It was all somehow so normal and I just didn't know how to fit in. I only stayed for a few days over Christmas; I couldn't wait to leave. I hadn't stopped loving my family – I just didn't feel part of their daily lives any more.

In the three years since I had left school I had achieved my ambition to become a model. I had also unwittingly set the pattern for the alcoholism and co-dependency problems that were to dog my life from then onwards. Others had recognized it in me, but back then I was more interested in having a good time and building my career – whatever the cost to myself.

CHAPTER TWO

Fight and Flight

At the age of twenty-one I was living in Germany with a boyfriend, Tom, and his mother, Anna. She had recognized some years earlier that she had had a problem with addiction. She had managed to stop herself from falling any further into the abyss of full-blown substance abuse. She could see the same symptoms in me and pointed them out. However, I chose to ignore this advice and instead ran away from the safe haven of her home. I was simply too ashamed to face her, because I knew I did not have the strength to deal with my life in the same way she had dealt with hers. All through the early days of my modelling career the same pattern kept rearing its ugly head – I spent seven years constantly running away.

When I was eighteen, I was living in South Kensington with Andrew, a relationship that had lasted for two years. We shared the house with his parents. After I had been living with him for about three months, someone sent him a clipping they'd cut out from *Mayfair*. Andrew had gone down to make some tea one morning and he'd brought up a tray, which was very rare indeed. On this tray was a letter; it was addressed to both of us. When he opened it, there I was: legs wide apart, head thrown back and long, pink false nails clawing at my inner thighs.

My stomach constricting, I flew out of bed and vomited violently in the bedroom sink. I was shaking, panting, gasping for breath, sweat pouring down my face.

I turned and looked at Andrew. He just sat there, his eyes glued to the photograph, this photograph that had smashed its way into our home. He looked at me, with hate in that look, and disgust in his eyes. He looked at me as if I were a stranger.

'You whore, you fucking little whore,' he screamed.

'No, Andrew, no. Please, please; you must listen.'

'You fucking tricked me, I thought you were a decent girl. You're nothing but a fucking whore.'

My head spun and I felt myself disappearing. I couldn't believe his words, I just saw his face as he screamed obscenities, then everything went black.

When I came to, Andrew was standing over me. He had flung a glass of water in my face. Sobs racked their way through my body, my wounds gaped open, and I mourned and cried like an animal.

'Get up, for God's sake, get up.'

I did so on shaking legs.

'Get dressed, pack your bags, then get the fuck out.'

My head whiplashed as he slapped my face. Spots danced in front of my eyes. Somehow – and I don't remember how – I washed and packed, tears streaming down my face. I sat on the bed and numbly stared out of the window.

The bedroom door opened; Andrew, now showered, shaved and immaculately dressed in a clean, white, button-down Oxford shirt and grey slacks, looked at me. I couldn't read his face.

'Andrew, please let me explain.'

He stopped me. 'No. You don't say another word. You can stay, but I'll never think of you as I did before. You ask nothing of me, you stay in the house with my mother, and you only go out with me. You are nothing.'

'Why don't you let me leave, then?'

'Because I want you to stay,' he replied.

'Why?'

'Because I do, that's why.'

Even though I had witnessed how much Andrew and his father controlled his mother Catherine, I myself became Andrew's victim for a while, losing myself, 'people pleasing', putting him before my own needs. Spending days copying down notes of lectures he hadn't attended for his law degree, when I should have been concentrating on getting my own career in modelling off the ground. He found the idea a threat, and would put me off at every opportunity, pointing out my faults to the point of making me doubt myself and my abilities. His smiles of praise became my rewards. I fell victim to Andrew's charm. It was only when the hurt got too great that I began to see how he treated his mother. I became painfully aware of her predicament as a way of escaping and ignoring my own.

I didn't leave because I believed I could win his trust, his respect. I believed that if I was very, very good, and did as I was told, he would love me again. He was my first serious boyfriend and I believed I loved him. I now know that I didn't know what love was, and that I didn't find it for many years to come. I was trying to earn respect from Andrew, even though he had never been taught to respect women, and had been brought up watching his father treat his mother without respect. I never understood that he was emotionally unavailable to me. This inability to realize which men I could like and which I couldn't, would lead me to make the same mistake time and time again.

I became Andrew's pet, his slave. I spent hours waiting for affection, watching him like a hungry animal waiting for a morsel of food, at his beck and call. He was genuinely fond of me, and would sometimes let up and forget that awful morning. Those were the moments I lived for. Twice a week we would go out and dance, I lived for those times as well. His world became my world. I had nothing without him, my mind told me. I gave myself away those two years, tossed myself aside. When we went out we drank a bottle of wine; I loved the feeling it gave me. I felt beautiful, confident and danced provocatively to hide all my pain. He loved the admiring stares of the men all around me. I had to be careful not to catch their eyes or he would become cold and still towards me. Even through the warmth of the alcohol, I would shrink inside. Oh yes, I was Andrew's victim, and I didn't even know it was out of choice.

One morning after yet another row, I woke up and finally made the decision to leave. I phoned my mother's solicitor and arranged to get my hands on my trust fund. Then I padded downstairs and opened the French doors. I could hear Andrew's mother in the kitchen. Andrew – beautiful Andrew, selfish Andrew, shaming Andrew. He had finally delivered the last blow. He'd successfully mutilated my confidence for months until last night. 'Oh God,' I groaned. I'd bitten him, telling him he was a selfish, cold bore, that there was more to being a man than blond hair and blue eyes. I thought of his face when I told him he was the most boring lover I'd ever had, and that his penis was so ugly and inadequate it made me vomit. I had wanted to wound him deeply, and I had. My words had hung on the air like floating bee stings, attacking and leaving red, angry marks; he was frightened to move in case they turned around in mid-air and stung him again.

He was so humiliated, his face red with anger and effort and I could tell he was struggling not to strike back. He got out of bed, dramatically whiplashing the door after him. As an afterthought he returned and took two pillows, his back muscles erect and proud. Andrew had a beautiful body, and he knew it. Sickening – right down to his perfect feet. No marks, no corns, toenails like pink shells. Perfect insteps leading to even more perfectly formed calves. Looking down at my own crunched toes and twisted nails, I saw my two ugly corns wink at me. He turned around, his head angled, his blue eyes looking up from under his – yes, perfectly straight – eyebrows as they burned into me. I opened my legs wide and, without a word, made an obscene gesture. He slammed the door shut. I lay back, my thoughts closed. Tears, ancient tears, flowed, not for him, not for this, but for the ache that had always been with me, the ache that kept on reminding me, every now and then, that happiness, peace, contentment were not to be mine. It seemed I was unlovable, defective, craving to be adored, yet sabotaging any chance of it ever happening. Even as I fell asleep this sense of shame towards myself began to fade. Gulping it back down, feeling it slide like a slug back where it came from to lurk inside, ready and waiting for the next opportunity to come writhing back up and take bite-size chunks out of my heart.

It wouldn't be until years later that I would gain insight into why this pattern of allowing people to control me kept occurring. I always handed over too much control and then found myself resenting it. The only way I knew how to stop feeling this way was to sabotage *it*, whether *it* was a relationship, a friendship, work or another project. The skill in keeping one's independence in any relationship was unknown to me then.

The drawing-room door opened. 'Good morning, Paula.'
   'Good morning, Catherine.'
   'I've made us a pot of coffee – you know how I love coffee and a ciggie.'
   Oh, how I would miss this simple woman. We moved to the French doors that led down to the perfectly manicured lawns of Rutland Gate, went out, lit fags and sat on the steps like two girls sneaking a puff behind the school shed. Catherine had been told strictly not to smoke. I had been told not to encourage her, or to smoke in front of her. Well, bugger them – selfish pair. We sat in silence, puffing and sipping rich, dark coffee.
   'I'm leaving.'
   'Yes, dear. Will you pick up some fish on your return?'
   'You may have a long wait.'
   She looked at me, not understanding.
   'I'm going away on holiday.'
   'You really should wait. Andrew's year is nearly up.'
   'I'm leaving Andrew.'
   'Why?' She looked so young, so scared. She adored Andrew. God knows why, he barely acknowledged her. Watching her washing his shirts by hand so tenderly, humming under her

breath, her eyes never leaving her work. Washing his clothes as if they were as delicate as his christening gown. Andrew, twenty-nine years old, who might well have been twenty-nine months. He had betrayed her by growing up, a fact she couldn't, and would never, accept.

'Paula, he needs you. Who will write up his lecture notes? Who will make him laugh? He won't exist without you. Paula, you can't do this to him.'

'I can, Catherine, and I am,' I said gently. 'He doesn't love me.'

'Oh, but he does.'

I realized I couldn't expect her to understand. Her own husband treated her like a maid; not once in two years had I heard him say anything that resembled a compliment. He was always complaining she hadn't done things right, bullying her. He wasn't her friend. Why did one-time lovers always seem to end like this? Well, it wasn't for me. Each time her husband opened his mouth some sort of put-down came out of it. No amount of love could hoodwink me into accepting that sort of behaviour, no amount. I'd stamp on it before it ever knocked me down, devouring me to nothing as it had done Catherine. Dear sweet Catherine, who had never known love, warmth, acceptance of who she was, not once, not ever. Always accommodating: first to be what her mother and father wanted, then a slave to her brothers and now a slave to her man and her son.

The more I looked at her life, the more I panicked. The force of it brought me abruptly to my feet. I put my cup down and ground out my cigarette. Taking two more from the packet, I reached over gently for her hand. Without taking her eyes off the garden, she closed her hand around mine.

I packed my few belongings and took a train to the airport. I had a friend, Angel, who lived in Spain. She was spending the summer with her mother. They had a house in the mountains behind Marbella. The plane ride was magical. I splashed out and bought a bottle of champagne to celebrate, and felt lighter than I had for ages. I enjoyed the admiring stares of the men on the plane and thought, Look, you can want me, you can dream, but you can't have me. None of you will ever have me. I'll have you, but you'll never have me.

I wasn't anti-men, but I hated the idea of losing sight of myself within a relationship. At that point, I could see this only in other women, who had allowed themselves to become controlled by men to the point where they had lost themselves. I did not then know that I also had problems, which would only be revealed by going through one painful experience after another.

I knew I needed to believe in myself in order to feel safe. If I never gave in, I'd never be hurt, never used and tossed aside, or worse, trapped and beaten down into nothing. I didn't want to be like Catherine, watching all her dreams dying a little each day as each one was picked up and tossed aside like a peach stone. How many women live like that and why do they allow themselves to be beaten down?

I was only eighteen, but I was already pushing to find the answers. I would find them; I didn't know then that it would take years, and be a long slow painful process, but I knew I'd find them. I didn't have a role model who was going to teach me. The structure of my family was dysfunctional. I would only be able to find answers when I had explored all the avenues, not knowing then that I was an alcoholic or an addict, but eventually realizing and, more importantly, admitting that I needed help.

From Spain and my first real modelling jobs, I went back to England and was accepted by Bobton's Modelling Agency. The next few months passed in a blur; by the time I was nineteen, I was living in Japan. By this stage I was drinking all the time; it was part of everyone's social life. There were quite a few models in Japan and we really did live a life of luxury, getting into clubs free, meeting all the other 'beautiful people'. We all tended to congregate together because work was so strict and regulated that we just wanted to go out and enjoy ourselves in our free time.

I found out just how strict my working life was going to be as soon as I arrived at the agency. I took the lift to the top floor. The doors of the lift opened straight on to the office where there were huge booking tables off to one side. At least eight bookers sat at each, with clipboards with the individual girl's names, details and job lists. Very much run like a London agency. Covers and covers of girls in frames smiled down at me from the walls.

'You must be Paula. Welcome to Folio. Have you had a good journey?'

'Yes, thank you.'

'My name is Kajos. I'm your booker. I have six girls. You'll get all the details of work from me. Now we received your portfolio and cards. Your working papers are in order?'

'Yes, yes, they are. At least I didn't seem to have a problem in Hong Kong.'

'Good, last week they were being difficult and sent six girls back. Very annoying.'

I didn't know it was up to the discretion of the agent to hand out work papers. 'Gosh, so I was lucky?'

'Well, you're here. Paul Rose would like to see you. You met him briefly in London a few weeks ago. Take the stairs to the top floor. He's waiting for you.'

I opened the door to Paul Rose's office.

He stood and chuckled, 'Well, well, Miss Hamilton, you made it. Sit down, come on, sit down.'

I liked this man immediately. He was warm, friendly and had a mischievous twinkle in his eye.

'Now we've got you an apartment on the other side of Repponi Cosatini. It's expensive, but they all are. Let me run through some of the ground rules whilst you are here:

'One: if you are late three times in a row, due to your own fault, your contract will be terminated.

'Two: if you gain more than five pounds, your contract will be terminated.

'Three: if we get more than three complaints from clients because of your attitude, condition of skin or being difficult, your contract will be terminated.

'Four: if you cut or colour your hair without first consulting with the agency, your contract will be . . .'

I echoed him, ' . . . terminated.'

He looked up at me, rested both elbows on his desk and laced his fingers together. 'I sincerely hope you will honour your contract. Being in Tokyo is hard work. You need to take responsibility for your own well-being. The nightclubs and certain restaurants are free to you models, including drink and food. You will be appointed a manager who will travel with you everywhere. You will be driven by limo at our expense. By the way, you are working tomorrow.'

'Already?'

'Yep. Big money, big campaign.'

I grinned from ear to ear. 'How much? Big?'

'Yes.'

I'd already forgotten the long list of dos and don'ts. This last bit of information I'd received made me feel fantastic. It's always a worry in the back of your mind that you're not going to work. I finished up my meeting with Paul who walked me out back to the lift.

'By the way, you can call me any time and come over to the house and meet my wife.'

'Thank you,' I responded.

He kissed me on the cheek. 'Remember,' he said like a fairy godmother, 'you are responsible for your own well-being.'

I saluted my response and headed for what was to be my home for over a year.

On the way to Japan I had got cold feet. We had to stop in Hong Kong to obtain our work permits for Japan. I felt scared. I hated Hong Kong, I couldn't understand anything. I couldn't tell if the Chinese were happy or angry. I felt lost; the noises, the smells, nothing was familiar. Self-doubt began to creep in. What the hell was I doing in Hong Kong? Did I even really want to be a model? I crept back to my hotel room, drank a bottle of wine, and lay looking at the damp patches on the ceiling. Six months.

If I left a day before, I would come home empty-handed. That was the deal, and even I knew a deal was a deal.

My apartment was large by Tokyo standards. It was well decorated with TV, telephone and a big double bed. I had windows on two walls looking out over a government building with beautiful gardens. I walked into a small, compact kitchen and put the kettle on. I unpacked Marmite, coffee and Earl Grey tea. For the next ten years these travelled with me on all assignments. Tokyo was tough going. My little apartment became a haven and I rarely had to share it. But from time to time they'd put a girl in who was new or scared, and before long I became known as Mama Polly. Some of the models were as young as fifteen.

Only occasionally did we smoke pot. One, it was extremely difficult to get hold of and two, anyone caught with it would be in prison for over a year, and every Japanese name in your address book would be investigated.

I did my six months in Japan, and it changed my life forever. I had never felt so free. So many models became instant friends. Surrounded by the Japanese, we banded together and hung out. We drank too much, danced too much, ate too much. Yet everything was superficial – we never got too close to each other, it seemed no one was capable of it. Work took up much of our time, and when we weren't working we were playing hard.

I got close to only one model in Japan, and we stuck together like glue. Her name was Mollie. I adored her. She was the only friend in my life, up to that point, who confronted me with my behaviour, and asked why I acted the way I did. We were having a Shiatsu massage when she hit me with a few home truths. I cried and cried. Firstly with humiliation, secondly with relief. I was to lose this relationship five years later. To this day I can truthfully say I don't know the exact reason – whether it was my fault or not. I've tracked her down to where she is living in Kenya with her husband and baby. I have tried to talk to her about it but never got to the bottom of it all. I lost a very dear friend yet again. One day I hope we will be able to sit down and talk about it. If not, I need to accept that too.

Mollie opened her doors to me, her friends and contacts. We partied nearly every night at different nightclubs. The Titanic had just opened and we spent many an evening there, drinking champagne by the bucketload and snorting cocaine. We were young, successful and wealthy in our own right. The men flocked around us. When we didn't go out, they would come over laden with goodies: champagne, cheeses, exotic fruits and plenty of drugs. I always bought my own. I didn't like the idea of relying on taking someone else's.

During the day I worked for *Vogue*, *Marie Claire*, *Elle* and *Cosmopolitan*. In the evenings I flirted and danced the night away. Not all my drinking and drug-taking was miserable. At the beginning it was wild fun and adventurous. If I'd known then what lay in the future, I wouldn't have believed it anyway. That's the insanity of addiction; each time taking the substance, each time thinking it would be a different result. I didn't have time to be lonely in Japan; if I was, I just drank. 'Why feel bad if you don't have to?' was my motto.

I met a very special man in Japan – Stephen. He was a footballer from America who'd come over some years previously. We met in a bizarre way. He was rather drunk and asked me to dance; I thought he was rather dashing. He had an old, white, Russian-style shirt with a laced front and ruffles on the cuff. He wore this with black, baggy pants, tucked into high black boots. He was well over six feet five inches tall, and had one of the most masculine, handsome faces I'd ever seen.

His mistake was that, as he was asking me to dance, he was already dragging me onto the floor. I wasn't having any of it and I stamped down hard on the side of his heel. He bellowed, let go, then swung for me, his face red with fury. I nipped past him, as nimble as a cat. He turned and gave chase. I ran as fast as I could down a spiral staircase, and out of the building into the street. The traffic was bumper to bumper, the pavement crowded. I pushed through the crowds; he was catching up and shouting for me to stop. No way! I turned towards the traffic. Only one thing for it – I jumped on the bonnet of a car, leapt on to the roof of the next one, then looked back. Damn, he was doing the same thing. Now the chase took place from car to car; people were shouting at us, a policeman blew his whistle. I just kept going, concentrating, waiting to see if the traffic would start to move.

About fifty yards on I dropped to the pavement, and ran as hard as I could until my apartment block came in sight, just a few yards away. I tore open the door and ran up the four flights of stairs to my apartment. I knew he was close on my heels; I just had to get to my apartment door. My hands fumbled in my pockets until I found my key, I turned it in the lock – please God, let it open. It did, just as he reached my landing. As he reached out, I ducked inside, slammed the door shut, turned the lock and bolted myself in. He banged furiously on the door for what seemed like hours, shouting for me to open the door, threatening to break it down. Eventually he went away and I went to bed, but sleep was a long time coming.

The next morning I looked outside the door. I saw he'd twisted the iron handle into the shape of a knot. There were red roses everywhere, and a note to say he'd be back. Staring at the roses, thoughts jumbled through my head: Why me? Why me? What did he want? Bending down, I touched their petals, perfect petals; roses, dozens of them. I'd never received flowers from a man before; a shiver ran up my spine. He was a man, he was huge and he wanted *me*. The game was on! I took the roses inside. I had no vases so every available empty red wine bottle had three roses in each of them. The apartment was blood red with huge velvet blooms. I giggled; I couldn't wait to show the girls next door.

The next day I went to the front door there were more roses, double the amount of the day before. I stood laughing and suddenly he was standing there, looking at me sternly.

'Makes you laugh, does it? Why?'

'I'm not talking to you,' I replied. 'You're rude and your be-haviour the other night was brutish.'

He took one purposeful step forward and was beside me. My stomach lurched. What did he want with me? Instead of pulling me to him and kissing me, as I expected, he squashed a cock-roach that had come out of its hole, and was crawling towards my head.

'What the hell are you doing?' I shouted before I realized what was happening. 'Yuk, that's revolting.' I saw him wipe the cockroach juice down the side of his trousers.

'Supper tonight,' was his response. 'Be ready at eight o'clock. I'll pick you up. Wear something decent.' He turned and was gone before I could think up a reason to refuse his invitation. Any normal woman would have said 'no'; I called 'yes' to his re-treating back; he didn't even turn his head. Why not? I reassured myself, I wasn't scared of this gorilla in trousers, and spent the rest of the day planning what I would wear.

Stephen, true to his word, picked me up at eight o'clock on the dot. He looked splendid, wearing a full-length fur coat and hat to match. He produced the same coat and hat in my size and, without a word, held them out for me. I didn't speak but turned around, so he hung the coat on my shoulders and plonked the hat on my head. I walked downstairs and outside into the chilly October night.

I immediately understood the necessity of the warm coats when I saw the car. It was a vintage Aston Martin convertible in racing green, and the hood was down. It was stunning. He opened the door for me and I climbed in. Sitting there, I grinned like a Cheshire cat, still not a word between us. He fired up the car and drove into the streets of Tokyo. As we drove through the streets we caused quite a stir and I enjoyed the attention. I soon found out that Stephen had a fleet of cars, including the Aston Martin and a Rolls Royce.

He parked the car outside a magnificent home, huge in com-parison to the little Japanese houses on either side. He got out, opened my door and, still not speaking, gestured me up the stone steps. He leapt on ahead, two steps at a time, pushed open the big wooden doors, took off his hat and dramatically bowed, inviting me in. I suppressed a giggle. I walked slowly inside and stopped; it took my breath away. What greeted me was a huge, round, stone room that had a magnificent, medieval chandelier dominating the ceiling and a fireplace large enough to stand in or even lie down, in which a fire was blazing, wood stacked on one side: an unusual sight for Japan. Faded tapestries lined the walls and candles flickered from large, wrought-iron candelabra, cleverly placed around the room. Rich oil paintings, obvious even to my ignorant eye, caught my attention – Rembrandts, Constables and Turners. Large sprawling ferns hung generously near windows covering one wall of the room, slightly bowed to follow the line. He flicked a button, the windows slid back, lights came on, and to my amazement I was looking at a golden eagle sitting on the branch of a mature tree. On closer inspection I saw there were four more. I walked over to the now open space. A twenty-foot-high waterfall tumbled from the rocks, falling into a pool below surrounded by pampas grass; it was breathtaking. I sat on a cushion on the floor, my eyes as big as saucers. Stephen clicked his tongue and the eagle I'd been watching swung around at the sound, angled his beak and took off directly towards me. He landed at my side, bunny-hopped over to Stephen and pulled on his boot lace. Stephen got down on all fours and the eagle took a piece of dried meat offered to him. I was mesmerized.

As if this were not enough, down the circular staircase trotted a female cheetah – Leala. She sat at the bottom of the stairs, observing us. The eagle, with the meat in his beak, flew back to the safety of the tree. Stephen walked over and sat down next to Leala, rubbing her ear absent-mindedly. 'You're the first woman I've brought here, apart from one other. This is Leala, she is seven years old and hand reared. Do you want to come and say hello?'

I'm very proud and didn't want to show that I was scared. I

quietly walked over, my heart thumping, and sat down next to him. Leala came over to me, blowing warm, meaty air into my ear while she nuzzled my neck. Then, just as quickly, she straddled me and peed. Stephen laughed – I must have looked shocked, covered in cheetah pee. 'She doesn't like you – that was meant for me. In other words, dear girl, you have competition.'

Stephen offered me a kimono to wear and, as I was to experience this jealous behaviour with Leala time and time again over the months of our extraordinary friendship, I learned to stay well clear of her.

Stephen behaved like a perfect gentleman that evening after a splendid meal. We arrived home, he walked me up the stairs and removed the fur hat and coat. 'I've called your agency and you're not working tomorrow. I'll pick you up at nine in the morning, and show you the rest of the family.'

I lay in bed that night going over the evening in my mind. He was rather wonderful and handsome. I liked him very, very much.

The next morning, dressed in riding boots and breeches, teamed with a suede jacket, I waited by the door to be picked up. Again he was punctual, knocking on the stroke of nine. I swung the door open.

'Good morning,' he grunted. 'Glad to see you respect time.'

'No fur coat?' I replied. He turned back and smiled.

It was a beautiful, blue October day. The Rolls glided through the city and I felt like a princess. The crystal-clear notes of Vivaldi played from the tape deck. I looked over at this man, wondering what he saw in me. We parked and he led the way through a beautifully designed office building to the elevators. We stopped on the top floor, which his friend, who owned the building, let him use. The doors opened and we were on a roof. I looked around and saw immense, open-plan cages, similar to the ones at his home, except less grand.

Two beautiful grey Canadian wolves, one female, one male, came to the bars to greet him. He opened the door and they rushed at him, jumping up, their great paws on his shoulders, and licking his face. 'Hello, my beauties. Come over and say hello.'

I did. They dropped to all fours and prowled around me, sniffing.

'They like you.'

'How can you tell?'

'Well, they haven't bitten you, have they?'

I looked at him and gave him a confident, cheeky grin.

We spent the entire afternoon there playing with and feeding the animals. Also in residence were an old male cheetah called Rocky, and a lynx that didn't come out of the log he was sleeping in.

'I meant what I said. You're the first female to meet our family besides one other, also very special to me. You have a way with animals that is very rare. Just because the animals know me does not mean they will automatically trust all humans. They have had very little contact with others besides myself. So you can think yourself quite special.'

And I did. For that moment, I really did. Little did I know then, that nearly a decade later, my love for animals would lead me to create my own charity – Tusk Force.

The animals had been rescued by Stephen. The wolves had been taken from the cellars of a rich Japanese who had bought them as a party attraction. When they grew and began to bite, he'd put them into a cellar. Stephen found them and hand-reared them. Later they were returned to the wild in Canada; he spent months out there with them to accomplish this successfully.

Stephen and I became lovers; our relationship was special. I spent a lot of time with him. He met my mother who came over for my twenty-first as a surprise. She brought with her my birthday cake. She stayed with me in my apartment and we had a wonderful time for those two short weeks. My mother danced all night with me. We had supper with my agent and friends.

Stephen treated her like a queen. We introduced her to the animals. She became the third woman to meet them. She walked into the cage with the lynx, put her nose gently to his, and stayed like that for a few moments. I had to walk away, I was so scared. Did Stephen know what he was doing? Even *I* didn't go into the cage with the lynx.

My mother came out with a dreamy look in her eyes, put her fingers to her lips and walked away from us. Hands on hips, I looked at Stephen. 'What was all that about?'

'She touched herself,' was all he would say.

I felt that my mother's presence in Japan brought us closer than we had been, but my use of alcohol kept my mistrust of her deep inside me and I still couldn't allow a more open relationship to develop.

I kept my relationship with Stephen separate from all my other acquaintances in Japan. I didn't confide in anyone around me about Stephen; he took me away from the madness of modelling and gave me an escape into his own private fantasy world. Here was a man who was in love with me and cared for me deeply, yet I didn't realize it at the time. Perhaps this is why I didn't fall in love with him. Perhaps I was too afraid to lose myself again, as I had with Andrew. The day I left he made me a card which I still have today. It reads as follows:

> In the end I hope you realize that I shall always attempt to understand you and shall remain a *friend*. I desire all the best for your future – perhaps you shall find a man to satisfy your needs!
>
> Stephen

When I left Japan I didn't know whether I would see him again. In fact I did, five years later, and was shocked at the amount he was drinking. When I had been with him, he never even smoked cigarettes; he had been one of the few people I knew who didn't indulge in any form of mood-altering substance. Looking back over my life, I have always been attracted to people who have this illness. Before the addiction kicks in, it's in our behaviour; this inability to live within reality.

One morning at five, on my way from Tokyo to Osaka, I stood at the train station, queuing up to catch the Bullet train (the Chin Kan San). It was supposedly one of the fastest trains in the world and travelled on an elevated track above the cities and towns. I was a few minutes early so I'd gone to the platform's vending machine and bought a can of hot cream corn soup and a packet of dried jellyfish; this had become a ritual. I always felt better after a night of drinking if I ate something – the cream corn soup and salty dried fish seemed to help.

I became aware that people were shuffling at the front of the platform. There was a shrill whistle which seemed to split my head in half, some of the soup spilt down the front of my coat and I jumped about a foot in the air. Feeling ruffled and agitated, I shuffled with the other commuters, and little by little I began to feel squashed, yet they kept moving closer until we were squashed like sardines. No one shouted, no one complained. I looked around and thought they were like polite robots, no one looking at each other even though men pressed up against women and women pressed up against men. At the best of times I don't *like* crowds, I *need* space around me. I began to feel agitated, to feel very warm and not too happy at all. I was even thinking of not going. When the train arrived, the crowd surged closer and the doors opened. A sea of people disembarked through a regimented channel that the waiting crowd had formed. They didn't move until the last commuter had got off. All of a sudden, as the crowd surged forward, I felt something flat press into the small of my back. With great effort I twisted round and saw, to my displeasure, that I was being herded forward by a guard. The pressure I felt in my back was his wooden shovel, shaped very much like a water-ski with a pole. The guard held on to the pole in front of him, and the horizontal paddle attached to it acted like a snow plough, pushing us into the train. I felt angry and indignant, confused and frightened. Scenes from Auschwitz went through my head. 'Back off, buddy,' I hissed through clenched teeth. 'Get the fuck off.'

This didn't seem to make any difference; he kept pushing until I was on the train. I couldn't move, I couldn't speak. I stood sandwiched, wedged in, my feet barely touching the floor. Could this possibly be legal? By this time I was acutely aware of my hangover and was feeling quite nauseated. My only thought was, Please God, don't let me be sick.

When we finally arrived I vowed I would never do the trip again. The weather in Osaka was bitterly cold. I looked forward to the warmth of the studio, a cup of coffee and a fag. What greeted me was not what I'd had in mind. The doors (the size of those found on aircraft hangars) to the studio, a converted warehouse, were wide open. The cold air blew in, and I hoped they had been left open to receive goods. No. They were open because the head photographer wasn't happy with his crew and as a punishment, he had made them strip down to their boxer shorts and ordered the doors to be left open.

'What's going on?' I asked the make-up artist, who filled me in with the details. An assistant the day before hadn't done his job properly, therefore the whole crew was made to suffer. After my hair and make-up session I went to the head photographer, told him I hadn't been working yesterday, was therefore not a part of this punishment, and would not model under these conditions. He looked at me with contempt, and told me I was to do as I was told. I told him, no way, and he had two minutes in which to close the doors, or I would leave. Two minutes later the doors remained open and I was back on the Chin Kan San. I would never allow myself to be under anyone's thumb.

When I got back I went to the agency and explained why I had left. They listened, nodding, their faces full of understanding, so when they did open their mouths I could have fallen off my seat backwards.

'You will have to pay for everything, including the studio, the photographer's fee, train ticket, make-up artist, the lot. You walked out of a contract.'

'But the conditions were ridiculous. I need a lawyer.'

They informed me that I would be working for nothing, as the entire cost was over seven thousand pounds. I couldn't believe it. I didn't have a leg to stand on. I did the next two weeks of work and never saw a penny. Ironically I had put myself under their thumbs. A valuable lesson indeed, and one I would never forget – professionally, at least.

Tony Curtis came over to Japan for Christmas, and we met – as there were so few foreigners it wasn't difficult – at a nightclub where I'd been invited to his dinner, along with a few other models. We got on famously. While we were talking, he looked at my hands.

'You, too, suffer from big hands. Cover them, my dear, with frilly shirt sleeves.'

I was embarrassed that he had pointed them out. Tony, by telling me I had big hands, confirmed the fact in my mind. Fourteen years later I would bump into him at the BAFTA awards. I repeated the story to him.

'Who told you that you had big hands?' I asked him.

'Errol Flynn.'

'And you believed him?'

'Yes.'

We both chuckled. For years, Tony Curtis and I had both hidden our big hands, believing them not to be perfect. All of this started by Errol Flynn – bugger him.

After supper, none too steady on our feet, we went back to his hotel for a night cap: my agent, Paul Rose, Tracey Lee and a few others. When we got to the Okura Hotel lobby, Tony Curtis spied a Christmas tree. He winked at me and grabbed the tree, pulling the light socket out of the wall. He shot into the elevator with the tree, which wasn't easy – it was over eight feet tall – while the concierge screamed at us. We all piled in, up to the seventh floor and ran down the corridor to Tony's room with the tree behind us. We opened the door, went inside and plugged in the tree. Pulling the sheets off the bed, we all got down on the floor and covered ourselves with them. When the hotel security guards burst in, Tony explained he HAD to have a Christmas tree to pray to, and in Muslim fashion started chanting, 'Alabalala, Christmas tree!'

We were in hysterics, high on life, young, beautiful and mad. What fun, what adventures.

In the morning after no sleep, Tony fell for my parachute jump suit and waddled off wearing it. He was overweight at this time and looked like the Pilsbury Doughboy. I went home, walking through the streets wearing a kimono belonging to the hotel. I wasn't to see Tony for another three years; when I did in Portafino, Italy, he hit the floor and greeted me in front of everyone, much to my embarrassment: 'Miss Hamilton – ALABALALA, CHRISTMAS TREE!'

I met Urs in 1981, when I was twenty, after my first contract in Japan had finished. I'd flown to Switzerland with a girlfriend whose lover was Rod Stewart. She was a tall, lanky blonde who was addicted to tennis and rock stars. We arrived in Zurich for work, joined a modelling agency, and lived in a room above a noisy pub filled with young students and bikers. I worked well in Switzerland, making a decent amount of money. Brenda didn't, and sank into a deep depression, deciding finally to return to her home in Florida. In the meanwhile, I had met a Swiss boy called Urs Arsenfrauts; translated into English, his name meant 'grinning rabbit'. Urs was tall, blond and blue-eyed, with a body like Michelangelo's *David*. He was a tennis coach, part-time model, and was studying psychiatry.

I moved in with him, but continued to work. After a short while cohabiting, he suggested we should get our own pad together. Exactly what I thought I wanted and needed – a home with someone to love me; someone to care and share with. We found a place I loved, and I spent the next two months renovating it. I found pine furniture – stripping and restoring each piece – in obscure little villages in the mountains. I slowly began to build a beautiful nest. I'd spend hours, when I wasn't working, at boot sales and markets, looking for bits and pieces. Urs was away most of the time, on courses for his studies.

But I began to run out of money, and knew the big bucks were in Tokyo. I loved Urs and my new home, but I needed to earn. I packed my bags, Urs drove me to the airport, and I told him I would send back rent money. He gave me a long, lingering kiss, and we said goodbye. That was in November.

On December 25th I called home to Urs.

'Hello,' a female voice answered.

'Hello, who's that?' I enquired.

'Marianne.'

My stomach flipped. It was Urs's old girlfriend. My mind raced. What was she doing there at eight-thirty on Christmas morning?

'Marianne, it's Polly. Is Urs there?'

'No, he's not. He's away skiing with his family.'

'Marianne, what are you doing there?'

'I live here.'

'What?'

'Yes. Urs has made a beautiful apartment for me. He said he would when I left for Spain a few months ago.'

I couldn't believe what was happening. 'But, Marianne, that's my home. I painted it, I decorated it. I bought the furniture, bedding – everything. My clothes, my belongings; they've got to be there.'

'No, there's nothing of yours here,' she replied.

I sank to the floor; I was four thousand miles away. 'Marianne, look in the cellar; see if you can find my stuff. I sent him two thousand pounds in rent money.'

'I don't know about that, I sent his mail on. I do remember a brown envelope from Japan.'

'Yes, yes. That was the one.'

'Call me back, I'll go and look.'

I put down the telephone, sitting on the floor with my back against my apartment wall. My heart cracked. The slug rose in my throat, choking off my air supply. I felt as if a knife was ripping its way through my innards, destroying my dreams as viciously as someone slashing a masterpiece.

My Urs wouldn't do this, he wouldn't. She's a nutter, she's broken in. Urs would call back, telling me everything was okay. It was all just a misunderstanding.

I called back after ten minutes.

Marianne answered. 'Yes, you were right,' – her voice was thick with emotion – 'I found your belongings in black garbage sacks. I'm so sorry. He's lied to both of us.'

'Oh, my God,' I cried. 'Marianne, that was my home.'

'I thought it was mine.'

We cried together.

I spent the rest of that Christmas day with my knees drawn up to my chest, lying on the floor, crying, shocked, paralysed. That night I got drunk, and stayed drunk for two days. Years later, while in New York, I found an old address book. I called Urs's number. We chatted for a long while. He said at that time he was really screwed up. He'd even changed his name from Arsenfrauts, 'grinning rabbit', to Urs Stoller. I had the last laugh. 'Urs,' I said, 'Stoller means fruitcake' and slammed the telephone down. It was the last I heard from him.

Six months later I left Japan, and went to Sydney. This was not a considered career move, but simply because I wanted to see Australia. I joined Peter Chadwick's modelling agency. I moved in with a fun group of people in a house on Point Piper: a fantastic location in an area that was very secluded with beautiful houses right on a private stretch of beach. I would come home after a day's work, light a joint, and go fishing peacefully off the end of our jetty. I learned to windsurf, and looking back, I learned to relax.

I was modelling one day at the Seable Town House Hotel, when I bumped into Tom Jacobi. I didn't recognize him.

'Hello, you're Paula, aren't you? I met you in Japan.'

I looked at him blankly.

'You remember, you managed to get me into the nightclub.'

'Oh, yes,' I said. 'What's your name again?'

'Tom – Tom Jacobi.'

'Oh, yes.'

'Can we meet later for drinks?'

'Sure.'

We did meet, he bubbled and talked non-stop. A very different man sat opposite me from the one I'd met back in Tokyo, when I'd found him pompous and boring. Tom, tall, good-looking, lived in Hamburg and was over here for *Stern* magazine. We met most days on the beach after work. After about a week he said he was going to New Caledonia, and would I join him? I said I'd think about it. I honestly had no feelings for this man, although I found his persistence flattering. I declined his offer, saying I was going to France to stay with friends before I went on to Germany for work. He flashed two business flight tickets at me.

'Polly, come on. You may never be in this part of the world again. New Caledonia is only a few hours away. It's a beautiful French colonial island. Why not come with me as an adventure?'

I said I'd think about it. I didn't know how to say that I would love to come – if there were separate rooms. My only experience with men, outside work, had been based around sexual relationships. After all, he was right. It was only a few hours away by plane, and I could see Mollie in Paris later. I had enough money to take some time off, and it was only for a matter of weeks.

We travelled in a minibus, and slept in it. New Caledonia was so very beautiful; mountainous, with hardly any tourists, the island was totally unspoilt. After our trek, we spent four days at a Club Med resort; I disliked it immensely.

One day, lying on the beach with Tom mooning over me, I felt suffocated. Suddenly I jumped up, shouting, 'Last one in the pool's a ninny' and charged into the hotel pool. Diving in, racing-style, I skimmed the surface; Tom, six feet four and weighing about eighty-five kilos, hit the water and disappeared, only to come up with his face smashed in. We had dived in at the shallow end, in about only two and a half feet of water. Poor Tom, his nose was badly gashed and broken. He nearly passed out. Since it would be quicker for me to take him to the hospital than wait for an ambulance, I got him into the minibus and drove, aware of every pothole and bump. At the hospital, they stitched his nose without anaesthetic and bandaged his face.

He rested for a few days, and then we flew back to Sydney. Tom asked if I would come and stay with him for a while in Germany. But I needed to go to France. We left Australia on a Hamburg flight with a Paris stop-over. I told him I would call him in a few days.

Instead, when I arrived, Tom called me.

'How did you get my number?' I asked.

'When you were talking to Mollie in Sydney,' he answered. 'You left the number on a hotel pad. How are you?'

'Well,' I answered, perturbed and a little annoyed.

'When are you coming to Hamburg?' he insisted.

'I don't know, Tom, I'll call you. I'm going to Fontainebleau to see Mollie. I haven't seen her for six months. I will call you when I've made some plans.' Putting the telephone down, I thought, What a bloody cheek!

Soon forgetting the incident, I took a train to see Mollie. I'd missed her so much, and we had a lot to talk about. Fontaine-bleau was beautiful, and so was the home of Mollie's sister and her new husband. We talked, laughed, and took long walks. I did love Mollie so.

One night before supper, the telephone rang. It was Tom. I couldn't believe it. 'Tom, how did you get this number?'

'I called Mollie's flat in Paris, and her flatmate gave it to me.'

'Tom, for Christ's sake, will you stop tracking me down? If I want to call you, I will.' I put the telephone down. Mollie had been standing next to me so I told her the whole story.

'Oh, Polly, poor guy. Look, it sounds as if he really likes you.

You are going to Hamburg for work, he could be a good friend. Call him back, tell him you're sorry.'

I did, and he was delighted.

In Hamburg, Tom met me at the airport, and told me he'd called Parker Zed, one of the top modelling agencies, and they'd said they would see me. I asked him where I would be staying; he replied, with him. He still didn't get it – I didn't want a relationship with him.

We went to his flat and it was charming. I put my bags down, and looked around. His photos lined the wall. 'These are very good.'

'Thank you,' he responded with obvious pride.

Why didn't I have any feelings for this guy? He was good looking, had taste and style, was well educated and obviously well off. Despite all of this, he just didn't do it for me.

'Come on. Parker Zed are expecting you.'

I freshened up, grabbed my portfolio, then went across to the agency.

'Hello,' said Dorothy. 'So this is Tom's golden girl.'

Tom blushed, and I felt very uncomfortable.

'Let's have a look at your portfolio.' Dorothy flipped the pages. 'Oh dear, oh dear, dear, dear. Darling girl, your book is a disaster. You'll never work with this book in Europe. My suggestion is, and it's only a suggestion: you go to Milan and try to work there. I can get you into an agency. The rest is up to you, and how hard you are prepared to work. When can you leave?'

Dorothy was right. My portfolio from Japan was irrelevant when it came to Western modelling. Although their magazines and catalogues carried western clothes, they were portrayed in the Japanese style: blue hair, black eyebrows, crazy poses, et-cetera. I had to go to the capital of the fashion world, Milan, and from there I could move into Paris fashion. The reason for this was that Germany and England rarely booked models who had not been to Milan and Paris. Once you had editorials in your portfolio from *Vogue, Elle* and *Marie Claire*, the top three magazines, you were recognized as a commodity; you'd proven yourself. If you could also model for the top designers, Versace, Valentino, Armani, you were definitely well on your way.

I looked at her. 'Now,' I replied.

'No,' Tom cried. 'You've only just got here.'

It was Friday, so I agreed to stay the weekend and leave on Monday.

Tom took me to stay with his mother in Kukels, a tiny village about an hour and a half outside Hamburg. We drove through the village, and on for about a mile before turning down a tiny little track for about two hundred yards. There were elder blossoms and a hedge on either side. On the right, at the bottom of the track was the house: the most enchanting little cottage, snuggled into the land. Wild flowers grew in abundance; it was a charming haven. Three-quarters of the way around the cottage was a beautiful lake. The house rested on the tip of the lake, jutting out over the water.

'Tom, it's beautiful,' I exclaimed. 'I love it.'

Tom's mother came out of the house. 'Tom, Tom, how wonderful for you to come, and who is this?'

Tom hadn't told his mother I was coming. 'Mama, this is Paula.'

'Poala, what a beautiful name. Come, come, you're just in time for tea, and I've made a cake. Yes I have, so lucky, I had no idea you were coming. Tom, Tom, you naughty boy, you didn't tell me she was so pretty.'

I blushed. So he had told her, he just didn't tell her I was coming.

I adored Tom's mother, Anna, the moment I met her. Her hair was thick and white, her face full of laughter lines, bright blue eyes and a charming smile. The inside of her home was breathtakingly simple. The kitchen overlooked the lake. Three cats slept on a sofa by the kitchen table. The warmth of baking filled the kitchen, making the air as soft as flour.

'Come, come, sit and tell me everything.' She gestured me to sit with her.

We talked for hours until eventually I said, 'So on Monday I leave for Italy.'

'Oh, such a shame, you've just got here. Well, maybe Tom can visit you at weekends, and you can come here whenever you like.' She was bewitching, warm, safe. I wanted to stay there forever.

The sky turned pink, I could hear gabbling geese.

'Ah, my babies want their supper.' She opened the kitchen door, the lawn was full of wild ducks and geese; all waddling up towards the house. 'Heeah, burra, burra, burra,' she cried, while scattering corn for them to eat.

'Gosh, Tom, there must be a hundred of them out there.'

'Probably, my mother feeds the geese and ducks, and knows them all by name, individually. She's been feeding them for years. Come and meet the hens.' Three fat, brown farm hens waddled up to Tom, and started pecking his toes. He giggled.

Maybe I could have feelings for this man after all.

Supper consisted of lettuce grown in the garden, roasted fennel with cheese sauce, and home-made brown bread. Sounds plain, but it was delicious. That night, tucked up in Tom's room under the eaves, I said, 'Thank you for bringing me here. Your mother is very special, and her home is beautiful.'

'I knew you'd like it,' replied Tom.

On Monday I left for Italy – as planned.

Parker Zed sent me to Milan. I needed this break to make it in Europe, and it happened in the most peculiar manner.

I was sent by the Milan agents to see Fabrizio Ferri, a famous photographer who would rarely give his time to newcomers. I'd only been in Milan twenty-four hours, didn't speak the language and the city was very strange to me. I took a taxi and arrived hot and flustered. I found Fabrizio in a studio surrounded by light boxes, negatives and contact sheets, with two assistants hovering in the background.

Armed with my portfolio, which had now been cut down to

only four pages – the rest of my photos were not acceptable and the agency felt they would hinder rather than help – I felt very empty and my confidence abandoned me.

'Fabrizio . . .' I said. He waved me away without looking up, his eye glued to a magnifying glass, studying a black and white photo. I stood back and waited patiently for a few minutes. I began to feel agitated, so I approached him again and this time he looked up.

'Short-haired girls only!' he barked.

My hand absent-mindedly went up to the ponytail that hung down my back.

'Couldn't you just look at my book, please?' I whispered.

'NO, short-haired girls only!' and he turned back to his photos with a dismissive gesture.

I felt my face grow hot. I'd bothered to come – the least he could do was look at my portfolio. I tried once more.

'Mr Ferri . . .'

'NO!'

I grabbed the scissors off his desk, cut off my ponytail at the nape of my neck, slammed it down in front of him, picked up my portfolio and tore it in two.

'Short-haired girl with no book!' I barked back.

The room fell silent. Fearful glances passed between the assistants and then, very slowly, this great bear of a photographer leaned back in his chair, picked up my hair, which was at least ten inches long and still held by its ribbon, and fingered it thoughtfully.

Fabrizio Ferri made my name in Europe, booked me solid for four months for *Donna* magazine, and gave me a memorable black and white cover that the fashion industry still remembers today. He taught me how to pose work and behave in a studio; he trained my eye for detail. He made me believe, in the hours I worked for him, that I was beautiful. He gave me work in a city where thousands of models fail every week. He made my dreams come true.

It was Fabrizio who developed my ability, not to model, but to *act* the clothes I was wearing, to portray and develop the character like a vignette. Each garment became a little scene in my head. I would become what I wore.

He used words: 'Your profile is aristocratic – use it.' So I would fantasize about being an English noblewoman and the harsh studio walls that encased us would melt away. I asked for classical music to be piped through and magically I would be able to slip into scenes, while soothing sounds from Fabrizio encouraged, cajoled and wooed me. I could transpose myself from the studio to the Alps of Switzerland, imagining the icy winds against my face, tugging at the fabric of my heavy coat, dogs at my feet waiting for their mistress as I boldly stared out over the land, my legacy left to me by my dying father. I had come here not to weep but to gaze upon my heritage. So through 'acting out' the clothes I was wearing, I taught myself to portray the image that was needed to illustrate them.

This is how I worked, and how I've always worked, in studios ever since. I need music and space, and whether it is for a simple catalogue or a shoot for *Vogue*, I give my all. I once remember asking a stylist in New York why I always got the crap stuff, and the reply was that I had got the ability to make any clothes look good. 'You make them belong, you can pull it off. That's the power of selling.'

At least in that situation my attitude was correct. I wouldn't let myself down by letting an outfit get the better of me, so I sold my heart out. Models would say to me, 'How can you be so enthusiastic, the clothes are ghastly?' But I felt it was a challenge to make the garments look good. My self-esteem was sometimes so low that a bad garment could sometimes make me feel as if I deserved nothing better. But I always had my fantasies and would just sell, sell, sell.

But Milan was a mixture of fantasy and frightful reality.

Model scouts would look all over the world for new young faces, who often came from the States, from provincial towns. They were naive, most of them had never travelled and some were as young as fourteen. The scouts would find them, convince their parents and, before they knew it, they were on a plane to Milan to an agency.

A portfolio was needed – immediately hair would be cut, faces and nails scrubbed and these young girls would be put in front of photographers. They would then be told they were in debt to the agency for flights, photos, accommodation and living expenses. If they were successful and worked immediately, they were out of the initial danger.

However, if this was not the case, the effects could and would be devastating. The agent would say something like: 'Well, we've invested all this into you, you're not working, so how are you going to pay us back?'

The young hopeful was penniless and powerless, and therefore easy prey for what would come next. I heard awful stories, such as agents telling youngsters they could spend the weekend on a friend's yacht. 'Get a tan, you'll feel better, and by the way, my friend has a large percentage of the agency – if he likes you, who knows?'

So off the girls would go, oblivious to what was being set up. They were seduced, given drugs and alcohol. The agent was then happy because his backers were being entertained; if the girls continued to do badly, they were sent back to the States.

I was lucky, I was working; successful and arrogant, the agents never approached me. My whole persona gave me a protective barrier. My nickname was 'The Ice Queen of Milan'. At the occasional dinners I attended, the playboys would joke that I was a lesbian and I never corrected them, just kept myself apart. I bought my own coke and belonged to myself.

I was able to help some of the younger unfortunate girls. Agents would only pay for their hotels during the week so that they would have no one but 'friends' to stay with at the weekends. Those who refused had nowhere to sleep so I stuffed my hotel room with mattresses at weekends and went travelling with Tom. I soon became Mama Polly again to the many girls who slept there.

Not all agents behaved this way, and today, twelve years later, Milan is finally cleaning up its act. When I was there it was horrendous. One agency who refused to pay a protection fee to the Mafia was blown up. Beauty and money are still a powerful combination, even today.

My life in Milan was hectic, yet all the time I worked there I was travelling back to Germany at weekends to be with Tom and Anna. I was torn by my success and by the home life that Tom and his mother represented. My life in Germany became tormented. At weekends Anna's home offered peace and tranquillity. Meals were prepared simply and grown from her vegetable garden. Books were read, flowers were planted and in the long winters we skated on the lake below the cottage, made snowmen, trekked across snowy fields to feed her animal friends, deer, birds and wild cats.

Then came Monday mornings, and along with them flight schedules and agents haggling over my time. Paris wanted me for *Marie Claire*, Milan wanted me for Italian *Vogue*, and Tom wanted me for himself. Half of me wanted the success and glamour, and half of me wanted a normal life with Anna.

I bought two horses and stabled them close to Anna's home. I desperately wanted both lives, I felt I was living them both. Yet not living them truly made me feel unfulfilled and torn in two. The constant pressure of magazine editors and agents all telling me to stay in Paris for three months at a time, and that Tom could visit, brought into sharp contrast Anna and Tom's advice to me not to model because the life was empty, and to do something else.

I soon discovered Anna's wine cellar and would take a bottle and my flute and walk across the fields to an isolated ridge, uncork the bottle and drink until I felt the warm peaceful glow hit my stomach, pushing all my worries, doubts and insecurities away. Surrounded by trees, hills and meadows I would play my flute, contented and at peace in my solitude. Then I would have to stop and face the thought of going back and seeing them both but, with the warm wine in my stomach, I could soon dig out my 'bravado' mask and could then walk home quite happily.

It wasn't long before Anna realized her wine supply was going down, and that, plus stories from Tom about my drinking, soon brought her to confront me.

We were sitting by the fire – Tom was out of the country that weekend – when Anna asked me gently why I was drinking so much. I laughed and tried to shrug it off. Anna was a vegetarian and had chosen a spiritual pathway ten years earlier when she divorced her husband for adultery. She had known about his affair with her best friend, but had chosen to ignore it with the help of anti-depressants and sleeping pills, hoping it would go away. When it didn't, she realized she had to take control of her life, so she stopped the pills, cleared her head and confronted her husband. When he had made his choice, she served him with divorce papers and set about building the life she had decided upon for herself. She had recognized her behavioural patterns, and had done something about them. This meant that, for me, there was no hiding from her knowledge. She knew what I did, deep down, which was that I had a problem – I didn't know how to stop drinking.

I ran away from Anna that day. I ran away from the love and support and the genuine care she offered me. I ran away because I was ashamed, because the feelings were too painful without alcohol. The idea of never again being able to medicate those feelings with alcohol was too overwhelming.

I truly understand those drunks on the streets that stagger and stink and have not an ounce of dignity. They ran away, too! The only difference between them and me are circumstances, luck, chance – call it what you will.

CHAPTER THREE

Burn Out

I literally packed my bags after my conversation with Anna, leaving behind me all the beautiful things I'd collected and bought for our Hamburg apartment. I left my horses with the kind farmer who'd looked after them. I just packed up and walked away.

I returned to London and spent a wild two months living there. One day I looked around. I found myself coked out of my head yet again.

The feeling coke gave me was fantastic. It made me feel beautiful, seductive, clever, queen of the castle; capable of doing anything I wanted. It made me feel excited, generous, loving. The feelings were intensified beyond belief. But the crash, oh God; the crashing-down feelings were directly from hell. My mind would say to me, 'Oh, oh, you're really fucking it up, Hamilton. Now you've got a whole day in the studio, with stylists pulling you around, make-up artists inches from your face. You're sweating, Hamilton. It's so hot inside, but you're sweating already. How will your make-up stay on?' I would lie frozen in my bed, unable to even shift position. I remembered how, when I was little, and really believed a bogeyman or a ghost was in my room, I pulled the covers right up to my chin, legs and arms frozen, unable to move. That's exactly what it felt like and yet I did it over and over again.

The little mews house where I was staying with a friend looked like a bomb had gone off in it. Clothes were strewn everywhere, ashtrays were overflowing, empty champagne and vodka bottles littered the floor. The curtains were still drawn, shutting out the day. When you are coked out of your head you want the night to last forever. Reality comes with the dawn, so if there was coke left, I'd take it; if there was booze left, I'd drink it; if whoever I was with crashed, I would pick up the phone and start calling friends, family, the States, Tokyo – it didn't matter who or where. I would try my best to get the time right. I had soon discovered that no one wanted to speak after being woken up in the middle of the night.

I didn't ask Christopher if he minded me using the phone. I suddenly picked up the receiver and dialled Elite's number in New York. Elite is a major modelling agency.

'May I speak to Monique Pillard?'

'Just one moment,' came the reply.

After about five minutes the voice asked, 'Who's calling?'

'Paula Hamilton.'

'Just one moment.' After a short while the voice said, 'I'm afraid Monique cannot take calls. Can you call back?'

'Yes,' I replied, 'after you tell her I'm a model. I'm in the March issue of the French *Marie Claire*, Italian *Vogue* and *Elle* magazines.' I gave all the page numbers, saying I would call back in half an hour. I added, if Monique would not pick up my call, I would be joining Fords, her competitor.

I put the phone down, and felt the adrenalin rush through my body. I checked my coke supply – two more grams left; very rarely did I have this amount left after being up all night. It was now two in the morning. I sat on the floor by the phone.

Christopher was snoring softly. I could never understand how anyone on a nose-load of coke could either sleep, eat or not talk. Crashing from coke was my biggest nightmare, it could last up to four or five hours.

I took up a credit card from the bedside table and used it to grind the crystals into powder, then scraped and divided them into two lines the size of two Swan Vesta matchsticks. Rolling a twenty-pound note into a straw, I lifted the mirror to my face, stuck the straw up my nose and sniffed up each nostril. The coke wasn't very good, it brought tears to my eyes. I looked around the room for something to drink. Nothing. I padded down the stairs to the kitchen, and opened up the fridge freezer. Bingo – a bottle of excellent Russian vodka, iced to perfection, and two little hit glasses. I pulled a bottle of champagne from the crate on the floor, picked up two champagne glasses and trotted back up the stairs. I unscrewed the top of the vodka bottle and poured myself a hit.

I picked up the phone and pressed the redial button.

Same receptionist, same request, only this time Monique Pillard came on the line. ''Allo,' she said in her French accent.

'Maybe you've seen my tear sheets.'

'Well, I know your name. You're with Gerard of Paris Planning. We've spoken of you.'

'Good.' My stomach was doing a wibble-wobble, yet nothing could be detected in my voice. 'Do you want me or not?'

'We do.'

'I need work papers, a visa and a flight that I want you to pick up the tab for, plus one week's stay at the Plaza.'

Monique didn't reply immediately, and it was several seconds before she said, 'That's not how we usually do things.'

'There's nothing usual about me or this deal.'

She laughed, warming to me. 'Quite demanding, aren't you?'

'Yes.'

'We'll put you in Model Management to promote you, then move you to the main top-booking board.'

'Wrong, I don't need promoting, I'm going straight to the top-booking board. I need your top booker to look after me, and I'll work my ass off.'

I asked how many clients I could see in a day. I would need to do a week of 'go-and-sees', to meet clients and photographers.

'About five.'

'Why so few?'

'It will take some time to work out the train system.'

'Wrong again, I'll see twenty a day, and you'll give me a chauffeur-driven car for one week. Do we have a deal?'

By now she was letting out full belly-laughs, and asked me why I hadn't let Gerard negotiate the deal for me. I said because Gerard was a prick, and he wouldn't have got what I was asking for; also, she then would have been tied to him, giving him five per cent of my first year's earnings.

'By the way,' I added, 'he's not having it and neither are you. So, instead of twenty per cent of my earnings, you can have me for fifteen per cent. If I make over a hundred and fifty thousand dollars my first and second year, it stays. Anything over and we'll negotiate it down.'

'Stop,' she called down the line, 'stop', yet all the while laughing.

'Oh, and one more thing. I fly first class and expect a car to pick me up at the airport. I have a booking in Arizona in two weeks' time for one week so you need to get me a national ticket only. I look forward to receiving my work papers. You're busy. If you put me back to reception, I'm sure someone can take the details. Monique, I look forward to meeting you soon.'

'You're tough, Paula.'

'I know. Till then.'

'Till then.'

The line between us was closed.

I poured myself another vodka, threw it down the hatch, and took up the warm bottle of champagne, which I thought needed chilling. I flew downstairs, yanked the fridge door open, pulled out a chilled bottle and ran back up the stairs. I shook the bottle and popped the cork which missed my friend Christopher, snoring in his bed, by an inch, spraying half the bottle of champagne over him.

'What the fuck?' he yelled, rudely awakened.

'Christopher, I did it, I did it.'

'Did what, you bloody idiot?'

'I've joined Elite – top division, work papers, flights, chauffeur, car, hotel, all expenses paid, and they're only getting fifteen per cent.'

Christopher looked at me and grinned. He'd been married to

61

a top agent in London, and knew I'd pulled off one hell of a deal. We drank to my success, had more coke and jumped in the bath. As I didn't have any clean clothes with me, and as he was only five feet eight inches, I dressed in one of his Savile Row suits: tie and shirt, crocodile shoes, cufflinks, the lot.

We left the mews, coked, drunk and high as kites, and went to Harry's Bar, and had breakfast which consisted of more champagne and coke. We were oblivious to everyone's stares and I revelled in the glow of what I had just done. How I would have loved to go back to all those schools who had said I wouldn't amount to anything. I was going to be famous and rich. Bugger the lot of them.

Monique was true to her word. Three weeks later I was at JFK, flying in from Arizona.

The week there had been a complete nightmare. The job boring, the weather relentlessly hot, and there was yet another stylist who couldn't understand why my size seven feet wouldn't fit into a size five shoe.

'Couldn't you just squash your feet into the shoes, just for the shot?'

These shots could last up to half an hour. It wasn't pretty; my feet were so sore I was in agony for a week after. If you complained, then the stylist would back-stab you and the client wouldn't book you again. I'd learnt this the hard way in Paris earlier on in my career. On my composite, which contains details of me and my vital statistics, it very clearly states what size feet I have. They're thick feet, and that, plus the combination of their size and the heat, meant they became swollen, making my toes look like chipolata sausages. At the end of each shoot, every toe had a corn plaster on it, my heels were rubbed raw and I'd written about three poems all about feet.

Walking out of JFK, or rather hobbling, my feet still a mess, the noise hit me, with people jostling, some not smelling so good, mixed with women in furs, luggage boys in tow. Blacks, whites, Mexicans, Chinese.

Customs hadn't been such a nice experience either. The official who stamped my passport looked at me. 'Model, eh?'

'Yes.'

'With or without your clothes on?'

I thought, If only you knew I was capable of twisting your nose off and feeding it to you, you jerk; you wouldn't say things like that. What I felt beneath my anger was shame and the *Mayfair* spread flashed before my eyes.

'With my clothes on,' I smiled sweetly, but thinking, You old fuck.

I took a taxi into New York, heading for the Plaza. I knew about the Plaza because I have a book called *Eloise*. It's the story of a precocious child who lived in the Plaza, causing havoc. This book had a big impact on me when I was a child because I had learnt to read with its help. Eloise was grand, arrogant and extremely mischievous, and caused chaos wherever she went. I had so identified with her character as a child, that I had always promised myself that I would stay at the Plaza on my first trip to New York. The taxi pulled up outside. At the entrance were doormen dripping with gold tassels, blue coats and white gloves. I walked in and my baggage followed me up to the front desk.

'My name's Paula Hamilton,' I announced. 'You have a booking for me.'

'Yes, Miss Hamilton, we were expecting you.'

They were expecting me! Now I felt that I had arrived. The bell captain showed me to my room. On our way we passed a portrait of Eloise. I asked the bell captain to stop. I walked up to the portrait and smiled at Eloise. 'Eloise,' I said, 'I'm here, I'm really here.' I swear she winked back at me.

My room was beautiful and overlooked Central Park. The weather was at its best, a sunny spring day. The bathroom was fantastic, with a four-legged bath, towels the size of sheets, and a basket full of goodies: soaps, shampoos, conditioners, lotions, perfumed powders and miniature bottles of scent. I looked in the mirror, my face stared back at me. My skin was flawless; my eyes were large, bright and excited. I looked and wondered what they saw in me. Had I imagined all this? I was twenty-four years old, and at the top of my profession, a profession that turned thousands of hopefuls away in Europe and the States. Yet here I was at the Plaza with one of the biggest and most powerful agencies in the world. Whatever did they see in me?

The phone rang and I ran to answer it.

'Paula?'

'Yes.'

'Monique here. How do you like your room?'

'Oh, it's beautiful.'

'No complaints then?'

'Not yet.'

'You must be tired.'

'I am.'

'Then why don't you take today off, have a look around? Come in tomorrow morning around eleven, we'll sign you in and perhaps you and I could get together over lunch?'

'That sounds great, Momo,' I replied.

'How did you know my pet name?' she asked, surprised.

'I didn't.'

'You're a funny girl, Paula, see you tomorrow.'

I put the phone down, and sat on the edge of the bed. The sun filled the room. The large windows had swagged curtains hanging from them. It's really happened, I thought. I'm here in New York, I'm a top international model.

I burst into tears, sobs hacking their way through me, knowing it wouldn't be long before they found out I was a fraud. I couldn't possibly keep fooling them, someone was going to realize soon that I wasn't beautiful, I wasn't even photogenic. I got up off the bed and walked over to the fridge. I pulled out a chilled vodka miniature and half a bottle of champagne – my two friends. The little bottle went down in one and the champagne I sipped in a bubble bath, soon feeling better.

I chose my favourite outfit – knee-length jodhpurs and a cashmere hacking jacket – and trotted downstairs. I had five hundred dollars in my back pocket and went straight to the tea room, where I ordered an Earl Grey and a vodka and tonic. A small orchestra in the corner was playing music from *Doctor Zhivago*; I felt like a million dollars. Suddenly my name was called. I looked up and there in front of me was a stunning brunette – Julie, another big name model from Fords.

'Hi,' she said. 'When did you get in?'

'Today.'

'Fantastic. Are you here long?'

'Couple of years.'

'You staying here?'

'The agency's paying.'

'Lucky you.' She was obviously impressed.

I asked her to join me. She promptly did and spied my drink.

'Vodka and tonic,' I responded to the question on her face.

She said she'd thought it was water, which we both laughed at. After a couple of drinks she asked if I needed to go to the Ladies, I said I did and we went, a little high and giggly. I passed the portrait of Eloise and I paused and saluted; this became a ritual gesture for me. In the rest room Julie pulled out a vial of coke. My face lit up and my heart gave a familiar jerk. Four little spoons went under four little nostrils – how I loved the rush. I gave her a big hug and asked where I could purchase the same. She said she'd get it for me, I handed over three hundred dollars and off she went. She was to meet me in my room in an hour.

Four hours later she returned. The waiting had been agony so I'd drunk a little too much, not wanting to crash, not wanting to believe she might not be back. When I heard her knock I flew off the bed and opened the door – bless her.

'Have you got it?'

'I have.'

'Oh brill, bloody brill.'

I took the packet from her, three whole grams. I picked up the house phone and ordered a bottle of Cristal and caviar. Julie asked me if she could take a bath.

'Be my guest, I'll line us up a few.'

The waiter arrived with the order and I served us up the champagne, caviar and coke. Julie lay in the bath and I sat on the floor. I'd never been happier than at that moment and I wanted it to last forever.

Julie looked at me. 'Come over here.'

I leant over and she touched my lips with her fingers, her eyes looked so sad.

'What's wrong?' I asked.

Two tears escaped from her eyes and fell on to her breasts. She pulled me towards her and kissed my mouth, ever so gently, then looked at my face to see my reaction. I wasn't turned on, but I knew she needed comfort – for what I didn't know, I just knew she needed comfort. Suddenly her expression changed; she slowly slid down the bath and disappeared under the bubbles. When she came up, it was as if the whole incident hadn't taken place.

'Do you want to go dancing?' she asked brightly. 'I know this fab club.'

'Love to.'

'Got something I can borrow?'

'Yep, anything you like.'

We spent a good two hours going through every outfit I owned. The room was in chaos, and an image of Eloise flashed through my mind. At last, both ready, both looking wickedly wonderful, we left the room, but not before I called housekeeping. I asked for the room to be cleaned and the clothes to be put away. What bliss. I could get used to this lifestyle very quickly. Julie and I danced the night away in a club called Limelight. I'd been to plenty of clubs but nothing like this. The club itself was in a huge converted church, massive. We got in by walking straight up to the bouncers, ignoring the huge queue that practically went halfway around the block. The bouncers took one look at us and let us in. We didn't pay and our egos soared a little higher.

Once inside we headed straight for the rest room, refilled our nostrils, applied more make-up and headed for the bar. As you are aware by now, my drink was vodka followed by champagne. It was Julie's also – it seemed the best thing when high on coke. I knocked a couple back, and we headed for the dance floor. Soon clearing a space for ourselves, we danced and danced. The music, the atmosphere, the effects of the coke and alcohol, made me feel that heaven could be like this, and if it was, I wouldn't mind dying at all. I felt financially secure, I was with a friend I liked, and in a profession I knew would last forever – wouldn't it?

After being in New York for about six weeks, I found my own apartment. It was a brownstone and I loved it. Wooden floors, shutters, fireplace, four-legged bath-tub and a view from the bedroom window of a small garden and trees. I began to furnish it slowly by visiting junk shops, going to garage sales in Connecticut, New England. I loved to drive alone and explore but this began to happen less and less.

Tom eventually tracked me down and followed me to New York to confront me. He was hurt, angry, disillusioned and confused. I sat with a bottle of wine; my body was there, but my mind and my heart were safely tucked away inside that bottle. I heard, felt and saw nothing except a man who had tried to stand in my way. It was only when Tom had left that I crawled into bed with my two Siamese kittens and cried and cried and cried.

I made my mind up quite early in my career that I was not going to do catwalk modelling. It was all because of my subconscious self-protection system, although I never really admitted the truth to myself.

To do catwalk, I'd be travelling, sleeping, eating and breathing the same people, the same girls, designers, stylists, choreographers, and they'd get to see me, know me and I'd be found out. Twelve years ago, coke was a common substance used in the fashion business, and I was already hooked. Champagne flowed by the bucketload, and I didn't have a control button, a 'stop, you've had enough' button. Subconsciously I knew that in catwalk modelling I'd get caught or some disastrous thing would happen. Also I lacked the ability to know how to behave, how to make friends and keep them. My inadequacies were hidden behind various masks – of anger, of arrogance, of aloofness – to ensure that no one got too close. I could control photographic work more easily, so I tended to stick with that.

I had learned some pretty tough lessons. My mentor, Momo, the president of Elite, would say to me, 'You can't catch flies with vinegar.' She meant that I had a reputation for being difficult and warned that if I brought it with me it would not be tolerated and I wouldn't work. Eventually I listened to her and started to become more aware of all the other people and jobs going on around me in the studio.

I had taken the stylists for granted, never thinking how the clothes, shoes, belts, and other accessories arrived at the studio. I had never realized how important the stylist was, or thought where they might be heading; most of the fashion-magazine editors started out as stylists. Sometimes they had just a day to find shoes and clothes for a model: the right styles, sizes, what was in and what was out of fashion. Some grumbled and pushed their ideas on to clients, sometimes they just delivered what was asked of them. Most don't have assistants, so if a button is missing, or a garment has a bad crease down the front, causing a re-shoot, the blame falls on the head of the stylist. So, if I covered their asses by being aware of what I was wearing, if I didn't scuff the shoes, or spill coffee on an outfit, or sit down in clothes prior to shooting, I would get big brownie points.

I became even more professional, and liked a little better. Comments began to come back to my agency: 'she's helpful', 'a great model', 'it's difficult to take a bad picture of her'. I made a point of being aware of photographers' assistants, realizing that one day they too might become big names. I started to include them into my day; before, I'm ashamed to say, I had been totally unaware of them.

Make-up and hair in New York is a rare luxury on set; you are meant to be able to do your own. Coming back to work in England was a real shock; by then I was used to doing my own, and being in control of my look. I have pissed off and upset many a make-up artist and hair stylist in my time by doing my own hair and face.

I had a drug problem. I knew this in my heart but I thought I could handle it. I began to spend my money before I earned it. The agency president became suspicious. 'Why do you need money, Pol?' The name Momo gave me. 'Do you do coke?'

'Yes.'

'Lots?'

'Not really.'

'But enough to ask for advances? Pol, you're making a lot of money, therefore you're doing a lot of coke.'

'Well, maybe a little more than I thought.'

'Listen, you owe the agency eleven thousand dollars, so you're going to learn to live on a budget until you square up and cut even. Okay? If you have a problem you'll soon know it.'

So I allowed the agency to put me on a budget. Enough food for me and my cats, Rigor Mortis and Moët Chandon, house and hotel bills, sundries and travel. It went well because I was proving I didn't have a problem and I enjoyed the challenge. In less than a month I'd paid back the agency. In that month I awoke every day with no hangover, no headache, no heebee-jeebees and I felt fresh and very much alive.

To celebrate my debt being paid off I called my girlfriend/coke dealer.

'Hey, Polly, where've you been?'

'I've been working my butt off. How about a little fun?'

'What do you want?'

'Couple of grams.'

'Why not meet me for supper and we'll hit a couple of night-clubs?'

'Sounds good to me.'

You see, at that point, no one really knew the extent of my addiction and how soon it would grow completely out of control. During the day I put on a good show for the clients, photographers, make-up artists, hairdressers, stylists and other models. During the night I would hang out with my dealer who would keep up and keep me company alongside the little white powder. No one knew me, I didn't even know myself any more. I didn't know how to get close to anyone, let alone myself. When you've so much to hide the last thing you want is intimacy. Yet the lonely side of oneself needs it. I struggled with this on a daily basis, letting people in only to push them out again.

If you got too close, I'd run before you found out I was a fake, that I was not who I portrayed. On the inside I felt tortured and lived in hell. You'd then relate stories back to me about the evening. You'd say, 'Gosh, you spoke all through dinner. Were you nervous?' My insides would crawl with sober shame. We could not have known each other very well anyway, because I never got close to anyone. So before you saw any more of the real me, I'd hide from you.

I heard people saying, 'I like being on my own. That way, I feel okay. It's when I'm with people that I have problems.' I started to convince myself that I liked being alone. So I started to go out on my own. This happened in New York, around 1985, a year after I'd arrived. Of course, I couldn't get through the front door without having drunk at least half a bottle of champagne, and perhaps a little vodka. I'd meet people in bars, nightclubs – and I'd meet my dealer. I'll call her Charlie.

Charlie came from a diplomatic family. She'd grown up in the Philippines. She'd had a good upbringing, and had found herself, aged twenty-seven, divorced and living in New York. Somehow she'd got hooked on coke and dealt a little to friends in order to maintain her own supply. Charlie had a comfortable apartment on the East Side and a zippy little English car. I was her best friend and her best customer.

I'd go to her on a Friday. At first we'd go out dancing, perhaps to a restaurant. But mostly we sat in her apartment, drinking, taking coke and talking. We talked for hours, days – non-stop, until we'd gone through however much she'd supplied me with. After a while I noticed her apartment was looking really good. Newly decorated, new carpets, curtains and furniture. I thought she must be doing really well. She'd temp for law firms, and supply lawyers, clerks and whoever else with her own little magic, that white powder.

One day I said to her, 'You must be doing really well. This must have cost you a fortune.'

I thought of my own apartment: brownstone, one bedroom, beautiful bathroom, fireplaces, wooden floors, high ceilings. I had cable TV, an indoor tree that was twelve feet tall, and antique desk and chair, a sofa and a bed – that was it. My walk-in wardrobe was quite sparse. Clothes weren't high on the agenda. During the day I lived in Levis, white shirts and cowboy boots. When I went out at night I'd wear a tuxedo.

Charlie looked at me. 'Polly, all this that you see, is from you.'

'What?' I looked around, confused. I didn't understand.

'Look, you dummy. You buy coke from me. This is the profit.'

I sat down. 'I'm stunned. How much am I spending?'

'Oh, a good one to one and a half thousand dollars per month.'

'You're kidding.'

'No, I'm not.'

'Bloody hell.' I laughed. 'Shit, are you sure?'

'Of course I'm sure.'

'So every time I score from you, you think – great, another pair of curtains.'

'Something like that.'

'Well, you've got it made. You get to do as much coke as you like and you get curtains –'

She cut me off. 'I don't like what you're getting at. This is what I do. This is how I make my living. If you can't afford coke and curtains, then quit buying the stuff.'

'Don't be ridiculous, a girl's got to have a couple of vices. Got a gram?'

When I did go to a party I would look with care at people who were relaxed, normal, having fun. I thought to myself, How do you do it? Then I'd put the thought out of my head and put my hand out for another vodka. Putting down drugs and alcohol is easy, not picking them up is difficult as hell, and painful, confusing. I go to AA now, not because every day I'm afraid to drink, but because I know I need to change my behaviour. If I don't continue daily to commit to change, I WILL slip back into my old thoughts, patterns and behaviour. It's only a matter of time. I know, because in the past, after a year of sobriety, I've picked up a drink and gotten drunk. Waking up all the past misery. Waking up with me.

It makes me shudder just to think about relapsing and having another drink. My head goes, my fear chokes me, my imagination runs away with me. Could I keep it a secret? If I talk about it in AA or NA, will someone shop me to the press? Will the press print? Will clients drop me? Will I be able to stand the ridicule, the low self-worth, the pain, the self-obsession? No, thank you, no way. I'd rather shoot myself and get it over with. Until I came into recovery and stayed (when this book is published I'll be five years clean), it was only then that I realized how painful my life had been, and how much time of it spent trying to shut out the agony I felt mentally.

I write this with a feeling of great tenderness towards myself. I say, 'Polly darling, we never, ever have to go back to that.'

Towards the end of my drug-taking days, I thought of suicide on an hourly/daily basis – please God, I want to die. No one should have to live like this. Somewhere deep inside – the part of me that hadn't been silenced with my fear – was a small flicker of hope and a tiny piece of sanity telling me there had to be a different way. Not knowing how to reach out for help, not knowing if I'd be heard, not knowing how to stop. Now that is agony.

Whilst working for Revlon on the 'Rich and Famous' campaign for lips and nails with Patrick Demarchelier – the photographer who took that beautiful photograph of the Princess of Wales – who would have believed that the face that stared out of that campaign, looking so distinguished and elegant, was as high as a kite and thought very little of herself. My client list was very impressive. Coty, Revlon, Clinique, Saks 5th Avenue, Bergdorf Goodman, The Gap, *Glamour, Vogue, Marie Claire, Elle, Harpers and Queen, Harpers' Bazaar*. I was working for the world's leading magazines, designers and fashion houses. But it just wasn't enough. Neither money nor fame gave me what I craved and needed. And when you have what I had, how could you complain, how could you be depressed? So out of shame I kept my mouth firmly shut. As long as I was kept busy, it was okay. But as soon as I had time on my hands, the ugly slug of pain came up, reminding me I was terribly damaged, unlovable and unlikeable. I instilled that message in myself every day in one way or another.

Both my brothers visited me in New York at different times. The youngest was only sixteen at the time. It wasn't until years later, perhaps ten, that he confessed to me how scared he felt and how afraid he was for me. I dragged him to nightclubs and dinners, and on occasions would send him home before me by cab, with my address on a scrap of paper and a few screwed-up dollar notes in his pocket. Sometimes I would do this in the early hours of the morning, thinking it perfectly okay. I look back now and think 'How could you have behaved like that?' But I did worse. My little brother, whom I adored, took second place to cocaine and alcohol in my fast lane.

We also had mad moments of fun thrown in, but always hanging over them was the shadow of whether I would go off the deep end. Would the mad moments turn into insanity? It was touch and go, never relaxing, never knowing which way I'd shoot. And all the time I thought we were having fun!

*

The Gap campaign, which was to last two years, was shot in the Teton Range of mountains in Wyoming. It was incredibly prestigious and I was considered unbelievably lucky to have got it.

I called Mummy. 'Fancy coming to Wyoming for two weeks?'

'Darling, how wonderful, of course I'd love to come.'

Famous last words!

I arrived a day early with Mummy, nervous because she was unpredictable when drunk. What a laugh, I was so deep in my own denial, that I could see her behaviour around alcohol, but not my own. So we had a little talk about it.

'Darling don't worry, just go and have some fun.'

The photographer was not amused in the least that Mummy had come and said so. I soothed his ruffled feathers. 'What exactly is it that you don't like?'

He didn't want her to come to sets or dinners. I told him that was fine and we'd dine alone.

'But you need to be with the client.'

'Why? I never have before.' This was true, for if I dined with the clients on trips they'd see the quantity of alcohol I drank. Then I'd drink more to try to forget how uncomfortable I felt. So the easiest way around it was to say I was tired; I'd been doing this for the last couple of years.

The shoot went well. The clothes were casual and fun and they suited me. The male model was delicious and uninterested in me – what a waste. I soon discovered he was gay. We shot on ranches with horses, camp fires and branding irons, on rivers in canoes and at camp sites with sunsets. During the shoot Mummy would go to Jackson Hole and shop. She soon made friends and we would meet and swap stories:

'The photographer threw his camera down the side of the mountain.'

'Why, for heaven's sake?'

'The battery went and he fired his assistant. Then they cried and made up.'

'Darling, how exhausting.'

'Not really, he throws wobblies all the time.'
The worse someone else behaved, the better I felt.

The last shoot over, Mummy and I decided to stay on for a week
and go dude riding, fishing, camping and white-water rafting.
We found a ranch called Six Hearts; it was authentic and the
horses were of good stock. There we met a wealthy family from
Texas whose money came from that thick amber stuff, oil.
Helen, the matriarch of this large gathering of people, was a
true out-and-out alcoholic who drank steadily from morning to
night. Mummy and she became good friends immediately!

Off we all went, horses packed. I had a bottle of Dimple
scotch slung on the front saddle horn and planned to nip at it as
I rode the five-hour journey. I don't remember much of that day.
I do remember waking up in the middle of nowhere, drunk,
horseless and alone, with a whacking great lump on my head. I
was alone in the mountains, confused and disorientated. I
began to wander, not knowing where I was going, only aware of
how thirsty, hungry and afraid I was – there's bears in them
there mountains. I whistled to keep up my spirits – I was shit
scared. My new cowboy boots I'd bought the day before were
killing me. The backs of the heels were folding, making my
journey twice as difficult.

After walking for over three hours, and now in total darkness,
I heard someone call my name. Oh joy of joy, I wasn't going to
die after all!

One of the dude ranch handlers rode up to me. 'You
okay?'

'Fine, absolutely fine.'

He looked down at me whilst chewing on a toothpick.

'Actually, I feel like a complete idiot. What happened?'

He told me that I'd been so drunk that I'd just taken it into
my head to ride off alone, had fallen off my horse and it had
gone back to camp alone. They'd had to send out search parties
and I wasn't very popular just then.

When we arrived, Mummy was standing on the edge of the

camp. Poor thing, she looked scared out of her wits. 'Oh, Polly darling, you had us all so worried. Are you all right?'

'I'm fine, really fine.' In fact I felt about two inches high and very sheepish.

The tents had been put up in my absence, fires lit and food cooked. I walked over to the fire and sat down. 'I'm very sorry, it was ridiculous and dangerous, and I feel awful. Please excuse me.'

Twelve faces looked back at me. No smiles. 'We're just glad you're okay.'

I was handed some hot food and realized how hungry I was.

That night, bedded down, Mummy hugged me. 'Polly, you gave me such a fright.'

'I'm sorry, Mum, I really am. I wanted this to be fun, not dangerous.'

'Don't worry, just take it easy with the booze, Pol. You just don't know when to stop.'

Back and forth this conversation had gone between us for years, often with me saying exactly the same to her.

The next day, blue, crisp and clear, the horses ready and saddled, we took our fishing tackle and went to the famous Blue Lake. Fishing, swimming and eating, the memories of the previous day began to fade. Mummy and I went white-water rafting and got the T-shirts to prove it. We drove through Yellowstone Park and all we saw were two chipmunks and the arse-end of a buffalo disappearing into the bushes. We bathed in sulphur pools.

Always underlying most meetings with my mother was the question that was burning my stomach lining. Here, it accompanied each movement of the car going over the cattle grids through the park. 'Who's my father, who was my father?'

I'd brought up this question repeatedly since I was eleven. I couldn't let it rest, I needed to know. I kept asking, knowing that each time I would be fobbed off. One night we went to town for dinner. The question sat there like heartburn. After dinner, we went to listen to live country and western music. The haunting, sad melodies moved me and I jugged down yet another beer. The tequila slammers came next. Each time the fiery liquid poured down my throat, it ignited the question: Who was my father?

Something exploded inside me and I stormed out, needing air. I don't remember what happened next. Mummy relayed the story to me.

Worried, she had followed me only to find a cowboy sitting on his butt, with his legs straight in front of him and holding his jaw. Mummy stopped in front of him. 'Did you see a blonde-haired girl go by wearing jeans?'

'Sure did, ma'am, and boy, what a right hook she has. I only asked her for a drink.'

'That's my girl.'

She found me sobbing in our rented car. 'Polly darling.'

'Shut the fuck up, Mum. I'm hurting, drunk and this isn't a good time to talk.'

Bruce, Helen's farmhand, had witnessed the whole thing and had stayed back, but kept at a distance, knowing somehow we needed him there. He offered to drive us back to the ranch. Mummy also had quite a lot to drink and was yakking away in the back of the car. I desperately wanted her to stop. 'Mummy, please be quiet, let it go.'

She wouldn't and put her head between the two front seats. I couldn't believe the stuff coming out of her mouth, and how deeply the words wounded me. My fist shot out – Mummy howled.

The next day I woke with a screaming hangover. The whole awful scene from the night before came back. For the first time in my life, I'd hit my mother – my God. I took a shower, packed and found Mummy sitting outside with Helen.

'Well, young lady, that's sure one hell of a shiner you gave your poor, wee mom over there.'

I had, too, and it made me feel sick inside with shame to look at her. 'Mum, here's your ticket. I'm going back to New York.'

She didn't say a word. We didn't speak for the next six months.

I went back to New York with three gashes from my mother's nails down the side of my face. The next day I had a shoot with Clinique for a campaign. They were seriously looking for another full-time face – it was very similar to the deal Elizabeth Hurley has now obtained with Estée Lauder. I made up a cock-and-bull story concerning a rodeo and how I got thrown but still won a prize of one thousand dollars.

I shot four campaigns. Then all the top executives got fired and, as I was their project, I was fired along with them. But I often wonder if my odd eccentric behaviour helped to get me axed. Why glamorize it? My alcoholic behaviour must have made them run a mile. Who knows?

After that, clients learned not to book me on trips and location shoots. My behaviour was unpredictable – even if my look was what they wanted, they would choose another girl rather than go through the aggro and possible misery of taking me along. I must say I don't blame them. Going to a foreign country with a team – hair, make-up, stylists, clients, photographers, assistants and models – can all add up to a lot of individuals and a lot of responsibilities. The last thing they needed was a model who was going to rock the boat.

Charlie no longer dealt me coke. 'No way, Polly. You're sick, you need to stop.'

The walls were closing in. Little by little I began to lose it. I started being late for work or I just didn't turn up. The agency suspended me from work. My twenty-fifth birthday was looming up. I sat in the apartment of a coke dealer, whose name I can't recall, for about four days. I did nothing but take coke in the form of what is known today as crack. Something I thought I would never do. It took just four days to bring me to my knees.

We'd consumed great quantities of vodka. I had not eaten or drunk anything for those four days. People came and went. I had spent over one thousand dollars and had put at least five hundred dollars' worth free from the dealer up my nose. I looked down at my feet. My boots were now on his feet and his were on mine. I couldn't remember the transaction.

I looked in the mirror and saw a death mask – mine. Eyes hollow, inhuman, haunted, dying. The light was no longer flickering behind them. Where was I going? Was this how I would die? In this room with people I didn't know. Sucking a glass pipe greedily. Flying high for a few minutes, then crashing, crashing with the ghost screaming in my way. Chill tendrils wrapped themselves around me. Cold, damp, wet snakes crawled in and out of my heart, leaving holes that freezing air whistled through. I sat down shaking. I had to get out, get home to Mummy. I picked up the phone and dialled her number. 'Mummy, I'm coming home this weekend – I'm dying.'

I'd hidden the extent of how mentally ill I was from my family. How far down the road of addiction I had gone. When I arrived home, Mummy was shocked at the amount of weight I'd lost and how tired I looked. I sat in the drawing-room, slowly getting drunk.

'Darling, what's the matter?'

'I can't stop taking cocaine. I use so much more and cut work. I can't stop. I need help, I can't do this alone.'

She replied with those all-too-familiar words, 'Darling, after a few days you'll feel better, you always land on your feet.'

In that split second I jumped from my chair and threw my glass through the closed window in front of me, overturned the coffee table, threw ornaments and books around the room in a blind rage; I was blind with fear.

'I won't land on my fucking feet. I am going to die if I don't get some help. I've been dying each and every fucking day of my life. I can't take it any more. I can't hope tomorrow will be better because it won't be.'

My entire family was standing looking at me, looking at me

as if I was a stranger they didn't know, a stranger standing in their drawing-room with the face of their sister.

Mummy gently led me to sit down. 'Darling, shush, shush, it's going to be okay. We'll get help. I promise we'll get the help you need.'

I cracked, sobbing. 'Help me, Mummy, every day has felt like slow suicide, every day. No more, Mummy, I can't take it any more.'

She cradled me, crying. My mother had lost her first husband to the disease of alcoholism and now her second daughter lay on her lap dying from it, masked by cocaine.

Alcohol secretly steals your soul, so slowly, so sneakily and full of glee. Because no one tells you until it's too fucking late. I wrote this book because I had to. If I knew there was a huge hole in the middle of the road at the dead of night, would I walk away and sit on the side of the road, waiting and watching for a car with a passenger to crash into it? No, it's in my nature to flag that car down. That's what this book is about. I'm just flagging you down. Take care, there is a huge hole. I know this hole. It would break my heart if you fell into it because you weren't warned. Perhaps this book can guide you away from that hole. Who knows? I hope so.

True to her word, my mother managed to get me into a treatment centre the very next day. Full of guilt, hung over, ashamed, I walked into that centre numb, not knowing anything any more.

CHAPTER FOUR

Tin Man

I met Danny in September 1986, six months after I'd come out of treatment in England. In that last month I'd started drinking again. I'd moved back to New York, and had a boyfriend called Peter, who was younger than me. I wasn't in love with him, but I felt safe and secure with that. I was able to maintain a relationship, and yet keep my independence. I carried on with my work, my friends. It wasn't until later on, when I was in my thirties, that I began to understand the meaning of the word 'co-dependency'.

With my past relationships, when I had been in love, I let go of my own independence without being consciously aware of doing so. I put the comforts and needs of my partner first. Their work, their social life, their dreams. I would fit myself into their plans, their lives. I would give the relationship my full attention, to the point of ignoring my own needs – my friends, my peace of mind and my recovery. My time was their time. I did this because I believed 'that's how it should be'.

I believe those thoughts were born from low self-worth, and that serving them was the only way I would receive the love and adoration I craved and so badly needed. I looked towards my partners for approval: I dressed for them, I made them complicated and difficult meals. By doing this, I believed they would love me more.

A few years ago, a partner living with me at the time said how much he missed his mother's garden, how he would love hanging baskets and lavender tubs. The very next day, that's what he got – and more. I transformed the back garden into something out of *House and Garden*. I thought he would love my efforts, and therefore love me, and that I could fix his feelings. He was going through a particularly bad patch at work and I wanted to make him feel better.

Instead I got the reverse. He acknowledged the garden, said it was lovely and walked away. I told him I'd done it for him, but now I felt empty. I'd done so much and was exhausted.

That evening I presented one of my complicated dishes, and placed it in front of him. He ate and got up from the table.

'Did you like it?'

'Oh, yeah. Thanks.'

'I made it specially for you.'

He smiled and left the room. I looked at the table. He hadn't offered to help, to clear up. I took the dishes noisily from the table to the sink. I became more unhappy, more empty, and then a feeling of resentment began to creep in.

That night when we retired for bed, I washed, brushed my teeth, lit a candle and got into bed. He declined from lovemaking, saying he was worried about work and needed to sleep. I lay on my side with his back towards me. I felt a terrible loneliness; I felt I had done something wrong.

The next few days continued in the same way. I kept thinking of the nice things I could do for him. But the more I did, the more he withdrew. Resentment kicked in hard. I'd had enough. I'd made him a garden, meals, sorted out his clothes, hadn't demanded his attention, left him to watch the news in peace; on and on went the list in my head.

The weekend came up and we decided to go away. Pulling out on to the motorway, I asked what was wrong, giving him the list of things I'd been doing for him. We got into a horrible fight, with hurt and anger from both sides. At the end of it I understood. Every time I did something for him, he felt guilty because he didn't have the time to do things for me. It made him feel inadequate. It had got to the point where he didn't appreciate anything I did; in fact, would have preferred it if I did nothing at all for him.

It took a while for me to understand this. I did things for him, so he'd do things for me. I started seeing a counsellor (who I had nicknamed 'my own personal head Hoover'!) after leaving treatment in 1989, and this was one of the problems I took to her. She told me, 'Only do for him what you want to do, with no other motive in mind. If you're doing it to score brownie points – to be loved more, for his approval – then don't do it. Only do it if *you* want to do it for *you*, because it makes *you* feel good.'

What a relief, what freedom. For a few days I didn't cook, clean or tend our garden. I learned how to get a balance, and to be aware when I did things out of co-dependency. Being aware, however painful, is the starting point of being able to change. For a while the relationship went well, with balanced emotions on both sides. He felt freer and so did I.

It was on my way to an assignment in the Seychelles, that I met the man who was soon to become my husband – Danny Mindel. He worked on films and commercials. His job was to assist the cameraman. He was dark, good looking, of medium height, raised in South Africa, smoked pot, hated the system, and generally rebelled against any authority. I fell for him the moment I set eyes on him.

Apparently I kissed him on the way out to the Seychelles, something I don't remember. I ignored him during the whole shoot until the end, then stayed alone with him for a week. We didn't touch, kiss, hold hands – nothing; just talked. I listened for once, and fell in love with this dark-eyed man. Apparently I got very drunk on the plane coming back with him and I felt so ashamed that I didn't call him again. He rang me a few days later, we met up, again on friendly terms only, and hung out together.

I went back to New York at the end of that week, to Peter

who was also a model. After a week of being back with him I missed Danny terribly. I called him, telling him I had a job to do in London, which was a complete lie. He invited me to stay with him. This went on over a period of weeks, with me flying in and out of London like a yo-yo. I always slept on the sofa. The last time I flew back before leaving Peter, I stayed at Danny's house. Instead of sleeping on the sofa I threw him the duvet and said, 'You sleep down here by all means, but I'm going to sleep in your bed.'

After howls of laughter and much teasing from his flat-mates, he climbed the stairs, and we became lovers. I was head over heels in love, when I flew back to New York.

I told Peter I was leaving; he stared at me, shocked and confused.

'When did this all happen?'

'When I went to the Seychelles.'

'My God, why didn't you tell me?'

'I didn't know at that point. I do now, and I'm telling you now.'

That was the extent of my – kindness. Poor Peter was tossed aside; I didn't give him more than a peck on the cheek and a hug. 'Cheer up, Peter, you'll soon find someone, too.'

'I thought I had.'

I looked at him and saw tears in his eyes. White-faced, he said goodbye. I walked down the hall to the elevator, I felt I was floating on air. I was going to marry the man I loved, I was going to live happily ever after – wasn't I?

I moved in with Danny, and settled into the routine. Every-one who lived in the house worked in the film industry; there were night shoots, and people slept during the day. We shared the house with Shane, Ben and Cecil. They all brought their girlfriends in from time to time. The house in London was large and accommodating; I had an instant family and friends.

I'd always had so much need for a sense of belonging. I needed to belong so much that I would adopt people, usually

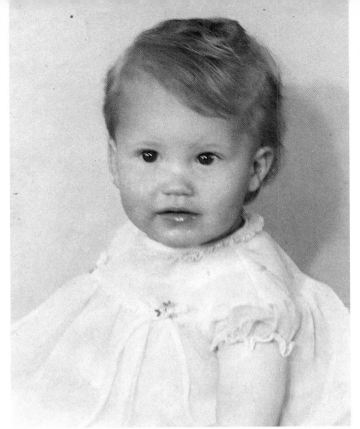

Who would have thought this baby would grow up to be an alcoholic?

My mother and her mother. Grandma sadly died from alcoholism in 1995

Polly aged two

The last photo of brothers, sisters and me
before leaving South Africa for England

Me aged four

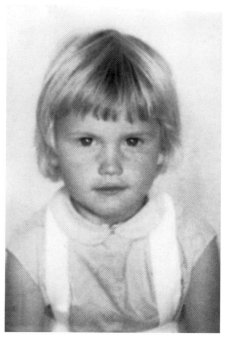

Aged eighteen in Marbella just before my modelling life began

Diego, Marbella 1979

Me, Stephen and Leala in Japan

This picture launched my career, aged twenty-one

The famous Volkswagen ad even gave rise to cartoons

Me and one of Stephen's wolves in Japan

Photograph by Patrick Demarchelier – the height of decadence

Up for three days and nights on coke in New York working on my campaign

Valentino: twenty-one years old and working my way to the top

Rebel, hungover, living with Tom in Hamburg

Tom's mother, Anna, with her beloved geese, outside her cottage in Hamburg

my boyfriends' families. I always involved myself in order to feel that I belonged to them. I felt that Danny's house, and his friends, had become mine overnight.

Now it is the house I live in that has given me a sense of belonging, of identity. It has become terribly important to me. Many times I struggled to meet the mortgage payments, fought the possibility of losing it through divorce, etcetera. Then I was frightened to let go of it. Now it is the place where I put my life back together, the place where I can truly be myself.

Those early days with Danny were filled with laughter, the house always supplied with booze and drugs – mainly soft. I stayed clear of any coke, I wasn't interested. I had knocked that one on the head in treatment, although I still hadn't tackled my alcoholism in any depth. I had been clear of drink and drugs for seven months, but when I met Danny I slipped easily back into my old ways. Anyway, Danny didn't believe I was an alcoholic, and introduced me to pot, which I loved. It made me feel relaxed, helped me to fit in, took away my hyperactivity, and made me feel like I belonged.

Work came in thick and fast. We had everything and more.

One day Danny and I decided we'd had enough of work, and decided to leave England. We decided to take all our money, pool it together, and travel the world without a goal or a plan. We just got up one day and left. We took this decision to travel because we'd both exhausted ourselves with our industries, and were becoming disillusioned with both our work and our lives. We planned eventually to buy a boat in order to hire it out until we could afford to buy another. The aim was to build a business of five yachts, based around the world, well crewed and fully equipped. Then we would travel the world in our own yacht, doing what we wanted to do, which was nothing, except having fun and enjoying life, simply living on the boat and sailing from island to island. It sounded idyllic.

The fact that neither of us had ever sailed, let alone owned a boat, didn't seem to bother us – we'd learn. We got every book we could find on sailing. Our first stop was Australia. We did the traditional travellers' route: we bought our Combie van and travelled the country.

When we first arrived in Australia, Danny had a job to shoot. An Ambre Solaire commercial. When they heard I was with him, they asked me to work for them. It was a very prestigious commercial, and I willingly accepted a contract on my own terms, meaning I wanted to be paid in full at the end of the shoot. This was a nightmare in itself. Roger Lyons – an egomaniac, who now is sadly dead – was the director. He bullied the crew, belittled the cast, generally made a fool out of himself and was just about everyone's enemy, including the cook and entire catering department.

Then Danny, who was the focus puller on the camera, had a run-in with Roger. Danny's job was to focus and say how much footage was left. 'Roger, fifteen feet. Roger, ten feet.'

Roger wasn't listening, so Danny, who wasn't going to let the film come off the spool, shouted, 'Cut!'

Roger went purple, slapped Danny on the back of the head, and screamed, 'I'm the only one who shouts "cut", you runt.'

There was complete silence on set. The atmosphere was thick. Flies could be heard buzzing and the ocean waves crashed on the shore, reminding us that life was still happening.

A voice piped up. 'You can tell the focus puller's a pommy – the director's still standing.'

Then I heard Roger screaming, 'Get the bitch back on set.'

I picked up the walkie-talkie. 'Roger, you asshole. Look at my contract, there's no deal on a reshoot. You only get what you get, and you've had the lot. Nothing, but nothing, will get me back on set with you, now or in the future.'

Danny and I walked off the set – paid.

By the time we got back to England, the episode had gone round the entire industry. Roger Lyons was a renowned asshole to work with. Danny and I were their heroes, or so we thought. Young, rebellious, hot-headed. I thought he and I were the perfect match. We both loved the countryside, hated cities, disliked our jobs and the people in the industry. We wanted out. We just didn't know how to do that.

With Danny and I both being addicts of marijuana and hash, we didn't know how to stop and look around us. We kept thinking it would be better, prettier, greener, further on. That's when I began to drink heavily again. I couldn't understand it. Here I was, travelling with the man I loved, yet when I had a drink, I wanted another and another. Danny would look at me. 'Come on, Pol, give it a rest, you need to share the driving.'

There was an incident at a hotel. Danny went to lie by the pool, I stayed in the room drunk, calling everyone I could think of to tell them what a great time we were having. I was getting more and more drunk by the minute. A waiter brought in some more ice; apparently I walked up to him and kissed him. Danny walked into the room at the same moment and went berserk.

The next thing I remember, it was evening and Danny was sitting on a rock. I looked around, seeing nothing except a blazing sunset and dry desert. He'd driven us off the road.

'I can't drive any further.' He looked terrible, he'd been crying.

'Danny, I'm so sorry. What happened?'

He looked at me in disbelief. 'You were fucking kissing a fucking waiter!'

I hid my head in my hands in shame. I didn't remember a thing. My mind raced – 'You're an alcoholic, see. The treatment centre said this would happen even though you kicked the cocaine.'

Deep down I already knew I was an alcoholic. That didn't

stop me drinking. Ironically, intelligence and knowledge of the disease won't stop you drinking. You have to admit it daily, at a gut level: to take action and go to meetings regularly. That's how I manage to stay sober now.

How different it all was in Australia. Then I was waking up at the side of a road to Danny's tears.

'I can't stop drinking, Danny. I want to, but I can't. I don't know how to stop.'

'We're going back. I'm dropping you off at the airport, and you're going home.'

We spent the night in silence. I felt at death's door, unable to believe that what I was craving was a drink. The next day, Danny drove five hundred miles non-stop; we sat in silence. He lit a joint, and passed it to me.

'I don't want to go back, Danny. Please, I won't drink again – please.'

He looked at me, and held out his hand. 'Deal – if you don't drink, we'll finish this trip together.'

We shook hands; we had an agreement and I felt some balance had been restored.

A few days later we went diving, staying for a while so I could get my PADI diving licence. I hadn't drunk and I passed my exam.

But afterwards Danny passed me a beer. 'Love, you deserve this.'

I looked at him.

'Go on, I trust you.'

I was confused. Was this a test? I thought we had a deal that I wouldn't drink.

I remembered my stepfather, Johnny. Mummy had married, when I was two, a man very much younger than herself. Johnny, twenty-two, Irish and fresh from the army, was himself carrying his own family legacies. My thoughts, my actions, my realities were so different and, for me as a child, confusing and frightening. As much as I tried, I just couldn't understand his actions, or become like him.

His punishments didn't make sense, they weren't consistent. I never knew what to expect, was never able to interpret the expressions on his face – not that of approval, nor that of danger. One afternoon Johnny was resting on the sofa, reading the newspaper. I, aged three, sidled up to him for a hug, and tried to lie next to him. Without looking at me, he elbowed me on to the floor. I thought it was a game so I got up and tried to lie next to him again. This time the poke from his elbow caught me under my ribs and I landed heavily on the floor. All the while he hadn't even looked at me – he just continued to read the paper.

Mummy had witnessed this from the hallway. Not wanting to make an issue out of this incident, she walked down the hallway to the bathroom, anger welling up inside her. This pattern of his rejection of me was already set but it was so monstrous, and so far from the plans she had for us all, that perhaps ignoring it was the only way she could cope with it. Many times I heard Mummy apologize for my stepfather's bizarre and cruel behaviour. She would say, 'He's just a little boy who doesn't know any better.'

That phrase came back to me all through my life, especially in my relationships with men. Now all sorts of questions were running through my mind. Could I trust Danny? Did he really know what was best for me?

In the end I took the beer. I felt trusted, but grown up and scared at the same time. That night we both got drunk.

The next morning we woke up with smiles, made love, dived together. It was all going to be okay, wasn't it? Maybe I'd gotten over my alcoholism – maybe I just needed to be loved.

For the next few weeks it was okay – until the next time.

After five months of travelling in Australia, Hawaii and the rest of the USA, we returned to England. We were none the wiser, broke and looking for work. This came quite quickly – sucking us back into the very thing we didn't want to do. However, we didn't have the tools to change ourselves. Our love, our lives and ourselves were all dysfunctional. Danny wanted to live in LA, I didn't. I wanted to cut loose from the business and live in Spain. Both of us wanted to sail into the sunset. All our dreams and ideas were there. We just didn't know how to make them happen.

During our travels together Danny and I were in each other's company for practically twenty-four hours a day. This wasn't natural for us, given the early days of our time together, when distance and work kept us apart.

Before Danny, I used to hide in my solitude. I had to convince myself that I liked being alone. Again this was something I learned in treatment. As I got older, I began to feel I couldn't keep up first impressions. I would fear that people would see I couldn't handle certain situations, like consistency in my behaviour; that I suffered major mood swings; that I was oversensitive and hyperactive; that I fabricated the truth. When nervous, I had the tendency to talk too loud, for too long, mainly telling stories relating to myself. I didn't know how to have a two-way conversation.

What I felt was that everyone had got it sussed and I hadn't. These feelings hurt like hell. They made me acutely aware there must be something terribly wrong with me. So I would drink to anaesthetize my feelings or have a joint. This would only make matters worse, except that then I was either drunk or stoned, and I didn't care.

The reason I found myself drinking heavily with Danny was because he had my company twenty-four hours a day, and I didn't feel adequate. I felt emotionally naked. So I drank – only sometimes I couldn't stop in time. There would be an argument. I was good at smashing my glass against a wall. That didn't work after a while. Looking back, I don't know how I got through those two years of being with Danny. I put him through hell. Being with someone who's an alcoholic is like living with someone who slips in and out of insanity. The sad thing about it is, I didn't know how to stop drinking and stay sober.

*

In May 1987 I was still spending a lot of time modelling in New York. Danny and I would fly back and forth between London and New York to see each other. I had a work permit for the States and Danny hadn't. So when he came to see me, he wasn't able to work. This meant he had to spend a lot of time on his own. At first this didn't seem to bother him. Then he would become frustrated because he wanted to get into the film industry in the States. Eventually work in England would beckon him and he would go back.

One night I got a phone call. 'Pol, I don't want a trans-atlantic relationship. What are we going to do?'

I remember replying, 'Danny, I make a lot of money here, I've reached the top of my profession. If I come back and work in England, I'll only make a quarter of what I make here. I'm twenty-seven years old. I've only a few more years left in the industry. Can't you see that? What if you and I don't work out, and then I find myself out of the circuit here?'

Danny was silent at the other end of the phone.

'Oi, Mindel, you still there?'

'Yeah. Well, what are we going to do?'

'Be patient,' I replied.

'I have been. Pol, let's go away for a while.'

'We've done that, Danny.'

'Pol.'

'Yes, Danny.'

'I don't really want a relationship where we're always separated.'

'Do you want to split?'

'NO!'

'Sure?'

'Sure. Pol?'

'Yes, Danny?'

'You coming home this weekend?'

'You want me to?'

'Yeah.'

'Okay, I will, Danny. I love you very much.'

'I know, Pol. Me, too, for you.'

It was the same as always. The man in my life clicked his fingers – I jumped. I just didn't have the skills to get what I wanted in a relationship. I had worked so hard to get what I wanted in my career. I had risen to the top of my profession by being assertive and by being well known for my unusual negotiating behaviour, which had got me some of the best modelling contracts going. Yet I couldn't control my personal life in the same way. I flew home that weekend, wondering how I was going to be able to jiggle with this.

Again, that weekend in England, the same discussion came up.

'Danny, if you want me to stay with you, buying the boats is going to be further away, because I can't make the money here that I can make in New York.'

'I don't care, as long as we're in the same country.'

'Why don't you get a work permit?' My immigration lawyer had told him it would take about eighteen months to get his work papers up and running. 'I mean, if you wanted to marry me, that would be different. At the moment, I just don't know, it's so much to risk.'

'Marry me, Pol.'

'When?' was my immediate reaction.

'Tomorrow.'

I looked at Danny. 'You're serious, aren't you?'

'Yep. What do you say?'

'I say YES.' I floated away on the never-never cloud again.

We married a few days later on his birthday, in a registry office in South London. My sister Tina and his best friend were our witnesses. That was it – small, quick and quiet.

We had lunch at Chelsea Harbour. I drank too much champagne and don't remember very much. What I do remember is feeling blissfully happy. I couldn't be all bad if Danny had wanted me enough to marry me. I loved Danny deeply at this point. I now had a valid reason to allow myself to stop modelling internationally on a regular basis. I knew the money would be less, yet he was also working. Our lifestyles didn't need that much financing, or so I thought at the time.

I was back in another perfect example of co-dependency. I believe today that I should have said that eighteen months wasn't so long. Our love, if true, would work out. However, once again, I was prepared to sacrifice my hard-earned career. I was buying into the myth that marriage was more import-ant, that somehow marriage would give me some sort of pro-tection. Only I'd married a man I didn't really know. Out of the eight months we'd been together, five of those months had been spent travelling, and the rest of the time, flying back and forth to the States. I was screwed up, without really knowing why. I brought all of that insecurity, and my alcohol-ism, into the marriage. It was doomed from the start.

Today I've learned that the 'behaviour' of alcoholism and drug addiction stole my choices. It prevented my maturity, stunted my ability to respond. For years later I blamed Danny. By then I was used to blaming: 'if only my childhood had been happy and stable'; 'my parents didn't understand me'; 'I had a rotten time at school'; 'modelling was the last profession I should have entered'; 'my work is so unstable'; 'my choice of partners has been so bad in the past'. If only I'd known how to make better choices, how to make decisions for the right reasons.

During my drinking days, I blamed everything on my par-ents, childhood, friends, boyfriends, work situations, always focusing the blame away from myself, until it was pointed out to me in recovery that I had to stop blaming others. Blaming is very counter-productive. Whether one is an alcoholic, or not, it makes victims of us. By blaming my parents until my late twenties, I was willing myself to be, and seeing myself as, their victim.

I was no longer a child, I needed to take responsibility for my life. I needed to bear the consequences of my behaviour if I ever stood the chance to change. 'I' needed to change my

behaviour or the vicious circle of active alcoholism and addiction would continue. To take responsibility, I needed the
ability to respond to everyday life appropriately, without
taking a drink to help me through. I needed to break down
everything I had built up for my own self-preservation. Tear-
ing this down would be the scariest thing I'd ever done, because behind the protective wall, which had become my
prison, lay a very vulnerable little girl; a little girl who had
never learned to trust and believe in herself.

At this point in my marriage, I hadn't learned the skills of
recovery. This enabled me to blame Danny too, by saying if
only he'd been this way, if only he'd been more understanding. But Danny was Danny. I had wanted a knight in shining
armour to fix me. Fix what? I wasn't quite sure. Instead of
the knight in shining armour, I got the Tin Man, and we held
hands and clung to each other as we stumbled along our own,
tortuous, Yellow Brick road. We were searching for ourselves,
for who were we, and where we belonged. We didn't have our
two-point-two children, but we had our two dogs. Danny had
Jake and I even had my Toto, in the form of Titch, at my side.

Titch is still with me now, a constant companion. Yet even
she and I need a break from each other now and then. She
made an unconventional entrance into my life, and I had to
take responsibility for a rash decision.

One day, Danny and I had gone to Harrods to pick out
some classical music for his father's birthday. I got bored with
hanging around waiting while Danny made his choice, and
walked over to the pet department.

'Oh, look at ya, ya adorable li'l thing.'

A huge bottom, threatening to burst itself out of a pair of
bright orange polyester stretch pants, bent over a cage, blocking the view of whatever it was this American woman was
talking to. Her hair would have made Joanna Lumley's in
Absolutely Fabulous look tame. It was backcombed into a
beehive nest, about a foot high. Huge purple Dallas-type ear-
rings dangled from her stretched ear lobes.

'I'm gonna take ya back to Florida with me and feed ya choccies.'

I peered over her shoulders. A tiny white dog, a West Highland terrier, was looking up at her. It was bored, uninterested and unimpressed.

'Now, do you want to come with me, you little cutie?'

Much to my surprise I piped up, 'Sorry, madam, the dog was sold about ten minutes ago.'

'Aw, what a shame.'

I shrugged my shoulders and smiled as she gave me a look and waddled off.

'Excuse me.'

I turned around. The manager of the pet department was standing behind me. 'Who bought the dog? Did you?'

'No, I just couldn't stand the idea of that dog going to Florida and growing fat and unhealthy on a diet of choccies.'

The manager began to move towards the disappearing bottom of the woman. It wasn't difficult to do.

'Hang on, I'll buy it. How much?'

'Two hundred and fifty pounds.'

I swallowed. Bloody hell.

So that was how Titch and I began our lives together.

I stuffed her inside my jacket and went to find my husband. It wasn't until we got outside that he saw her.

'Polly, what the hell is that?'

'A dog, Danny.'

'I can see that. But why have you bought it?'

I told him the story and we laughed all the way home. Those were happier days.

Initially I didn't like Titch very much. She was small and white. We already had a huge dog called Jake the Rake. He was a giant Schnauzer. Titch chewed my shoes and wasn't house trained until she was over ten months old.

One day she began to limp. I took her to the vet who said that Jake had probably landed on her badly. I knew Jake was very careful and protective of Titch, so something else must be wrong. I waited another month, and then took her to another vet who said he would X-ray her. The X-ray showed very clearly that her hip was disintegrating. It was a hereditary disease which affects this breed of dog. She would need to have the bone trimmed down, and would need at least eighteen stitches. Her leg would function again, but would be a little shorter. The vet assured me she would adapt to walking and running on it again.

I took her back the next day for the operation. I dropped her off, then drove back home. On the journey home I began to feel very uncomfortable. I pulled over on Clapham Common, and then it hit me hard. I was worried for her. I realized for the first time that I loved her, she meant a lot to me, that I cared about her. That whole day I sat and thought, How can a dog live with me for six months and I not know I loved it? That's how far removed I was from my feelings in those days. I couldn't connect to my emotions and when I did, it was rare for me to identify what the feelings were.

I picked Titch up the next morning. Her leg was shaved, and a huge incision, with the eighteen stitches, ran down her back leg to the ankle. She began to go everywhere with me after that, even to AA meetings. Today Titch and I are almost inseparable.

Despite all that was happening in my personal life I continued to work, unaware that an opportunity was soon to come my way. An opportunity that would change the direction of my career, and see me on the television sets of every home in the UK, in one of the most successful television commercials of the decade.

And I did it by being me.

CHAPTER FIVE

Changes

Nursing a hangover, up a ladder painting the drawing-room one blue October day, I heard the telephone ring. Bugger it, I thought, and let it ring. I was determined to finish this chore I'd set myself. Again the telephone rang and rang. Climbing down off the ladder, I picked up the receiver and snapped, 'Hello.'

'Pol, Models One here – Zoë. Are you busy?'

'Yes, what is it?'

'Did we get out of bed the wrong side this morning?'

'Yep.'

'David Bailey's requested to see you for an audition for a car commercial. Do you want to go?'

'Bugger. What time?'

'Two p.m.'

'Shit, that's in one hour.'

'Can you make it?'

'I'm covered in paint and look like shit.'

'Just go. Who knows? This could be the big one.'

'Yeah, yeah. Big, big, bloody annoying nuisance. All right, I'll go.'

Zoë gave me the address; it was right in the middle of Soho. Fabulous – nowhere to park, and everyone fighting to get back to their rabbit hutches after lunch.

Needless to say, I wasn't in the best of moods.

I grabbed the keys to my blue Beetle, snatched up my jacket and slammed the front door. Well, this was what they were going to get. I groaned as I looked at my face in the rear-view mirror. Donning sunglasses, I sped off.

Finally, after finding a parking space, I raced into the building at the address I'd been given, taking the stairs two at a time with the desk clerk shouting, 'Miss, oh, miss, you've got to sign in.'

'Later,' I shouted, equally loudly, over my shoulder.

I found the office on the third floor, and opened the door. Shit, shit, shit. The room was filled with leggy blondes in heels and minis. Serenely sitting pretty with portfolios held in their hands. Oh, fuck, I thought. I'd forgotten my portfolio.

'Yes, can I help you?'

'Yeah, Paula Hamilton – Models One, casting for VW.'

She looked me up and down. 'Take a seat, and fill out your details.' She dismissed me.

Snotty cow.

I didn't recognize any of the faces, so I put my head down, and filled in the form – Height: 5 ft 9 in. Hair: Blonde, short. State Commercials In The Last Three Years – I put a pen through a load of print, and wrote: Contracts signed for PH by Models One. I'd been caught out three years previously with Almay. I'd done a test job for them after being up all night, and had stupidly signed something, only to watch my face appear for the next three years on the inside of every magazine cover, for the meagre sum of sixty pounds. There was nothing I could do about it. Finishing the form I looked at the other models: freshly made-up faces, clean shining hair, clothes crisp, cool and business-like.

I looked at the brief:

Woman storms out of house – early morning – slams the front door – rips off ring, and posts it through the letter box – storms down street – flings fur coat over parking meter – sees drain, and contemplates dropping keys down it – STOP.

I looked down at my feet. I had on paint-spotted Doc Martens, green tartan trousers that were too big and snicked in at the waist, a white collarless shirt with the cuffs cut off and rolled back. My hair was back off my face, still finger waved haphazardly for the day before's job with L'Oréal. My nails were torn and ragged, and my face had paint crust on it. I shifted uncomfortably on the chair, and reached into my back pocket. I pulled out a wet paintbrush – great presentation!

'Paula Hamilton?'

'Yes.'

'You can go in now.'

Well, here goes, I thought.

I walked into the room that was cramped with cameras, lights, and executives from the advertising agency – including David Bailey.

'Glad to see you made an effort,' Bailey said, sarcastically. 'You still modelling?'

I turned to him full on, 'And will be until I've worked with Bailey on my own turf. My attire is such because I was in the middle of a project when I was rudely interrupted with this nonsense.'

He glared at me with those famous eyes, then threw back his head and laughed.

Taking this as approval, I searched for the white marker four feet from camera, and stood waiting.

'Have you read the brief?'

'Does a chicken have lips?'

'Okay, Hamilton – so you come around that corner – furious and feisty. What do you do with the keys? The VW is parked just ahead of you. Turn your back to the camera, then turn around, and give your interpretation.'

The cameraman focused, asked for name and agent. I turned around, waiting.

'ACTION!'

I slowly turned back and faced the camera. I looked down at the drain, held the key ring – letting the keys dangle for a few seconds – then lifted my head, threw the keys up in the air about a foot, and looking directly at the camera with a smile, said, 'BOLLOCKS!'

'CUT!'

The room was silent. The men looked from one to another. Smiles began, and then laughter broke out.

'She's our lady,' said Bailey. He opened the door and said, 'We've cast, thank you for coming,' and closed it.

He called my agent for availability. We had to move two jobs to accommodate the days he wanted to shoot. Never, in seven years of modelling, had I felt so good. I'd been completely me, and they'd cast me for myself. I didn't know then, or even after we shot 'Changes' – the title of the commercial – how big it would be, or how much it would change the direction of my career and future.

The commercial was to be shot in Eccleston Mews, in 1987, using forty-eight camera set-ups with the best crew in the country. I loved every moment. It was a pure acting part. Not just looking pretty, but fired with emotion and feelings.

Bailey nicknamed me 'One-take Garbo'. I felt I'd found my forte: acting. I felt warmth and approval coming thick and fast from the crew. Adrian Biddle lit the set with Hugh Johnson. They were both brilliant lighting men. Both, separately, came up to me and said, 'You should act, you really should.' They were both friends of my husband.

I was drinking at that point, but trying to stay sober. I was able to do so until the next flood of feelings overwhelmed me. Those two days made me feel back on top of the world. Alcoholism hadn't taken its powerful hold on me yet, that gripping illness that no amount of love can fix. No amount of cajoling, threats or promises can mend an alcoholic; in fact, it makes it worse. That's the irony of the illness.

I know why VW 'Changes' was a commercial made for me. In the past I had known how to look good, act good, be a success at my work, but when it came to intimacy, I couldn't handle it. Anger was the way I dealt with most things. A fuck-it attitude. So portraying a feisty woman on screen was so close to my own behaviour that it gave me the feeling I could walk away from anything, and that was totally acceptable. It was a way of behaviour with which I was now familiar. I'd walked away from a house in Switzerland with Urs; a home with two horses with Tom in Hamburg, and an apartment in New York with Peter.

What everyone else saw was a woman in control, a woman who knew her own mind. The career woman wasn't going to take any shit from anyone – least of all her lover, her boyfriend, her fiancé or husband.

Before the commercial came to TV I had a row with Danny and stormed out of the house, sober, but angry and very lonely. I went to my favourite restaurant, only to find it was closing. Two of the waiters who knew me offered to take me dancing and, feeling lost, I accepted. We arrived at the Hippodrome, and I went straight on to the dance floor. Alone in the lights, the atmosphere engulfed me and the music took over my thoughts. I never saw the two drunks dancing wildly behind me, legs flying out like karate kicks, and the next minute I was on the floor staring at my twisted leg, the bone sticking out through the ankle and a small pool of blood forming around it. In shock, I tried to stand up but collapsed back on the floor. My friends came to the rescue but couldn't persuade the nightclub staff to help in any way, in case of bad publicity. They wouldn't even call an ambulance, so my friends had to pick me up in a fireman's lift and carry me through the crowds to the car several streets away. Through all this I hadn't had a drink and the pain was appalling. As they put me into the back of their Mini, my tibia shattered. I begged my friends to stop and get me a bottle of brandy. By the time we arrived at St Stephen's Hospital, I'd polished off half of it.

I was vile to the nurses, telling them I had to work the next day, and ordering them to put only a splint on it. I tried to shove the bone back in, and kept looking away, willing it to mend. I could not see beyond the job I had to do the next day. It was an act of the insanity that comes with alcoholic drinking. I simply refused to see what was going on. Danny was called and he treated me with anger and contempt. He was disgusted with me and at the end of his tether. I managed to convince them that I wanted a splint and that's what I got. Two of the nurses were crying, saying that I'd lose my leg because I had touched the exposed bone, that I'd get gangrene. Danny managed to get me into his van and drove home, with me lying on the floor in excruciating pain. I had refused painkillers and still could not accept the situation, even through this raw agony. Danny dragged a mattress down to the living room and left me lying in the dark. The alcohol was slowly beginning to wear off, leaving me feeling like a tiger with its paw in a trap. The fight left me and I hardly had the strength to call out for Danny. He drove me back to the hospital and my leg was encased in over twenty pounds of plaster, from the top of my thigh to my toes.

By the time the VW commercial was aired, it was too late to do anything to cash in on its phenomenal success. The damage was done and I was unable to do any follow-up work for eight months, unable to benefit from any of the commercial's spin-offs. Bad luck follows bad luck, and mine was just beginning. I didn't have a leg to stand on, literally. I was in a cast for over eight months and my self-esteem dwindled to a big, fat zero. Crawling around on the floor matched my feelings towards myself.

I was isolated in a big empty house in Brixton and Danny was travelling eighty per cent of the time. Our marriage really deteriorated during those eight months. I didn't drink, I was too scared. So I smoked pot day in, day out, while waiting for my leg to mend. No jobs, no calls for work, no place to go and no one to turn to. When Danny came home he would look at me with contempt. I'd lost a lot of weight. I felt I was going mad. I didn't have the tools to cope with it. So I smoked enough dope each day to numb the pain, and the feelings of inadequacy, of helplessness. I was a shell of a person, not wanting to live, not wanting to die. In fact, the whole experience was so humiliating that I had blanked it from my mind until writing this, now seven years later.

*

In the summer of that year, I accompanied Danny to a film shoot in Rio de Janeiro. Staying at the Copacabana Hotel while Danny was on location outside the city, I lay on the bed, looking at the ceiling. I had a premonition that if I picked up the phone and called my mother, today would be the day she would tell me who my father was.

I dialled my mother's number and when she answered, I went straight in.

'Who was my father?'

There was a short intake of breath, then silence.

'I need to know, please?'

Then she told me.

Rage boiled up inside me. It was someone I'd met when I was eleven years old. My grandmother had said he was my real father. I already had a dead father, and a stepfather who showed contempt towards me, and now I had another one sitting opposite me. I was confused, but I kept in touch with him until my mother found his letters hidden in my 'treasure trunk'. That was when she explained to me that Granny had a drink problem and had been very cruel. I knew that my mother was lying but I chose to believe her; I was too afraid of her pain not to. I tried to push it to the back of my mind, but the trouble was that it wouldn't stay there and I became obsessed with the thought of finding out the truth one day.

Now I knew, and I felt my mother's betrayal. I screamed obscenities down the phone, pulled it out of the wall, and, hobbling over to the window, hurled it out, watching as it flew through the air with a magnificent sunset behind it. I finally knew who my father was, and I stood looking at the smashed phone outside as the sun sank into the sea.

I was back in Africa with my Nanny Maria. Over and over again, she saw me traumatized by events within my family.

One day, at the age of five, I remember her taking me behind her hut as the sun was going down. She pointed to the sky. 'You see how the sky begins to change colour?'

'Yes.'

'Now, little one; you mustn't let anyone break your spirit. I teach you how: stand on one leg and balance. Stand like this until the sun goes down behind those mountains, until the sky is dark. When the sky changes colour, concentrate on the colours, not on the pain in your legs and arms – forget your body. Follow your eyes, your mind will follow, and you will fly into the colours – the colours are your pain, your pain is those colours, the colours are your friends – they will be with you always.'

I can still see in my mind's eye the five-year-old girl with sun-bleached hair and gangly limbs, arms outstretched to balance, standing on one leg, very much like a stork, and staring into the sunset – a sunset I've never forgotten. As the sun left the sky, I was unaware of the chill in the air as the temperature dropped because I was no longer there, I felt nothing. I was flying up amongst the colours of the sunset.

Finally, when dusk turned to night, my nanny, who had been sitting to one side, came over to me and wrapped me in a blanket. As she carried me inside she said, 'You have the courage and the heart of a Zulu warrior, little one. Now no one will ever break you, you belong to yourself, now you have a protector.'

I didn't speak to my mother for a year after that. When I was in treatment in early 1989 she wrote me a long letter explaining all that had happened, and how I was conceived. I still didn't want to see her or hear her on the subject, I was too caught up in my own pain. It would be another three years before I forgave her, and forgave myself for shutting her out.

My leg eventually healed; I still had no work, so when Danny asked me to join him in Mexico where he was filming, I decided to go. The film, called *Revenge*, starred Kevin Costner, Madeline Stowe and Anthony Quinn. Conavaca was a beautiful town. Our house had sunny grounds with palms and wild flowers. A huge pool with a pool house for barbecues and parties. I took a friend with us; she was an artist who was also deep in the throes of anorexia. Danny had known her for years and slowly she became my friend. The first month passed without much problem. My girlfriend and I would explore the town and country-side. We swam, wrote and partied. Danny would come home with the crew at all hours of the morning, so we rarely saw each other, and rarely ate together. The dope in Mexico was strong, but not strong enough – my feelings of shame, inadequacy and low self-worth started to come up again.

One day we stopped off in a café. I ordered a white wine alongside hers. She looked at me, but said nothing. My reply to her silent stare was, 'One's not going to kill me.'

Five years earlier she'd been left by Danny's best friend, whom she'd loved, cherished and adored. She never got over it and that's when her illness came out. Anorexia at that time, and still today, is a very misunderstood illness. Doctors and profes-sionals still see it as self-induced, in the same way as alcoholism, obesity and drug abuse. It is very shaming when told, 'You can stop this. Why do you do it? Do you know how much it hurts your family to see you like this?'

All these comments are useless. Shaming the person with an illness or addiction is for me and for many others who all come under this umbrella, horrendous. We feel alone, isolated, bad, wrong, sick, self-pitying. This in turn spirals us further into the feeling of low self-worth. Those lucky enough to seek and receive help see that, in treatment or the fellowship, we're not alone. We find a family of people who have these illnesses. We talk about them without shame, learn to live with ourselves and others. It is a great gift to receive this.

I had been in treatment in Salisbury for eight weeks in 1986, for drug addiction and alcoholism. I wasn't ready at that time to hear about the underlying causes and the tools which I would need to acquire to counteract my reaction to the disease. Then, treatment centres were very tough, very hard. They cracked you, broke you down in order to reach the person who had hidden behind the denial; ripping off the masks and the beliefs we covered ourselves with in order to protect ourselves. I left that treatment centre six weeks later, like a worm crawling, believing I was still bad, believing I was worse than anyone else. I hadn't understood what they were trying to achieve. Perhaps if I had been able to accept that I had to change in order to recover, I would have made a start sooner. But it didn't happen like that.

Therefore, in Mexico, two and a half years on, I still didn't understand my addiction.

I began to drink during the day. Just wine, but it was enough. Danny smelled it on my breath. Too afraid of the consequences to confront me, he put up a wall and we avoided each other. Sometimes I would go on set and watch them filming. I'd talk to Kevin, laugh. Be interesting, funny. Other times I'd sit around watching, feeling shut out, thick, stupid, uninteresting.

The film location moved to Mexico City. One night when shooting was over, Kevin was in the bar and I walked over and ordered a tequila. We sat, drank and talked about the film industry, his wife and children. I kept ordering. Kevin asked where Danny was. I told him Danny had joined the camera crew for a drink. Kevin invited me to join him for dinner with the director and producers.

I went upstairs to change. Danny saw me.

'You're drunk.'

'No shit, Sherlock.'

'Fuck you, Polly. You're not going to fuck this up for me.'

The anger between us was tangible.

The telephone rang. It was Kevin. I said I'd be five minutes.

Danny reacted badly. 'You're going nowhere.'

I remember shouting, 'What you going to do?'

He pulled the telephone from the wall. I picked up a lamp, threw it and was about to walk out the door when he grabbed me. I punched him. He went down.

'Leave me alone, Danny, just leave me alone.'

He went to the bathroom mirror. His lip was bleeding. The twinge in my gut lasted but a few seconds. He lunged at me again. I pushed him into the bathtub and walked out.

I couldn't find Kevin, or the rest of his party. I sat in the bar and drank until I saw double.

*

I went back to the room at around five in the morning. Danny wasn't there, but the blood was, and so was the broken lamp and telephone. I didn't see any of it until I woke the next day at four in the afternoon. Danny was still absent. I thought he was filming. I looked around the room and the horror of the night hit me with such force that I retched for over an hour.

I sat in a chair for two days, only leaving it to pee. I left the 'Do Not Disturb' sign on the door, and ate no food. I was in shock. I knew my marriage was over unless I took some action. I had destroyed everything in my life and kept doing so. I wanted to die but didn't have the guts to do so.

After two days I booked a flight back to England, leaving a note for Danny. On my return I called the treatment centre in Salisbury and scheduled myself to go in on 4 January 1989.

Two days before that, Danny came home. I told him what I was doing. I told him I couldn't believe I'd hit him, and had almost sabotaged his work. That I needed help, I was sick. Danny told me that if I went into treatment, he'd leave me. I slapped his face, he slapped me back.

A couple of days later, I entered the same treatment centre. This time I knew I was a drug addict and an alcoholic: that I needed help and was prepared to go to any lengths to get that help, even if it meant giving up the only man I had ever loved. Treatment this time was very different. I was totally receptive to what I was being told. I was accepting and willing: willing to change my beliefs: willing to change my approach, and willing to listen and accept what was being said to me.

That was until they suggested I give up my work, sell my house and go to a halfway house for one year. That's when I put the brakes on. I instinctively knew Danny would not stand by me. I felt that the home I'd created was too precious to sell. It would mean coming out of treatment to no work, no husband, and no home. It was too much at that time for me to let go of. They tried for weeks to help me see why they had made these suggestions. It even made sense to me, but to let go of my identities, in the form of work, wife and homemaker, was too much.

When I came out of treatment in early spring 1989, Danny collected me. I felt so small, vulnerable and shy. I remember we went for a pizza on the Fulham Road. I tried holding Danny's hand as we crossed the road – a hand that was limp and cold. I felt the rejection, the hurt that went too deep. My heart ached. I needed a hug, a kind word, some reassurance. I needed something – anything. Instead, I found myself having one of the most revealing conversations of our relationship.

We ordered pizza.

'Danny, what's going on, are you still angry with me?'

'Yes.'

'About me being an alcoholic?'

'Yes.'

'You don't think I am one, do you?'

'Nope.'

'Why?'

'I don't know why, Polly.'

'Danny, I need you, need your love, need your support. You're being so horrible towards me. I can't change what's happened. If I turned back the clock, we'd still be living in a nightmare. I can't make today a nightmare too. Can't you give me some indication that there's still hope? Do you have any hope left?'

'I don't know.'

'Do you need time to answer that?'

'Jesus, talk to me like you used to talk. You sound like a fucking robot.'

'I feel like a fucking robot.'

I didn't feel comfortable yet with the new me, and I dared not revert back to the old behaviour, which I knew would lead to drink. 'Dan, give us a break – please. I'm doing the best I can.'

'I don't know any other way, damn it.'

'Please.'

'Let's go.'

We paid up, and walked back to the car.

'Dan, I love you so much. I really want this to work. I can't do it alone. Maybe if you got some support. You know they've got these meetings called Al-Anon. Meetings for the people who are involved with alcoholics.'

'You mean victims.'

'Is that how you feel – like my victim?'

He didn't answer, his mouth set in a line, his knuckles white as he gripped the steering wheel.

'I felt like your victim before I went into treatment, I felt like a scapegoat. Polly was to blame for everything. Because I drank I couldn't argue. I accepted all the blame. I can't go on doing that. Did you stop and ask yourself why you were attracted to me, even though you knew I had a problem with alcohol?'

'I thought you would get over it.'

'What were you attracted to, Dan? My face, my body, my money, my status, or me?'

'Well, who the fuck were you? I never knew what you were going to do, what you were going to say next.'

'So why were you attracted to me? It takes two to tango, Danny.'

'Polly, let's sell up – move.'

'I can't, Danny, I need to face life, and I need support. I'm not brave enough to sell up and go with you to LA where I don't know anyone. What if you dump me out there? What do you think my chances would be of staying sober?'

'What are your chances here?'

'Good, if I have some supportive loving people around me. Not good if I hang out with people who smoke pot, judge me, openly dislike me, and are hostile towards me. Then my chances would be pretty slim, don't you think?'

We were glaring at each other, then the lights changed and he looked back at the road.

'I'm sorry, Danny, I just can't move to LA.'

'I'm not staying in England, Polly, I hate the place. I want to go away, to start afresh.'

'With me, Danny? You know what really hurts, Danny? When you came to treatment, and the counsellor asked you what your ideal world was, you said you wanted a shack on the beach with a window and a view. He asked you if you wanted anything else and you answered – a peaceful life. When he asked you where I fitted into the picture, you looked at him as if you'd forgotten I was there, or maybe you hadn't. Is that how it is, Dan?'

He didn't answer me.

We arrived home. Opening my door after two months, seemed so odd. The house was void of flowers and plants. 'What happened to the plants?'

'They died.'

Jake and Titch, our two dogs, bounded up to me, Jake nearly knocking me down.

'I've gotta go.'

'Where?'

'Meeting some friends about work.'

'About Peru?'

'Yes.'

'So when do we go?'

'Ten days or so.'

He closed the door. I put down the suitcase and bags. My family were in India. At that time I didn't have any other friends apart from Danny's, and they all smoked pot or drank.

I picked up the phone and called my counsellor back at treatment. 'I can't go through with this.'

'Yes, you can.'

'What do I do? I'm so scared. He's so angry and hurt, I can't talk to him.'

'Where is he?'

'He's gone out with friends. I feel so alone, I can't do this.'

'Polly, go unpack your stuff, take a hot bath, get dressed, then go and find a meeting.'

'I want to come back.'

'I know. It's going to be tough. Take it one moment at a time.'

'I thought it would be so easy, so different. I thought there would be food in the fridge – flowers, hugs, kisses. I thought he'd hold me, tell me he was proud of me. Oh fuck, Jesus, I hurt so damned much. Why do I hurt so much?'

'Polly, we all set ourselves up with expectations. Don't. Then when things don't happen, we don't get hurt and when things do happen, it's a bonus. Now, bathe, dress, and go find people like you who are dealing with this. This is real, your hurt is real; it would be real easy to go and drink now. Instead, just put one foot in front of the other and don't expect a miracle.'

I put the phone down, walked upstairs, entered the bedroom, looked at the bed and lay down. It was four o'clock in the afternoon. When I woke up it was six o'clock the following morning. I was still dressed, and didn't know at first where I was – I was home. I lay there listening to the birds, then I felt along the bed and sat up. Danny wasn't there.

I got up, walked down the hall and gently opened the guest-room door. Danny was asleep on the futon. Jake, lying next to him, raised his big head, looking at me uninterestedly before flopping down again. I went back to our room, got back into bed, pulled the duvet over my head, stuffed my face in the pillow, and felt my heart crack in two.

There is a recommendation, on entering recovery, that the recovering alcoholic, upon leaving treatment, doesn't start an intimate relationship for a year or two, if they aren't already in one. The reason? In those new tender years, we are getting to know who we are, what our likes and dislikes are, how we stand emotionally. A lot of childhood issues are worked on. We may have had a whole list of destructive relationships in the past, which failed due to our inability to communicate our feelings positively. We may have lost our work, our homes, our families. If we rush headlong into a relationship, it may be with the wrong motives.

Relationships at the best of times are hard work. I believe great skills are required for a successful relationship. Addicts and alcoholics are driven a lot of the time by fear. Fear of not wanting to be alone, fear of failure, fear of commitment – the list is endless. The bottom line is to keep the focus on our recovery, to make sure our recovery comes before work and relationships. Without our sobriety, without our recovery, how do we expect to be able to give large parts of our attention to someone else, someone who means the world to us?

In the early days of sobriety, we need simplicity. Our past lives have been filled with chaos. We are still trying desperately to keep our ducks in a row. This doesn't mean that to remain in recovery, you have to be a nun or a monk. I know through personal experience what happens when I tried to juggle a relationship with a career, home, friends, family and recovery. I also have experienced a two-year celibacy, staying away from a relationship, and the rewards that this brings.

Today I have a healthy, long-term relationship through patience and learning new skills. I owed that much to myself. I want to know about life, but most of all, I want to know about me.

The two years of celibacy taught me so much. At times it was terribly painful and lonely. But I learned some valuable lessons. I learned to be alone, and value and enjoy my own company. I learned to reach out more and more to other women in recovery. Early on in this time, when I desperately needed to feel loved and held by a man, I found myself subconsciously dressing more and more provocatively, focusing my time on my looks and hair. I noticed myself doing this, and I realized I still didn't value the person who was me enough. I began to wear less and less make-up, spent less time on my hair and clothes, and started to present a real me to the opposite sex. Then I found myself gradually less threatened by them, felt less the need to defend myself. It was a very positive time. I'm grateful I allowed myself to have that experience.

I now realize that, because Danny couldn't accept that I had a problem, he was trying to punish me for my illness by withdrawing his sexual favours, his closeness: 'I'll sleep with you and show you love again if you put aside your recovery and come to LA with me.'

The relationship between us was disintegrating. I couldn't take the rejection. We now slept in separate rooms. Danny wanted to sell up and leave, which made me feel anxious and scared. I'd bought Danny in the past by giving him money to set up an account to buy our boat. Each time I got drunk and screwed up, I'd hand over large sums of money. When I broke my leg before going into treatment and couldn't work, I said to Danny that at least we'd have that to fall back on. He looked at me and said that we didn't.

It turned out that Danny had been paying his share of the mortgage with the money I'd given him for the boat. He couldn't see, or wouldn't admit, his fault or betrayal.

So when I came out of treatment I stopped giving Danny *carte blanche* with my money and took financial control back. He didn't like that. I didn't let him use my car. I stopped taking care of his dog. I set my boundaries and he fought them on a daily basis, trying to wear me down. He threw me the line I had been told to expect.

'I liked you better when you were drinking.'

Danny and I did not separate immediately. Before going into treatment, Danny and I had been working together on a project. I'd found the contacts, the money and the proposal for a documentary in Peru about horses. Whilst I was in treatment, it all came together.

Danny didn't want me to go. I reminded him that, without me, he wouldn't have a project to go on. So I went for six weeks. I spent the time with the crew, who drank and smoked dope. They were initially Danny's friends. Danny made me redundant out there, he didn't allow me to do anything. I watched whilst everyone else worked, watching my project and not being included, feeling lost and left out.

We travelled all over Peru. A girl who went with her boyfriend to photograph and document the event became, and is still today, my friend, and sober. Then she was drinking and using. I felt completely rejected and isolated. There was no one there who knew what I was going through, no one who could help me get through each day. I had to cope all by myself, so I wrote a diary and got through each day, each meal, without a drug or a drink. Doing all this alone made me realize, once and for all, that no one was going to help with my recovery, but for the first time it dawned on me that I could stand on my own two feet.

Even so, I decided to make a last-ditch attempt to save my marriage. When we got back to England, I asked Danny to come and see a counsellor with me. Reluctantly he went. After we'd been a few times, the counsellor said to Danny, 'Danny, you're very blaming and punishing of Polly. She's very well aware of the hurt and betrayal she's put you through. By staying clean and coming here she is showing you she's serious about her recovery and acceptance of the wrongs she has done to you. There are two people in this marriage, Danny. Focusing all the problems and blame on Polly is very convenient, but you need to start looking at what you contributed also.

'I understand you once had a long relationship with someone who had a heroin problem. You helped that person off it. Now you're married to an alcoholic drug addict in recovery.

'What's your attraction? What attracted you to Polly? Why do you set yourself up as the sane one who can rescue and fix? Why do you smoke dope every day, saying you can control it? A social user, which is what you claim yourself to be, doesn't think of the concept of control.'

That was the day I began to let go. I knew then that he would never have the courage to go into recovery and that I would never have the Danny I so much wanted him to be. That was when my grief came up, hitting me hard with the realization that he would never be the knight in shining armour I had always envisioned him as.

Five months after coming out of treatment, Danny and I finally separated. There had been so much hurt that there was very little trust left. The relationship had been damaged by a lack of communication, a lack of the right tools to cope with situations. There wasn't enough maturity on either side that would enable us to cope with what was an intensely stressful, and destructive, relationship. So two children in adult bodies had to deal with our marriage, and failed.

I didn't expect this part of my book to be so painful to write. I'd blanked out a lot of this. Now as I write, I realize that most of my life I've been unhappy. It's been six years since I split up with Danny and so much has happened since. Now I feel a great sense of sadness; so much of my life has been pain, and how hard I have fought life. A lot of blame is mine. Danny wasn't loving, supportive, kind or caring; he didn't have the tools, either. I can still catch a glimpse between the chinks of my armour and see a victim. Lordy, lordy – how much I have to learn, and how grateful I am that I have the ability today to face this with support and understanding, with tools that have so generously been given to me, passed on by brave and courageous people who came before me.

Addicts, alcoholics – anyone with an addiction who goes into treatment is taught the disease concept. Therefore, they come out with a different perception of themselves, different attitudes. We come out with more self-worth, less shame, more understanding, and a faith that if we stay on a path to recovery, eventually, a day at a time, life will get better. We are not the same people who went into recovery. People who were full of shame, low self-worth, confused and desperately unhappy. Worse still – not knowing why. Most people enter the programme believing they are bad to the core.

Recovery and relationships are very painful. Both parties need to look at themselves. Why do husbands or wives, for so many years, put up with the abusive behaviour of the alcoholic? I know, from experience, that my husband Danny believed his love could cure me. He would say to me, 'If you loved me, you wouldn't drink.'

I knew I loved him, but I couldn't stay sober. He did not want to accept I was an alcoholic. He asked me to see a psychiatrist, which I did. He asked me to smoke dope instead, which I was able to do for a short time. I always went back to sneak-drinking behind his back.

There is a support group for those who are closely affected by the alcoholic – Al-Anon. This support system is there whether the recovering alcoholic is drinking or not. Again, through the power of example, those affected can see and learn how to look after themselves, and can get support in how to deal with difficult situations as and when they arise. AA and Al-Anon give suggestions only. There are no rules. The only obligation one has is to one's own sobriety and an awareness of the effect alcoholism has on the ones we love.

AA has been around, worldwide, since the 1930s. I learned so much about alcohol while I was in recovery – things which would probably have stopped me drinking in the first place had I been educated in my schooldays about them. A knowledge of alcohol abuse is as necessary to young people as awareness of the AIDS virus and how to practise safe sex. The latter is taught in school, as is, to a certain extent, awareness of drugs. This knowledge will not stop young people from going out and trying sex, drugs and booze. But if they have the knowledge to recognize when to stop, perhaps fewer young people will have to learn the hard way, as I and countless others did.

When I told Danny I was going into treatment, and he told me he would leave me, I couldn't understand it. Why was he opposed to me receiving help I so desperately needed for an illness that was destructive to us both, that would eventually kill me if I didn't seek and achieve sobriety, that I didn't understand?

It was suggested that Danny came into Family Therapy with me while I was at the treatment centre. He refused. It was then proposed that he attend Al-Anon, where he could talk about our relationship without me present. Again he rejected this. Was he scared? Of course he was. Did he blame himself? Did he think they would point the finger at him, tell him it was his fault I was unhappy, and that was why I drank?

I could see why it was so difficult for Danny to make this commitment to my recovery and our marriage. A few of the women in treatment were in the same predicament. It *is* a lot to ask of someone who is already trying to come to terms with the fact that his wife is an alcoholic. For instance, some had to cope with looking after the children and running the house in their wife's absence, all the time coping with difficult and embarrassing questions: what man likes to admit that his wife is a drunk? If he can find the courage to come to these family groups, he soon realizes what a long, slow process he has become involved in. The art of trusting again has to start slowly – the concept that alcoholism is a disease is a difficult one to grasp. By working together on a daily basis, the family begin to change their old behaviour, and little by little, day by day, the family members grow well together as a unit, and as individuals. But some cases don't work out. Danny did not want to get help, did not want to go to family groups, did not want to accept I had an illness.

Danny wanted Polly back the way she was when she was drinking. He just didn't want me to drink. I came out of treatment, was assertive and went to my AA meetings. This was foreign to him. He hadn't learned the disease concept. He operated out of fear of losing control over me. He spent less and less time focusing on me. This meant he had to look at himself and he didn't want to. I knew if we stayed together, I would drink.

It all came to such an ugly end. We agreed after many nasty, hurtful fights, to separate and eventually divorce. It was the saddest and most painful part of my life. I loved him very much. However, I also knew, unless he received help, his belief system would not allow him to see things with new eyes. He fought me all the way in a long drawn-out divorce.

I cried non-stop for a year, I felt abandoned, confused, lost and hopeless. I threw myself headlong into my work and had my best financial year. Every night I would come home and cry, praying he'd call, praying he'd come back from LA: that one day I would hear his key in the door, and he'd come in and pick me up in a bear hug. He did in my dreams. He'd kiss me lovingly and say he couldn't live without me. I still had the knight-in-shining-armour belief that, if I worked hard, stopped drinking, worked on my recovery, somehow Danny would come back, forgive all and we'd live happily ever after.

I kept up that dream for two and a half years.

Today, six years later, I understand why he behaved in the way he did. The choice was to stay with what was familiar, or take a risk, and say, 'Okay, what is this thing called alcoholism?'

Alcoholism is a disease I didn't knowingly choose, or want. No one wants to be an alcoholic or an addict. No one wants to love one, or marry one. It just happens. I could have been a diabetic, or had cancer or leukaemia. I wonder how he would have reacted to that. Would he have wanted to learn how to support me, and more importantly, get help for himself? When I broke my leg, I willingly used a crutch to help me walk. Why is it that for something like alcoholism, people still believe it's weak willed, shameful and one shouldn't ask for help?

Today, I ask for help. 'Please help me, I don't know how to do this on my own. These tools are new to me. I don't always know how to use them to their best advantage. Their instructions are not included.'

I will continue to go to AA meetings for the rest of my life. I love my meetings. You just pick up a telephone book in any country, and there are those comforting initials – AA.

I live in London, where there are many meetings all through the day, so I have little excuse not to fit them into my daily life. I go and I witness newcomers walking through the doors, shaking and feeling spiritually bankrupt. A little piece of their dignity is returned to them. I know because it happened to me. I watch that newcomer, and he or she reminds me of how it used to be for me. When I see people who are more than three years into recovery, it gives me hope. When I share, the newcomer sees I'm staying sober, dealing with life and all its obstacles – without alcohol; it gives them hope and encouragement. When the ten-years-into-recovery AA member shares with me, he can remember how far he's come and it reminds him how difficult it was, yet he got through it. Recovery is maintained by power of example. It's a wonderful fellowship, and my gratitude to them will be with me for the rest of my life.

It is very healing to be with people who have this illness, and have survived and understood it. We don't need to explain what it's like, justify ourselves, or fear we're going to be judged. A A and Al-Anon are also a bridge to 'normal' living.

Alcohol – cunning, baffling, powerful. The different excuses it supplies to needs:

'I'm nervous, I'll have a drink.'
'I'm under the weather.'
'I need to relax.'
'I need to sleep.'
'I need perking up.'
'I need Dutch courage.'
'I'll have one for the road.'
'I'll keep you company.'
'I'm feeling lonely.'
'It helps me forget.'

Yes, it helps you forget. Forget the frightening statistics. Alcoholics have a four-per-cent chance of outliving the illness; some forms of cancer and leukaemia have a survival rate of ninety-five percent. Only one in a hundred find help and recover. Nine times out of ten, a man will leave a female alcoholic who finds help and recovers. Alcohol is the world's third leading killer, behind heart attacks and cancer – it has claimed three million lives in the UK alone in the last decade. Alcohol consumed in excessive quantities will kill and yet there is no warning on the side of the bottle, unlike cigarettes. There are about 350 thousand alcohol-related accidents per year, that's about one thousand per day. But there are also a hundred alcohol-related deaths every day. A high percentage of those in prison are there because of alcohol-related crimes.

Oh yes, it helps you forget . . .

CHAPTER SIX

The Ark

After Danny left, I put my heart and soul into work, and 1990 proved to be my best financial year. What made it successful was my determination to bury my grief. The more I worked, the less I felt. I didn't take any time off in 1989, which was just as well, because divorcing Danny was a huge financial drain on my income. He wanted to maintain the lifestyle to which he had grown accustomed. I'm so grateful for his bitter, hurtful words because the anger from them kept me going.

I'd always hated modelling. It gave nothing of substance back, other than money and an ego boost. For me, personally, while in the midst of modelling, I felt spiritually bankrupt. The feeling sneaks up on you. You are up there earning huge amounts of money; your agents, worldwide, are fighting for your time. You begin to feel desperately needed and important. The global travelling on a daily basis drains you physically, and giving all your emotions to the camera leaves you feeling empty. So when I saw a beautiful photograph of myself, I felt a brief lift, and then unfulfilled and empty. I took travel and money for granted – easily done when you are on a plane every other day. Men would say I was beautiful, but add: I guess you hear that all the time, so you won't want to hear that from me. Yes, I'd heard it professionally, but I wanted it said about me as a person, me on the inside, not the coating on the outside, which I didn't see anyway.

On the positive side, over the years, modelling has given plenty back. I've learned so much in many directions: a head for business, a deeper understanding of myself, and other opportunities to open doors, lots of contacts. The list is endless.

But every profession must have its drawbacks. Since January 1989, I've been known publicly as an alcoholic. I was first sold to the press by a patient who'd relapsed, using me as a cheque book, making themselves a bob or two by breaking my anonymity. Then the letters and the flowers from newspaper editors. 'Miss Hamilton', they read, 'we just want to say what a courageous thing to face. You have a responsibility to others, you can reach them through the press.'

When this first happens, you are so shocked, appalled. It leaves you feeling sick, ashamed and very alone. It is traumatic when you're going out and the press jump in front of you. I can put my hand on my heart and say that I have never called the press to set up an article or employed a press officer. I now have a manager and we have worked together over the years. We've learned what to accept and what not to. We've made some ghastly mistakes and, as a result, suffered greatly. He calls that a learning curve, I call it – hell.

After that huge and public relapse that found me in Brixton Prison, I had the international press and TV on my lawn. Being on the news for days on the trot, then disappearing to the States for a year – knowing I had to come back and face the press again was terrifying.

But this is jumping too far ahead. Back in 1989, I was one of the first models named in their own right, without being seen on the arm of a rock star. I had my own fame. I'd made a commercial that was nominated as one of the most remembered of the decade. I had always controlled my own deals and had learned how to get things done.

So while I was basically working alone, something extraordinary happened to me.

Although I had lived in Africa as a child, my main involvement had been with the animals I encountered around the homestead. I would bring home all kinds of hor-hors, a South African name for insects. We had three nannies called Unis, Beauty and Maria. They would click their tongues at me, and shoo me outside. I didn't put the insects in jars but would set them free, asking them to come back to visit – one, a chameleon minus its tail, always did.

My pets were my friends, and these came in many shapes and sizes. We kept Great Danes; my constant companion was a one-eyed dog called Igme. Other friends consisted of the chameleon minus its tail, three striped zebra field mice, and black worms with red legs called shongalooloos that curled up in your hands like Liquorice Allsorts and, when made nervous, leaked peed orange, staining your hands. I loved those days of freedom: hot and dry blue skies, the sounds of the insects and birds, so loud it was like an old jazz group, only all the instrumentalists were competing instead of playing in harmony. I would take long walks alone with a menagerie of animals. Sometimes I would crawl along the ground, writhing from side to side like a snake, so that I could feel what it was like. I was fascinated with the idea that each animal saw different things. How differently the birds, as opposed to ants, saw things. I would lose myself like this for hours.

Looking back long and hard, it's taken a number of years to work out why the plight of the elephants was so important to me. My interest began after seeing elephants being slaughtered on the television. I was in my late twenties.

I became more and more obsessed with the fact that we were killing off the elephants. Millions were being slaughtered for their tusks. I knew about as much as the next person, so I made it my life, for the next three years, to learn everything I could.

I now realize why I identified with the elephants. Their tusks represented so much money that the elephants weren't being seen or valued for the creatures they were. At the time I was being hounded by the press and publicly being known and written about as an alcoholic; I felt devalued. Behind the alcoholism and public persona was a person who dreamed, and had achieved. But what I felt, heard and read was not who I was. I, too, wanted to scream my fear and rage, just like the elephants, all across Africa, who were screaming their rage, and their fear of dying for the sake of a bracelet or garish ornament. I had no protector and I felt that neither did the elephants. Somewhere deep inside me something woke up. Call it my fighting spirit, maybe my ancestral voice called to me. I pulled through those two years by focusing my hurt (which could have so easily turned me into a victim) on the elephants who were fighting every hour for their lives, their destiny.

However, fighting battles on a daily basis, and giving my all in doing so, left me vulnerable, drained and cost me dearly. So, when Kenneth Oakhouse came along on his white steed, wearing his shining armour, charging to my rescue, I fell, exhausted, for his strong, powerful, protective image. I now realize I was too exhausted to think straight. Today, as a result of all my experiences, I have learned to put myself first; that way I am strong for me – therefore strong for you. Without putting ourselves first, we are no good for anyone.

Anyway, it all started at my kitchen table. What did they, the people protecting the elephants, need? My brother's girlfriend at the time, Sarah, helped me. At first I thought of, and researched thoroughly, a drive across Africa in a Volkswagen Transporter to give the money to Dr Richard Leakey, the Wildlife Director of Kenya. The drive did not take place, but what did happen was a million times more productive and helpful. The idea came to ask VW to donate a number of their Transporters, to be used as relief vehicles and ambulances, and to carry supplies.

I went to a meeting with VW and asked for help. They told me we needed to register as a charity. Then, if I was serious, they told me they were sure they could help. Remember, I couldn't read or write until I was eleven, and left school at fifteen. What skills did I think I had? I didn't think I had any, except a strong desire to help. I just wanted to do something and I did. I wanted the elephants to remain on earth.

The charity was formed and registered with a strong arm of trustees – young professionals who lent their time and dedication one hundred per cent. I begged for a computer, which was kindly donated to us by a company, plus a laser printer and paper. Ernst and Young designed our first logo and were incredibly supportive. Along with the charity, I decided a documentary about the elephants would be a good idea. Almost every angle had been done, so new ones had to be thought of to keep the elephants in the limelight. I didn't want them to become yesterday's news.

I went back up to Johnny Meszaros, the marketing manager at VW, and said I wanted to make a documentary. A wonderful man called Jim Cossick helped me put together a script. It was called 'Mothers of Nature'. It was about the women, who, after seventeen years of research, brought all their knowledge to us, allowing us to know these magnificent beasts. I wanted to go to Africa and film them, to wake up a sleeping audience. I didn't want this documentary to go on *Nature Watch* or BBC 2. I wanted to grab the attention of, and wake up, people who didn't watch nature programmes, to inspire them. I was egotistical enough to think they'd see it in the *TV Times* and think 'What's that VW girl doing in Africa?' Then I could grab their attention and hope that the knowledge would move and motivate them.

Around the same time, Dr Richard Leakey had caught the attention of the world's press concerning the ivory trade. He'd done this by burning confiscated ivory. A mountain of it was burned in front of worldwide television and press. His pledge was that he would fight the battle between the poachers and the elephants. The burning of the ivory was a symbol and message to all ivory traders and poachers that the trade in ivory was over. Today Dr Leakey has taken his fight for Africa into the political arena, an arena that has cost him dearly. The loss of his legs in an air crash and a government that fails to recognize his belief and empathy for both the people and wildlife of its country have proved obstacles in his path. But, little by little, ivory has disappeared from trading sources worldwide. The media now regularly hounds the Hong Kong traders in particular.

In the meantime, while Jim put my ideas, and a few of his, down on paper, I got a call from Port Lyme Zoo, from a man called Martin Smith, their head elephant keeper. He'd heard about my interest, and asked if I'd go down and meet with him. He was working on a project, and needed money to put it into action. He told me the African elephant, which didn't reproduce in captivity, was getting all the publicity, yet the Asian elephant was also in grave danger. So far, only one zoo, in Oregon, USA, had managed to have any consistent success. He told me there were only about forty thousand Asian elephants left.

Still modelling through all of this, because I had to survive financially and pay salaries, communication and administration costs, I found myself in Italy doing a commercial. When that was finished, wearing blue jeans, white shirt, cowboy boots and a dark blue, cashmere blazer – my signature – and armed with a very expensive present, a bottle of brandy, I set off to meet with Dr Chelansia, the marketing director for Volkswagen Italy. The meeting was a great success. He loved my idea and pledged fifty thousand pounds if I could involve Germany and four other European countries. This would mean that the documentary would be broadcast internationally. He also sponsored my ticket, and Jim's, to Germany where I met with the German Volkswagen director. He was not so excited, but was interested. I promised Dr Chelansia I would attend a VW conference in Milan, which turned out to be a godsend. They got me an interpreter and I asked nine hundred salesmen for their help. I received a huge round of applause and support, also a pledge that they would be prepared to raise funds, and help with the awareness campaign! The interpreter said she worked on a live documentary show which dealt with all kinds of issues, and was sure the director of that show would be interested in my crusade.

That's how I met Mino Dimento. I went on the show and, with the help of the interpreter, discussed my plans and hopes and that I needed help from industries, schools, mums and dads, people from all walks of life. Many times my alcoholism was brought up and I used it to my advantage. The pressure of my struggle with alcoholism was always there, as it can still be at times today. I am what I am and no less. But a few years ago I had to wear it painfully on my sleeve. What was there to be ashamed of? I had to say to myself over and over again, before going to shows or being interviewed. It's human nature. We've been told it's awful. Alcoholics live in ragged, dirty clothes and have big, red noses. Oh, hum!

I had an idea. With the help of the press office at the zoo and a dear girlfriend, Carolyn Cowan, who was, amongst other things, a brilliant body painter, I put my mad idea into action. I went back to Port Lyme in March 1990. Carolyn painted me from head to toe, like an elephant, plastering my hair back with mud, and all that covered my bits was a chamois leather. The press release read – *Paula Hamilton appearing nude with the elephants at Port Lyme*. I cannot tell you the press turnout we had. French, Italian, English, Dutch – it was extraordinary. After the photographers had their fill, then came the interviews.

'Did you know there are only forty thousand Asian elephants left?'

'No.'

'Well you do now, so put it in your paper!'

We got more coverage than any story I'd ever seen. We made the covers of the newspapers, and the six o'clock news in four countries. It was a roaring success. Looking back now, I realize I missed a great opportunity to raise the money Martin Smith needed for his project. Yet the awareness vehicle began to roll forward and we went from strength to strength.

An extraordinary young journalist, Andy Wilman, from *Auto Express*, came to interview me and said he'd like to do something to help. He ended up becoming a trustee, and still is. Incredibly dedicated, he convinced the magazine he worked for to give their support. He put together a European proposal and approached his bosses, saying he would like to get Holland and Germany, who both had auto magazines, involved in joining with VW to put together VW relief vehicles. We started to raise the money for these vehicles for Kenya's Stvavo National Park. This was ten thousand square acres, with only eight hundred or so rangers to protect it. Their equipment situation was pathetic and they were in desperate need of support. We found out exactly what they needed, and then VW supplied the vehicles and the hunt was on to get all the parts sponsored. Andy's efforts were tireless. He was brilliant. We were young, we believed in our dreams and we turned them into reality.

VW gave us two vehicles, and the genuine parts – every nut, bolt and screw – were donated by companies. That also enabled us to get coverage in all those countries from the media. The enthusiasm created was extraordinary. Without the help of these people and the equipment and monies raised, Tusk Force would never have happened. It was a global chain-reaction.

A book called *E was for Elephant* was dreamed up. Children were contacted through schools all over the world and were asked to send in their reasons for wanting the elephants to continue to share our planet. The reaction was phenomenal. Intelligent, heartrending and sometimes shamingly sensible drawings, poems and replies flooded in. Publishers were approached. Sadly, today, I hear from Tusk Force that the names and addresses of the children who sent in their work have been lost, therefore, without their permission, their works cannot be printed.

Tusk Force was now registered. Kate, who assisted me, worked long hours for a pittance. A string of unqualified, but dedicated, people worked for us. Those of you who came and went, forgive me for omitting your names, but my records have been destroyed, and I write this from memory.

I drove those people very hard and I can remember them saying, 'Ease up, Polly.' I exploded and said I didn't want a fan club, I wanted dedication, and anyone who wasn't dedicated could jolly well leave. We had a trustees' meeting every Monday night without fail. Minutes were taken, and each person allocated a project. There would be hell to pay if someone did not deliver what they promised; excuses didn't help, either. We were working against the clock. The elephants at that time, if taken off Appendix One – which was a protection status, meaning that they weren't to be shot or culled – had about eight years without it.

I gave many interviews. 'Why the elephant?' was the question always asked. I never seemed to say what they wanted. Now I know why, but I also felt that if we allow these magnificent beasts to become extinct, then as human beings we are truly lost. I just knew I wanted to do something. To raise awareness. Let's face it, there are so many good causes, so many, in fact, that I for one would feel overwhelmed by them. I would wonder how my little contribution could possibly help. I would then turn a deaf ear because I felt so guilty. How could I break through that barrier in others? I knew I would have to grab their support, keep them enthused so that our membership and support network would grow. We needed to give wildlife officials our support. Not to get politically involved, which was an art in itself. Each day I attacked projects, pushed people to breaking point. But all the while I was beginning to neglect my one priority – sobriety. Without that I had nothing to offer, nothing at all.

The organization grew and grew. People began to write in asking how they could help. Individuals and companies were incredibly generous, donating their skills and time – for example, the person who designed our logo; and Anglia Television, who found the famous image of Boadicea – a huge old matriarch elephant, making her last charge before being shot, which was used on the front of our packs.

I realized quite quickly I'd have to go to Africa. Communication between the charity and the people we were trying to help in Africa was very difficult and I wasn't being taken seriously. I asked VW to sponsor my ticket, and to loan me a VW Transporter. It was late 1990. My trip was for two reasons – the first, to contact the women I needed to interview for my documentary, to find out whether they would be willing to do it. The second reason was to talk to Dr Richard Leakey, Head of Wildlife, Dr Ian Douglas Hamilton and his wife Oria, who had researched the elephants for nearly twenty years, and Daphne Sheldrich, who had her own elephant charity looking after and rehabilitating orphaned baby elephants that needed constant contact in their first three years. They woke regularly from nightmares, extremely traumatized after seeing their mothers killed. They say an elephant never forgets. Daphne had proved that over and over again. Eleanor, an old matriarch, had grown up with and been cared for by Daphne, then had become a foster mother to the baby elephants. Once these elephants reached the age of ten, they were moved down to Stvavo National Park where Eleanor would watch out for them, teaching them the ins and outs of the bush. It was a fascinating story, and moving too.

Other women involved in caring for the elephants were Joyce Poole and Cynthia Moss, who lived in the elephant camp at Ambersali. There was also Eva Abe, who was a young woman in Uganda, working and studying the elephants. These were all older women who were highly suspicious of my motives in wanting to help the elephants. Was I seeking publicity for myself? So there I was, thinking that on my first trip out to Africa I would arrive to eager, open arms and ears for my efforts and ideas. Instead I found the opposite: suspicion, hard-heartedness and cold uninviting conversations like pulling teeth. I felt furious; here I was trying to help, but my efforts, yet again, were being questioned. Their past experiences with unfulfilled offers of help meant I would have to earn their trust.

With the hard work of the Tusk Force crew, Kate and Andy Wilman (key workers at that time, and for little financial reward), we would have to deliver what was promised in the form of the two relief vehicles; only then would we earn the trust we needed in Africa. It would take nearly a year to deliver the promise, but in the meantime the awareness campaign continued. Little by little the funds began to come in.

Because the money for 'Mothers of Nature' was coming from VW International, I was able to approach worldwide TV and media. VW was happy also in having a sponsorship title in the credits. However, unaware of the reaction of those very people I wanted to support, I was very nervous and very excited at the prospect of going to Africa to meet them. Ian Douglas

Hamilton asked me to bring out a suitcase which I picked up from his mother in London, and a printing bar for his photo-copying machine. Laden down, I boarded the plane. I sat in my seat and waited for take off. As soon as we were airborne, the stewardess asked if I would like something to drink.

'Champagne, please,' just popped out of my mouth.

I squirmed in my seat. Just one wouldn't harm me. Would it? The stewardess brought my drink over, and in slow motion I took it and thanked her. I looked at it, took a sip and thought, Bugger it, I've earned it, I'm off to Africa. It was the first time I could relax and feel pure relief.

I arrived at Nairobi airport at six in the morning. Oria greeted me. A powerful-looking woman with a face that held authority, she said I must stay over with them that night, but was afraid that I would have to go to a hotel the next day. Her children were returning from safari sooner than expected. My heart leaped.

The Douglas Hamiltons' home was beautiful, it reminded me of a tree house. A safari tent was pitched up in the garden and that's where I was to sleep. The bed was comfy, it had a little table and an oil lamp. Exhausted from the flight, and the long days before that organizing the trip, I fell into a deep sleep almost immediately.

I was wakened by a warthog's snout, snuffling outside the tent. I could see the bulge of its body against the canvas. I quickly got up and peeked out. He was huge. There were also quite a few young ones snorting and snuffling the ground. He caught my scent, looked directly at me, swung round quickly and was gone with squeaks, squeals and dust. I dressed, poured some water from the pitcher and washed my face. I wondered if I would be able to take a shower before leaving. I wandered across the lawn to the house and opened the door leading straight into the drawing-room. A fire crackled in the corner and in the most enormous armchair I've ever seen, curled up, lay Oria. She stirred and looked at me, stretched and yawned, then asked if I had slept well. I replied that I had and was I disturbing her? She said I wasn't, and invited me in.

I sat down by the fire.

She looked long and hard at me. 'Why the elephants?'

Oh, here we go again, I thought. I felt clumsy and tongue-tied. I took a deep breath.

'I just feel deep in my gut that if we allow the elephant to be slaughtered, to become extinct, I have a foreboding sense that Africa will never be Africa again, I have a strong belief it will have a knock-on effect. Am I right in thinking that the African elephants keep watering holes open?'

'Very much so.'

'And that each clan of elephants migrates from one to the other?'

'Yes.'

'And if these holes close up, then the surrounding land will become like a desert and all the wildlife and people will dry up, too?'

'Correct.'

'Is it also true that the elephant's digestive system is the only one able to digest the tree seeds in the forest, and its droppings deposit these seeds, enabling them to grow?'

'Correct again.'

'So, without them, deforestation could and would happen within about eighteen months.'

'Mmm.'

'Is it true that about forty per cent of our oxygen comes from these forests or thereabouts? Would tourists come to Africa if there were no elephants, and there was only a dried-up desert?'

'I don't think so.'

'Well, that's why I want to help these elephants. They are the jugular vein of Africa, they pulse out life. Without them, as I said before, Africa wouldn't be Africa.'

She looked at me suspiciously. 'So you think you can help. How?'

'I have a profile I can exploit in England. I can get to a large audience through television, newspapers and radio. The elephants are very much in the limelight. People are horrified at what's happening. I'm afraid that they feel helpless and look on with horror and sadness, but I believe if you motivate people, give them a voice, empower them, they will help. So many documentaries talk at you, are slow and sometimes condescending. I want to make a documentary that wakes up a sleeping audience. People who wouldn't normally watch documentaries would be motivated. The charity is set up, and will be highlighted in the film; people will want to do something and will be shown how. It's awful to just look and feel so helpless. I really believe in what I'm doing. I need your help. I need to meet people who I know will think all sorts of things: that I'm seeking publicity, that I'm egotistical, that I won't be able to follow through. I'm not giving charity balls back in England, it's not some sort of kick for me. I know people have let you down in the past. Ian told me of the months you've spent researching projects only for the money to fall through and interest peter off.'

She looked at me. 'Eat your toast.'

We moved on from Kenya to Tanzania, then over to Uganda. This part of my life was extraordinary. To meet these women and to see the film develop were beyond my wildest dreams: waking up in the elephant camps, going out with researchers through the bush; learning how to monitor the amount of elephants by the distance of dung droppings, and the paths and grasses torn out for food; travelling hundreds of miles by vehicle through bush and rain forests; staying in safari camps, small watering holes called hotels.

The director, Jeffrey Hadden, and the line producer had to deal with the fact that I was drinking in Africa. They both knew. I brushed it off and did my drinking alone. Why had I relapsed? Simple – I still hadn't accepted at gut level that I was an alcoholic. I kept my drinking out of sight and only openly got drunk once. The result was that Carolyn – my girlfriend and the photographer – ended up screaming at me, telling me I would lose everything and that if I didn't pull myself together the documentary wouldn't happen. I had no idea how I affected people around me.

The long and short of this was that the recce was concluded after three weeks. The material needed had been gathered. We went back to England. The next step was to place it in front of the TV networks. We had a lot of interest, both in Europe and the States. Sadly, a letter from VW International came through the post one day and everything was brought to a halt. They apologized but they could not find the money to fund the documentary because of the current financial climate. It was a massive blow. Who knows if the documentary will ever be made? The recession had hit hard.

When that project burned out, I turned a hundred per cent of my energy into keeping the charity afloat through the recession. If we could get through that, we could get through anything. Or so I thought.

Slowly but surely I gained the trust and respect of people. My efforts began to be recognized. I received an Italian award called the Ark, in the shape of a wooden Noah's ark. This award had only been given to three other people – the Queen of Jordan, Prince Charles and Sting. It was given in recognition of my achievements and efforts for the environment. I am extremely proud of this award and feel very honoured to have it in my possession.

I kept up my commitment to Tusk Force and didn't have a personal life. I worked, ate and slept elephants. My time outside work, became work. A means to finance my dreams. No social dinners unless they could help with the charity. Dates – definitely not. I was still pining for Danny. The harder I worked, the less I felt.

When I started the charity I had made a rather naïve pledge to the public not to use public funds for administration costs. This was now becoming a personal drain on my own finances. Up to this point I had covered all the costs out of my own pocket. One day, near financial and spiritual exhaustion, I put an SOS out in the *Daily Express* for an administrator guardian. It was a double-page spread. I appealed for a guardian to cover all costs, so that every penny the public donated would be used on the projects themselves.

The day before that I had appeared in the Femail pages of the *Daily Mail*, dressed in a Hardy Amies outfit, and had talked about trivial things that seem to interest us all. My favourite restaurant, my dreams, likes and dislikes. In New York, a man stared at this interview and tore it out. The next day, by pure chance, wearing the same outfit at a charity ball at the Savoy, this man saw me. He hadn't been in England for eighteen months. He walked over to my table.

'Miss Hamilton. For two hundred pounds, will you dance with me?' I nearly slapped him but he then quickly added, 'For your charity – Tusk Force.'

I took the money from his hand, placed it in my bag, stood up, took his arm and walked on to the dance floor.

'Are you willing to compete in events,' he asked, 'to raise money for your charity?'

'Yes, I suppose I would.'

'Call me. Events can usually raise a thousand pounds.'

'Good heavens, that's a brilliant idea. Thank you so much. By the way, I don't even know your name.'

'It's Kenneth, Kenneth Oakhouse.'

The next day I called him. 'Mr Oakhouse. Would you help us further? That's if you're still interested?'

'Well, I'm out of the country for the next few days.'

'So am I,' I retorted.

'Where?'

'Germany, Munich.'

'Me too. Give me your return flight details and my secretary will make sure we return together and perhaps you can tell me then.'

By the time I'd put the phone down I was standing on my

chair. 'Katie, Katie,' I shouted. 'Oh, Katie, I think I've found our administrator guardian.'

'Polly, don't build up your hopes.'

'Katie, I just know he's going to help us.'

I packed and left for Germany. My feet hardly touched the ground. I can't even remember the job. I had been contacted by Brenda, Kenneth Oakhouse's secretary, and she gave me the details. I took a taxi at the end of the day to the airport, giving the driver the directions. We went around the back of the airport and I walked into a small building. I sat and waited until a pilot came over.

'Miss Hamilton, this way please.'

He took my bag and I followed. Out we went on to the tarmac. I was escorted on to a Lear jet, and there he sat.

'Welcome on board.' I giggled. What fun.

Once airborne, he made me some coffee.

'Now, let me see, you need one hundred and eighty thousand pounds, or thereabouts, for administration costs.'

'How did you know that? No one knows that about us.'

He produced a cheque, already made out. I took it with shaking hands.

'Excuse me.' I got up, went to the loo, sat down and burst into tears. At that point I didn't care how he knew. It was like magic: we had the money we needed, and Tusk Force wasn't going to go under. I'd started this charity at my kitchen table with a girl of eighteen, in the middle of a recession, and with the public label of being an alcoholic. Now here I was, sitting in a Lear jet, with a cheque that would build Tusk Force into the organization I had dreamt WAS possible. But I'd also found a shoulder to lean on, as well as the finances to rely on, for the charity. I grabbed on to it like a swimmer in distress grabs on to a life raft.

It wasn't until later that I found out how Kenneth knew about the charity and who he was. Kenneth was a powerful business-man who believed in my dreams. He'd had me vetted from the age of ten to thirty – he knew everything about me, even my school reports. He knew that I was an alcoholic and addict. He knew everything, yet he still believed in what I was doing – so much so that he paid for the administration costs. In the meantime, for me, he filled the part of old dreams and ideas. He was yet another of my knights in shining armour.

I'd always fantasized about the man I loved being at my side, supporting my dreams and plans, believing in me. Kenneth fitted the bill. He was good looking, had a certain charm and made me feel incredibly special. We would meet in obscure places like Amsterdam, dodging the press, so we could have a secret friendship. This had to stay secret because of Kenneth's political ambitions. His support for Tusk Force showed his compassionate side.

All the while I kept up the lifestyle I had created. I continued working on the BBC *Good Sport* programme with John Fashanu, which took me all over the world; I modelled, ran my charity and film company. But little by little, Kenneth wanted more of me. He offered me a salary to work for my charity, saying any modelling jobs I did, I could donate to the charity. By this time I was so mentally and physically exhausted, it was easy to wear me down. I bought more and more into a very unreal world again, flying to Canada or Aruba at the weekend in his private jet. He had lent me a Mercedes and driver and I felt more and more disconnected from myself.

The pressure began to build up and I found I wasn't being true to myself. Every day I felt more and more drained and exhausted, yet felt I didn't have the right to take a day off to be with just me, to stay sober, go to meetings, see my friends who were also in recovery. When they called I was too busy to see them. My support system crumbled, I forgot how to ask for advice and started dealing with things undermining my own willpower.

Everything seemed to get on top of me. I felt pulled in all directions: the charity had media events, I'd be appearing on TV, up and down the country, never eating properly. Sleep had become a luxury – I was getting an average of about four to five hours a night. The day before my relapse I'd received a letter from one of my old schools, asking me to hand out prizes to their pupils who aspired to be me. A well-to-do shop had asked me to design a Christmas table alongside a number of the aristocracy and a royal. I was famous and was accepted in society. I felt I had finally arrived. You would have thought I'd feel fantastic, but I didn't. I felt awful, and I couldn't understand why.

Kenneth wanted me to spend more time with him. I felt torn, obliged to him for his support, but at the same time not willing to give up or delegate any of my duties at Tusk Force. Kenneth suggested that I get a manager to put some distance between me and the day-to-day running of the charity. I didn't want to seem ungrateful, and agreed to this proposal, but the more I thought about it, the more I felt Kenneth was trying to control me. Everything I had built up was slowly slipping from my own control; how was it all going to end? My thoughts became more and more confused, and I had a lunchtime meeting to get through before the interview of the new manager for Tusk Force. I had three glasses of champagne at lunch, and felt so relieved that the alcohol had temporarily taken away my fear and confusion that I spent the rest of the afternoon in the pub. By the time I arrived at the interview, I was sozzled. Even so, I was still able to realize what I had done, and I ended up telling the manager that whatever happened to me in the future, and I didn't know then just how bad it would be, that her one priority was the charity. Katie, my assistant, had been worried about me all day, and called a taxi to take me home.

CHAPTER SEVEN

Holding On

After the craziness at Brixton and the dramatic escape from my house, I flew to New York, chaperoned by Brenda, Kenneth's PA, and landed at night. I was taken by personnel from the plane through sections of JFK I hadn't known existed, then back on to the tarmac, and there he was. He was standing by his jet, hands in his pockets, in those bloody old blue trousers, at least two inches too short, making him look vulnerable, lost. He always made me want to look after him.

Looking back over my life, my need to change both what I don't accept and the people around me has caused me a lot of heartache. I kept seeing the potential in a partner, brother, mother, sister, friend and so on, and thought that by offering help and advice I was doing good. But when this was not asked for, I eventually realized it made people feel resentful and inadequate. Today, when I find myself giving advice, I stop and remind myself how I would feel if this person was giving me advice I hadn't asked for. I guess the old-fashioned word for it is meddling. Today it is called controlling. I still do it out of habit, but far less than I used to – and I find that my relationships are better. The moral of this for me is that other people's lives are not my business. If my partner or family members are having a bad time of things, I am still able to get on with my own life.

I hadn't really changed Kenneth, not even the trousers, and when he hugged me to him, his arms around me made me feel safe for the first time in two days. His special quality engulfed me, I just wanted to stay like that forever. He was so gentle, as if I were a broken doll, and I suppose I was. He led me to the plane.

'Hello, John,' I said to the pilot.

'Hello, Miss Milton.'

I had used that name since I had first travelled with Kenneth –
H. A. Milton. It protected me from the press when I was travelling. Airlines let it slip when celebrities travel. How else do you
think the press know when we fly in and out of the country?
Certainly no manager would let it out. Let's face it, coming in
on the red eye from LA, the last thing you want is your picture
taken.

We sat on the plane and Kenneth adjusted the seats so that
we could sit together. I held on to his hand like a lost child.
Suddenly exhaustion caught up with me, I couldn't keep
my eyes open. I dozed all the way, waking up sometimes to
see Brenda and Kenneth huddled close together, talking, and
then going back to sleep almost immediately. Brenda was
only one of Kenneth's personal assistants. She handled all
his travel and hotel arrangements, dealt with the press and
had been appointed to me to headhunt the manager we needed
to take over the day-to-day running of Tusk Force. She was
one of the few who knew of our friendship and circumstances
and I trusted her entirely.

Finally we arrived at our destination. I was to find myself
staying in the States for the next eight and a half months, away
from my home, family and friends.

We arrived at a hotel. It never occurred to me to ask where we
were.

He was so kind and loving, saying, 'Peanut, it's going to be all
right, you're all right.'

I cried myself to sleep. What right had I to hurt this gentle
giant of a man who was still prepared to protect me? I hated
myself, and felt that I had no right to live: that I should die, then
the pain would stop, not only my pain, but that of everyone else
who came into contact with me.

I woke up and I let these memories float in my mind as the
horrors of reality flooded back. I suppressed hysterical giggles.

Was the press still on my lawn, two days later? I wouldn't doubt it. Oh God, how I hated them at that time.

Kenneth woke, and I ordered breakfast. I remembered breakfasting with Danny, my ex-husband, after I'd had a bout of drinking, and how the room had hung heavy with unfinished conversations. The look of betrayal: me shaking and trying to get through breakfast without spilling anything or breaking something out of nerves and anxiety, feeling dreadfully hung over. Then the long painful lectures, as I saw them, from Danny, praying he'd be quiet, praying at the same time for his arms to go around me, hug me and tell me everything was going to be all right – knowing that it wouldn't.

In that hotel room with Kenneth, the situation seemed just the same. All I said was 'I'm so sorry' over and over again.

It was obvious to all that I was still in shock; I was trembling from head to toe. I had been clean for seven months before that – seven months. I started to cry again, knowing that everything would change, but not knowing what would change. A one-night relapse and it had brought me to this state. People sometimes innocently offer me a drink, knowing I'm an alcoholic. They say, 'Just one, this wine's such a beautiful vintage.'

I have to refuse. They try to insist.

My reply is always, now, 'One too many and a thousand never enough.' Are you an ex-smoker? If you are, you know you can't have 'just one'. It's the same for me and alcohol. It is not the amount, it is the effect. There are so many types of alcoholics, just as there are many different forms of cancer.

There is the maintenance drunk. Never makes a fool of himself. Keeps himself tanked up to take the edge off life. Then there's the binge drinker who goes off on occasions. Depending how he carries that off, he can go on for years. Then you have the net-curtain drinkers. Literally, she who drinks at home. Maybe white wine to get her through boring days. The classic excuses:

'I was bored.' 'The kids are at school all day, I was lonely.' Or perhaps there is a bad marriage, an abusive partner. Then there was me. I managed to humiliate and embarrass myself and whomever I was with. I thought it was hilarious at the time, they thought me sad and pathetic, and a pain in the ass.

Don't forget, no one teaches us to drink, or how to drink. So why should we know better? There's a saying, 'Don't drink alone.' So deep down one feels shame, and perhaps for that reason hides the alcohol in innovative places. I have heard wonderful stories over the years. The travelling salesman who connected his windscreen-wiper bottle to a tube that ran up the side of his car door, just about head high. The tube stuck out so when he pressed a button on the floor, he got a shot of chilled vodka in the winter and a wonderful warm brandy in the summer. Or was it the other way around?

Then there was the wife who couldn't understand how every time her husband went to lie on the lounger in the garden, he'd come back tanked. There wasn't a potting shed, just a square patch of lawn and his lounger. What he'd done was dig a hole in the lawn beneath the lounger, put a bottle of vodka in it with a tube and attached it to the lounger frame. He just sucked his way through the afternoons.

There was a dear relative of a friend. She was in her sixties and every afternoon, following her nap, she'd come down for tea, pickled. The house staff couldn't work it out, they'd gone through her room with a fine tooth comb looking for bottles. Eventually, on her death bed, she said, 'So, you weren't so clever after all.' She'd had a ritual that went with her afternoon nap, and an accomplice in the shape of a young maid, who would fill her hot-water bottle half-full of gin and warm water. Joe, a friend of mine I met at the treatment centre, had a few mad ideas, too. He would empty a Windex bottle of its light blue chemical cleaner and fill it with vodka and blue food dye, and spend the day happily doing the housework right under the nose of his partner.

All of these stories are true. There is a funny side to them, but a tragic side too. Broken marriages, children who grow up without trust or feeling devalued because the alcoholic parent, without knowing it or wanting to know it, puts the bottle before anything else. But do we have to wait until we are a chronic alcoholic before we stop? There is not yet enough education about this disease for people to recognize the early stages of a problem. We used to make children who were left handed use their right, thinking this was better for them. I know my older sister was made to feel inadequate because she wrote naturally with her left hand. In the same way, my dyslexia was not recognized and I didn't receive the teaching I required. Today we know and understand the functions of the brain and we leave the children be. Perhaps if we recognized alcoholism, co-dependency, and all other addictions in the same way, we might be able to help ourselves and others better.

If this book helps people because they identify with it, then my goal has been accomplished. Be a fly on the wall and read this. People, friends, families, loved ones, partners, have all said, 'Why do you want others to know parts of your life? Aren't they yours, private and precious?'

I reply, 'I feel I have the ability and guts to share my experiences and I should do so because there's no instructions out there. To share my truth is a privilege; do with it as you will.'

We drove to the treatment centre in Pensacola. I still had no idea where I was, and to this day, even after living in the town, I still don't know which hotel we stayed in. The drive was tense. Every fibre in my body said – you can't go through this again; they'll break you into pieces. I had been in treatment before in England, as far back as 1986. In those days they humiliated you, broke you. Thank God, methods have changed, and a deeper understanding of alcoholism is being reached today. Yet all I had were past memories. I felt so trapped. I couldn't go back, and going forwards filled me with cold terror.

'Oh God, please make this stop, please tell me it's just a nightmare.'

Kenneth assured me that it was going to be all right. I wanted to believe him, I wanted to make things right again. As long as I had Kenneth standing by me, it *would* be all right.

At that time I believed that if I had a Kenneth by my side – a partner – I would be fine. Having a partner who cared for me would give me the feeling I was valued as a person because they had chosen to be with me. To need to get our self-worth from outside ourselves is a very dangerous affair. That gives the other person all the power. I believed as long as Kenneth stood by me I'd be all right. It was the same before. A lot of women feel they cannot manage alone.

Recently I knew of a friend who was being badly treated by her partner. He would make plans with her then change everything, expecting her to adjust, to fit in. She would try to keep up with his inconsistencies in her day. Each time he let her down she'd fight a little harder with herself to be more flexible. The message she was receiving on a daily basis was: 'I do not value you enough to include you in any change of plans. This is how it is. Like it or lump it.' What she needed to hear was: 'Plans need to be changed, I do apologize, what do you think? Will you be able to manage?'

When she brought this up, he was unable to see he was treating her like a parcel, without a thought for her. She felt he was the relationship, she was the outsider.

One day I asked my friend, 'Why do you put up with it?'

Her reply astounded me. 'I don't think I could manage on my own.'

I looked at her in disbelief. She dealt with all the accounts, the children, their schooling, the running of the house, keeping up with his ever-changing plans, yet she honestly believed she wouldn't be able to manage. When I pointed out to her that perhaps time away from this man would give her back her energy, she did exactly that. She was able to step back, look at how far down the road of self-destruction she had gone. She had run herself down, trying to make the relationship work by accommodating his mood swings and inconsistencies in order to keep the peace. At first, as her strength and power came back, she was angry – angry at herself, angry at him. But little by little she owned up to her part in it – why she put up with it. It all came down to self-worth.

A person with a healthy sense of self-respect doesn't allow another to undermine, to be blatantly disrespectful, to discard another's emotions. My friend managed, with the help of a counsellor, to talk to her husband and make it clear that the abusive behaviour towards her had to stop and remain stopped. There is a happy ending to this story. Today they are two people who are not only together, but also friends. They support each other, give each other space. It has taken hard work on both sides, but there is clearly love and respect. It gives me, personally, a lot of hope.

But that day with Kenneth, as the cab pulled up outside the treatment centre, I was a long way from knowing all this. Kenneth was in control and I allowed him to be, for I knew no other way. It was 22 October 1991. I would remain at the treatment centre until 8 December 1991.

We followed the woman who met us into a tiny office. The questions began, the forms came out and my name was changed to protect Kenneth and myself. I had been sold to the press before by patients in treatment centres, who saw me as a walking cheque for themselves. Normally, at the centre, they took a Polaroid picture of you to show you, four weeks later, how much you've changed. My photo was not taken. They knew they had someone in their office who had come a long way for privacy.

Kenneth left the office, and spoke to the Director of Treatment. He was standing outside the window and I thought how tired he looked. All the forms were signed, and they suggested I go and say goodbye to Kenneth. We walked the length of the gardens, and down the long dock. I looked about and began to focus on my surroundings; there was sea all around me. I held Kenneth and kissed him.

He smiled, saying, 'Peanut, I wish it were me staying here, I need a rest, Poppet.'

If I could have swapped places with him, I would have. I knew the journey that lay ahead of me; I knew what I had to face; I knew the large lumps of truth about myself I had to digest. As I walked back up the dock, I felt I was walking into a lion's den.

The tears streamed down my face, we kissed goodbye and he left. I stood alone for a moment, then began to shake. I felt nauseated. I wasn't allowed telephone calls for eight days or visits for fifteen days.

Mercifully I met no one on the way to my room. I told the woman that I didn't have any cases, that I had left in just what I was standing in.

The severity of what had happened overwhelmed me. I lay on the bed with my head turned to the pillow, and cried and cried. I felt so abandoned – a feeling, a message I had picked up as a child. My mother had been my world, and to a child that means life and death. When Danny and I divorced I felt so completely alone, at times it felt like death. The fear of abandonment had kept me trapped in relationships that were destructive, because the fear was so great. I would enter a childlike state, and feel I wouldn't be able to survive if I didn't have love and approval. It took me two years of non-stop heartache to get over Danny. The thought that I'd never see him again seemed so unreal.

Today, I have fallen in love twice and stayed loving. But I have managed also to end relationships that were at times very destructive. So I have managed to develop skills and tools to identify the destructive behaviour, own my feelings and move on. Little by little I choose healthier partners. But then, in that room in the treatment centre, I was so very far from this stage. Exhausted, I eventually dozed off.

I was wakened by a gentle voice asking me if I had any mirrors. I couldn't think what she was talking about.

'My make-up bag has compact mirrors.'

'Well, you need to give them up, your razors as well.'

Take away the few things I had – no. I opened my make-up

case, and tore out the mirrors, leaving myself with my eye shadows and powder, much to her dismay.

'Oh, Polly, those look expensive, we would have given them back to you to use. You just had to ask.'

I was too proud. I couldn't go up to someone and say that I wanted to put some make-up on, please. I couldn't. I gave her the mirrors and the disposable razor. I'd go hairy before I asked to use it. To take away my mirrors and make-up, for me at that time, was hell. I was forever touching up my make-up, making the outside presentable in order to cover up my feelings of inadequacy. When I was without make-up I was not in control and feared everyone would learn of my insecurity. My mirror image was how I saw myself. I couldn't negotiate a badly lit mirror that gives you bags and shadows. There are the other mirrors that make you look fresh. It all depends on the lighting. But because I didn't have a feeling of self, I was a victim of the mirror. If I saw a good image, I'd have a good day; a bad one, and I'd have a bad day.

The woman continued. 'Do you have any hair spray?'

'No.' The few belongings I had with me were strewn over the bed; she could see for herself what I had. You could inhale hair spray, drink mouthwash and perfume – they all contained alcohol. I never did, but plenty of others have. I began to feel so humiliated, my anger began to rise up, as it always did when I began to feel scared. I'd get arrogant and grandiose.

'Please leave me now, I just want to be alone. I've had a hell of a couple of days, I need to gather my thoughts together.'

She smiled and left.

I walked over to the mirror on the wall. What would stop me taking off my shoe, smashing it, and then use the slivers of glass to cut my wrists? Why in hell's name did they take my mirrors? There was a camera on the wall directed at my bed. I got on a chair and pointed it towards the ceiling. I got down, replaced the chair and stood by the window.

There was a long porch outside with people smiling, laughing and drinking coffee. It appeared that everybody smoked. These would be my fellow companions for some four to six weeks. Rednecks, I thought. They will never relate to me or I to them. Where the hell was I? I knew I was in Florida, but where?

I took a deep breath and ventured out of my room. I walked towards the porch. The conversations stopped. I didn't, and kept walking through them, pretending they didn't exist. My legs were shaking; I was in denial of even being there. I went to the patients' kitchen and got a cup of coffee.

'Hello, my name's Dan, and this is Sandra, she will be your Buddy for the next few days.'

A Buddy is a patient who has been in treatment for a few weeks. They show you the ropes. You are very disorientated when you arrive in treatment, and your Buddy makes you feel welcome, shows you where everything is, what you can do and what you can't do.

At that particular moment I was unreceptive, and I gave a tight-lipped smile and walked back to my room, back past the other patients, my hands shaking. I just wanted to run the rest of the way. In my room I placed my coffee beside the bed. I needed more air and flung the window open. I could hear the voices below.

'Snob.'

'Nah, she's just scared.'

'Who is she? Is she somebody?'

'Snubbed poor Sandra in the kitchen.'

'Leave her alone, she's just scared.'

'Nah, she's a snob.'

I hadn't even met them, and here I was being discussed. Rarely had I heard negative things about myself. *Snob!* I'd bloody well show those rednecks. I wouldn't leave my room for supper and just lay on my bed. I heard a knock on my door, and tried to ignore it. The door opened and a head appeared.

Dr Terry sat down on the opposite bed, and fired a few friendly questions at me. I then asked him why I was in detox; I hadn't drunk before the relapse for seven months. He replied that it was purely for observation.

Some people need detoxing when they come to treatment. The levels of substance in the body, be it alcohol or pills, can be dangerously high. To suddenly reduce the levels can have devastating effects – such as fits, or what is commonly known as the D Ts – in some cases leading to death. So a careful, monitored detox is vital. The alcohol is replaced by pills, and a gentle process of weaning the body off these is needed. Detox, in most cases, lasts about two to three weeks. This is the most traumatic time for the patient's mind and body. Therapy doesn't normally get going for a few weeks to allow the person to get to know their environment, and feel safe.

I have been in treatment four times, and on none of these occasions have I needed detoxing. This is because I was what is known as a binge drinker. This meant that at the end of my binges, which didn't go on for days or weeks, only hours, I had horrendous hangovers, occasionally the dry heaves, anxiety and depression, but I would then stay away from alcohol, sometimes for months at a time, until my emotions, or pressure of work, got the better of me and the insanity started all over again. Each time my illness has been arrested by going back into recovery, I no longer crave alcohol, and rarely do, to this day. Now, at The Friary, after only one night's drinking, I felt physically fit and knew I did not need a drink.

I turned to Dr Terry and mentioned the camera, which he saw was pointed towards the ceiling. He explained they needed to observe me for a period of seventy-two hours for insurance reasons.

'I will not have that camera pointed at me. I've lived at the end of a lens for ten years, and I refuse to have it pointed at me.'

The camera had become my focus; I started to shake again. He didn't know my profession, he didn't know what I'd been through the last few days, but I could tell he was intrigued. He left me, and I must have fallen asleep again, because the next thing I knew, when I opened my eyes, it was four in the morning.

I eventually woke at six-thirty. My stomach was doing backward somersaults. Shame covered me like a mantle, I couldn't shake it, but I couldn't hide in this room for much longer. There was a knock at the door.

'Breakfast, Polly.' It was the mouse, shy Sandra.

'Thank you.'

She hesitated, not knowing whether I would follow her or not. I left the room with my legs shaking, my hands sweating. How would they be? After hearing them discuss me on the porch the previous evening, I still felt they were a bunch of insensitive rednecks.

'Polly, we need to take your blood pressure and your temperature.'

'Why?'

'We'll need to do it twice a day for as long as you are with us.'

Again I felt trapped and humiliated. I was always so scared of illness and doctors, so out of control.

'Very good, everything's normal.'

Normal, I thought. If everything is normal, why am I here? I wanted to scream. Why did everything make me so on edge, so defensive?

After breakfast I headed down to the patients' kitchen. The coffee pot was empty so I poked around. One sachet of coffee didn't seem enough for me so I doubled the amount. Ten minutes later I had a decent cup of coffee, a fag and a quiet corner in which to have a peaceful five minutes. Just as I lit up Sandra came over and said that until I was out of detox and out of the observation room, I couldn't go beyond the deck. I looked at her as if she were totally mad.

'Don't be ridiculous, I need five minutes alone.'

'Rules are rules,' she countered.

'Fuck off, leave the fuck alone, you moron,' I hissed at her.

She looked genuinely shocked, shoved her hands into her skin-tight jeans, turned on her heel and was off. Great, Pol, I thought to myself, how to win friends and influence people. I couldn't relax now, so I picked myself up, and walked back into my zone area, feeling angrier than was good for me.

The bell that regulated our days shattered what peace was left. I grew to hate that bell. I followed the other patients into a round room with a cathedral-style ceiling. Everyone grabbed a big square cushion, promptly dropped it on the floor and sat down on it. Great, now I felt sure I had arrived at some weird place.

So there we sat, cross-legged on cushions, while my mind flashed back to kindergarten days in South Africa. Only these people weren't children, the youngest seventeen, the oldest in her sixties. I looked down and picked at the carpet. The door opened, a counsellor came in. 'Good morning, everyone.'

'Good morning,' chanted back the group. I just looked and sat in silence.

'There are a few new faces here today. Would you like to introduce yourselves?'

A young girl looked up. 'Hi.'

'Hi,' replied the group, once more in unison. Someone asked her name.

'Sandy.'

I looked around; all the faces were fixed on me. 'Hi, I'm Polly,' and gave a curt nod to the predictable reply.

'What's your drug of choice, Polly?'

'Alcohol, dope, used to take coke.'

Feeling trapped and exceedingly uncomfortable, I sat wishing I could just get up and leave.

'Well, are we ready to work?' The counsellor looked expectantly at the group.

I scanned their faces. No one answered.

'David, still not asking for help from the group?'

'Damn right,' replied a man of about twenty-five. 'Why should I?'

'David, we're all in the same boat, we all need each other. This work you are doing is important to your recovery. What would it take for you to ask for help from the group? How can we show that we care for you?'

'Don't know,' came his sulky reply.

'Well, I have an idea. I want you to think about it. I want to put it to the group that we blindfold David for the day. No one is to offer him help unless he asks for it.'

One voice after another said it was a good idea because he would have to risk, to ask, to see whether he would get the help he needed. I felt so much for this man who had been cornered by the counsellor and the group. I wanted to protest, but instead sat in silence, waiting to see what he would do. God, I had six weeks of this shit.

Out came the blindfold and the counsellor walked over to David.

'David, are you willing to do this?'

'No, I am not.'

'David,' cautioned the counsellor, 'if you continue to block your treatment, you will be asked to leave. If you leave, you will not have completed your programme. You made a commitment to the judge to complete your treatment, or face a two-year prison sentence. The choice is yours. What will it be?'

I sat, mesmerized. A little blue vein was fluttering on the side of David's temple; his eyes stared out with hostility. His shoulders squared, he looked directly at the counsellor. 'You sons of bitches. What choice?' He snatched the blindfold from the counsellor and tied it around his head. The counsellor pulled it down around David's neck.

'David, you forgot these.' She showed him two cotton pads and a reel of adhesive tape. He let the counsellor tape his eyes, snatched up the blindfold and tied it around his head. My heart ached for him and I hated everyone in that room. They were breaking him, they were breaking him. I hung my head, felt his shame, and felt hopeless. I wanted to die. I didn't think that I could take a moment more of this place. All I could think was: I had to endure another six weeks and I'd only been there twenty-four hours.

'Polly, Polly.' I looked up, it was the counsellor speaking.

'What are you feeling?'

'I'm feeling nothing.'

'Well, you look very angry.'

'I always look angry. I always look angry when I'm feeling nothing.'

'Why are you here, Polly?'

'I'm here because I was put here, that's why.'

'Polly, the same goes for you as for David. You don't have to be here, the doors aren't locked, you can leave any time you want, just walk out. If you don't change your attitude, you will be asked to leave. People here want to get better. They will go to any lengths to achieve that.'

That last sentence turned my blood to ice – any lengths. What did she mean?

'Are you angry?'

'Yes,' I replied through clenched teeth.

'Why?'

'Because I fucking am. I don't want to be here, I don't know where the fuck I am. I don't know exactly how long I'm supposed to be here. I can't relate to any of you. I think what you just did to that man is inhuman.' By now I had really worked myself up, I was beginning to sweat. I felt a familiar feeling in my head, as if it were going to explode.

'Are you scared, Polly?'

'No.'

'Are you scared, Polly?'

'Leave me alone.'

'Are you scared, Polly?' Her voice was controlled and insistent.

'Yes, fuck you, yes, yes, yes,' I yelled back at her.

'Well, that's good, you're angry and you're scared, those are two pretty powerful feelings. That's good, Polly, very good.'

I numbed her out, blanked my mind and concentrated on a thread on my cushion.

A patient piped up. 'My name's Tommy. I know how you feel,

Polly, I was scared and angry too. It's okay, you're in the right place. This is a good place.'

I don't remember the rest of that group session, I just sat in silence, sat up in the rooms of my head until it was over. I found myself back in Africa, standing on one leg like a stork, as I had been taught by my nanny when she knew I needed to protect myself.

After the session, we all got up, including David, and went out into the October sun. I was shaking and feeling a little sick. David walked unsteadily on his feet towards the door. He nearly made it through, but his shoulder whacked the door frame loudly and painfully. I went up to him, and put my hand on his arm. 'Want me to get you a coffee?'

'Fuck you,' he replied vehemently, and went to sit on a bench. I left him. I went to the kitchen and poured myself a cup of coffee. It was so weak. 'Does anyone want some stronger coffee?' I called. No one answered, so I simply did the same trick as I had done that morning, doubling up on the filters, and poured myself a large mugful. I walked out on to the deck, past the zoned area. Sandra saw me. She was about to say something, but I gave her a look that made her change her mind.

I concentrated on my coffee and lit a fag. I looked over the lawns and my eyes rested on the sea. There was a flock of pelicans landing, they looked like clumsy seaplanes, it was so peaceful. Spanish moss hung from huge pecan trees, dropping occasionally as the wind blew.

'Hello.' It was Tommy. She came and stood beside me.

'Hi,' was all I could respond.

'You're pretty shook up, aren't you?'

'Suppose so.'

'I know what happened back there shocked you. I know you're feeling confused right now, but we love David very much.'

'How long have you known him?'

'I've been here for six weeks, and have known David for three.'

'And you love him?' Sarcasm crept into my voice.

She looked directly back at me. 'Yes. He's afraid, he hurts, he doesn't trust anyone. I've heard his life story – it's horrendous. No one was ever there for him. Before we get well we have to trust each other, that can be tough.'

'We all have a problem with trust,' I thrust back at her.

'You've been in treatment before, haven't you?'

I nodded.

'Well, you know your work doesn't really start until you let people in, start to trust them. David wants to get well but he doesn't know how.'

'What's the point of blindfolding him?' I needed to know why.

'So he'll ask for help in order to get him to be aware of his vulnerability.'

I looked over to where David was sitting. Someone had lit a cigarette for him, he had a mug of coffee in his hand, but was not talking, just sitting.

'See, he had to ask for that, and he got it. It's a small gesture, but it's a beginning. Just wait, Polly, just wait and see what happens during the day. Have faith, trust the process.'

Learn to trust – my past didn't allow me that luxury at that point in my life. Today I know that eighty per cent of feelings belong to the past. To learn to interpret one's needs, one must first know and accept the past, and then grow to understand how powerful those feelings and needs are. A sense of low self-worth will always lurk beneath the surface. Sometimes it is so much a part of us, only the change of habit will move us on. Every day I have to work on my feeling of self-worth. The more I trust I will do that, the more trust I will have. The more trust I have in myself, the more I will trust you. This enables me to sift through what's good for me and what is not. David was at the beginning of this process. Even though it was out of fear of the consequences of his refusal, he had begun.

Tommy continued. 'You'll see some miracles being worked here, Polly, it's a magical place.'

'How much longer will you be here?'

'About another week.'

'Lucky you. What then?'

'Then I go back to my husband who doesn't think I'm an alcoholic. He thinks that I just got unhappy – that hurts.'

'What hurts?'

'That he doesn't believe in the illness. I think he's ashamed his wife is an alcoholic. I think he's ashamed of me.'

'He'll come round to it.'

'Maybe, maybe not. Come and sit and talk to the rest of the patients, they're a great bunch once you get to know them.'

I stood looking over the lawns of The Friary; if I had been there under different circumstances, I would have appreciated my surroundings: the pecan trees swaying gently in the breeze that floated in from the Gulf, October skies, blue and clear with enormous white clouds, the air crisp and warm. I couldn't feel any of this; in fact, I felt as if I were seeing it through glass and couldn't touch it. I was cut off, isolated, but even within this isolation I began to understand what Tommy was saying. I looked across at David and felt a huge lump come into my throat.

'You'll be all right, Polly, just let us in. We know you're hurting.'

Well, that did it, I broke down, turned my back and cried. Tommy placed her hand over mine and patted it gently.

I had been at The Friary for about four days when slowly I became more comfortable and began to know the patients. Sandra was shy, as fragile as her blonde hair. She had lost her home, her third husband and custody of her children through alcoholism. Her self-esteem was very low; I would say dangerously low because she felt hopeless, depressed and couldn't see a reason for living any more. I knew how she felt.

I was now out of the zoned area and Bruni Emanuelle, the Director of Treatment, found me sitting on a stone bench on the edge of the lawn, looking out to sea. He asked if he could join me, I invited him to sit down. He sat down and placed both his hands on his knees. My grandfather used to sit like that; it made me feel uncomfortable. He didn't say anything, he just sat there. I looked at him, wondering if he expected me to begin the conversation. When he finally spoke he asked me a question to which I had no answer.

'Do you know why you sabotage yourself?'

'No.'

'Has it never crossed your mind?'

I thought about the question, about the words. 'Is that how you see it?'

'Very much so. It would appear so from what I've read in your treatment assessment. Seems you get well, work hard, and at the peak of success you sabotage it each time. Don't you think you are worth it? What frightens you about it? Do you sabotage it before anyone else gets the chance to take it away from you? If you can figure that out, you'll never have to do this work again, never have to relapse again, never have to feel what you feel right now.'

His words were like a riddle. Since 1986 I'd been working on recovery. The first time I stayed clean was for seven months. I never accepted that I was an alcoholic. I had accepted that I was a coke addict, I'd got enough proof that coke wasn't good for you, but at twenty-five years old I couldn't accept I was an alcoholic. Consequently, after I'd been seven months clean, I went into the Chelsea Potter and ordered a pint, of all things; not vodka, not champagne – just an ordinary, harmless pint of beer. That pint cost me three more years, as I fell straight back into active drinking. It was during this time that I met and married Danny.

In 1989 I went back to the treatment centre in Salisbury, and it was there I truly accepted the fact that I was an alcoholic. I had proof and I was ready to hear it. I stayed clean for a year, then began drinking again. I got back to AA almost immediately, but had a succession of relapses. In 1991, when I went to the Charter Clinic to do a relapse prevention course, I learnt my trigger points. In other words, I learnt to look out for the telltale signs of a relapse. Relapses start to build way before one picks up a drink. There are behavioural changes. But I began to lose track of my guideline: sobriety is my priority. Work became my priority because I was then at the pinnacle of my success, and gradually I started to miss my meetings. My head began to tell me I didn't need those meetings: 'You feel good today, you don't need a meeting'; 'You're too busy to go to a meeting.' Soon, rather than missing meetings daily, I began to miss them weekly, and the longer I stayed away, the harder it was to go back. In doing this I sabotaged myself, and had the most horrendous relapse yet. It was this relapse that had brought me to The Friary.

Bruni's words bounced around inside my head over and over again. I wanted to know the answer to his question. I wanted to know the answer myself – why? As always when asked a difficult question, my mind went blank and I retreated into the room inside my head where the memory of my African nannies comforted me and blocked out all the pain of confrontation.

I looked at Bruni. 'I want to know the answer too.'

He looked back at me. 'You know somewhere inside of you there is the answer, you already know it. Our job is to help you find it, but without your help, without your hard work, without your courage, whatever we do, we can't find the answer for you.'

Bruni then spoke the words that turned my heart to ice. 'Are you willing to go to any lengths?'

'What does that mean?'

'Well, to begin with, if you are willing to go to any lengths you don't have to ask that. To go to any lengths you need to hand your will and your life over to a power greater than yourself. To know in your heart that, whatever happens, you will be all right.'

His words began to jumble in my head. I wanted to bargain with this 'any lengths'; to find a compromise.

'Tell me,' I insisted. 'What does it mean?'

He told me it meant following suggestions. They had said that to me in England. They wanted me to go to a halfway house for a year. This would have meant that I would have lost my work contracts and my home, because there was no one to pay my mortgage for me. There was too much for me to lose. My heart began to jump. If I agreed to go to any lengths, would they ask me to give up my work? Would they tell me to sell my house? Would they tell me to go to a halfway house for the next two years? My mind began to rebel and silently scream. I couldn't let them break me. I felt like a wild filly with a noose around my neck – the warm, damp Florida earth became rock and dust and the noose pulled tighter and tighter as my hooves began to slip – unaware that I was holding my breath. Bruni put his hand on the back of my neck.

'Breathe, Polly, breathe.' His fingers were the rope, the rope began to loosen, the muscles hunched in my back began to shiver and jump of their own accord. My hands were damp with sweat and I began to shake. I felt exhausted. My filly began to fade like a mirage and the scene I'd been staring at became once more the sea.

'Where were you just then?' Bruni asked.

'Here,' I replied, looking down at the ground and pushing a pecan nut with my toe.

'Yes, but where was your head? Where were your thoughts?'

You're not having them, I thought. You can have everything else but I'm not sharing those with you.

'I don't know,' I eventually responded.

'You've got a lot of work to do. Your walls are solid, Polly, you need to take the bricks away one by one. You're alone with all of this behind your walls, we can help you only if you, not us, break down those walls.'

He left me sitting there, cornered, by thoughts rebounding inside. Then I became aware of the African 'click-click' song playing softly in my head and the images and smells of my nannies came back to me. I wanted to lose myself in the memory. Bruni pushed me on and, like a child's soapsud bubble, the memory rudely burst in my face and I was back.

*

My days at the treatment centre continued. Patients came and went. Then one day Ruth arrived, white hair framing a face full of fun and mischief, flirting like mad with Bruni, unsteady on her feet, talking non-stop, every now and then giggling, and placing her hand on his arm to reinforce whatever she was saying. Bruni asked me to come over and meet her, then introduced me to Ruth and told her that I was to be her Buddy. He responded to Ruth's character by telling her he was going to keep an eye on her, that she was to be a good girl. Ruth loved the attention and gave him her prettiest smile as her blue eyes twinkled.

She looked at me. 'Well, dear, aren't you beautiful.'

'So are you,' I responded.

She threw back her head and chuckled. She must have been in her early sixties.

'How long have you been here?'

'About a week, a week too long.'

'You're British, my dear, aren't you? Is that a London accent I detect?'

'Very much so.'

I asked her to come with me for lunch and told her the food wasn't too bad. She asked if we could eat outside, and I realized she was a woman after my own heart. I told her we could, and we went to find food. Our lunch consisted of two large plates of salad, corn fritters, plenty of mustard and a bottle of hot sauce – a passion we both shared. We sat outside, sipping Coke and nibbling while Ruth vividly described why and how she came to be at The Friary.

'Well, Blake, my ex-husband, is the alcoholic, not me. My children overreacted, it's my diabetes. I just got the levels wrong and went into a coma, frightened them, I suppose.'

'Are you not supposed to drink if you have diabetes?'

'No, dear girl, these days they're very advanced. As long as you're careful.'

I looked at her nose with its broken veins and the telltale signs of rheumy eyes, the premature ageing of her otherwise beautiful skin. Ruth at the age of sixty was still a beautiful woman – she must have been stunning when younger. I found myself strangely drawn to her and spent a lot of time in her company in our shared room. I related to her more than anyone else. She was from New Orleans; she knew everything there was to know about music and the arts. I couldn't relate to the rednecks at all although I did find myself relating to their feelings and what we shared. That is why it wouldn't have mattered if they were from the farthest points of the earth.

Addiction is indiscriminate. It knows no boundaries of religion, colour, intellect, wealth or poverty. Like all illnesses it is a classless disease that is an epidemic throughout the world.

One morning at group therapy in the round room, sitting in our usual places on the floor on cushions, the counsellor came in with a tennis ball and sat down.

He threw me the ball. 'How do you like it here, Polly, getting on with everyone?'

'Yes,' I replied, wondering about the significance of the ball, but knowing at the same time that something was up.

'Why don't you throw the ball to someone?'

I threw the ball to David.

'How's Polly fitting in, David? Do you like having her here?'

'Not really.'

'Why?'

'She thinks she can come in here all high and mighty. She changes the coffee system without asking. It's just her manner, it gets to me.'

'Throw the ball to someone else.'

David threw the ball and Tommy caught it.

'Well, Tommy, what do you think?'

'I think Polly's scared, feeling lost. I mean she's in a strange country, with new people, no family, no friends to visit her. I think it's hard on her. I think we need to give her time to settle in.'

'Throw the ball, Tommy.'

I wanted to run from the room; my heart pounded. Tommy threw the ball, Sandra caught it. She was scathing. 'I think you think a lot of yourself. Twice I've tried to be nice and friendly towards you, and twice you've ignored me. I think, you think you're more important than anyone else here.'

The ball was thrown to every member. I felt crushed, devastated, ganged up on.

'Polly, we felt the community was upset, we thought you should know why. How do you feel?'

I wanted to say 'Fuck you all' and walk out. I thought, You bunch of jealous bastards. However, I just sat there and gave one hell of a performance. 'I am very upset that I have caused everyone so much trouble. I had no idea that was how you were feeling. Please excuse me.'

'Very clever, Polly. Now tell us how you really feel.'

Another performance. 'Hurt, a little shocked but everyone's entitled to their opinions.' Inside my heart felt turned inside out. All I wanted was to be liked, to be sought out, to be trusted, to be loved. I asked myself what it was that made people dislike me so much.

The counsellor sat and looked at me. 'Everyone can act sometimes, Polly, but you managed to do it in record time. I happen to know you're a very caring person. I've seen how you care for David. How do you feel about that, David?'

'I wasn't aware of it,' he replied.

'Well, she does, she wrote about you and how concerned she is about you in her significant-event form.'

David hung his head in shame. I thought they were bastards, that they were playing games. I wanted to know why.

'Polly,' the counsellor continued. 'Start risking, start caring openly about people in your group. Show them that you care, listen to them. Make room for them, do things for them, start being aware of your behaviour.'

I began to cry. I understood what he was saying. I looked at the faces of the group, I knew that I did care about them. I noticed that a few of them were upset, a few cried. I felt the ice melt around my heart. I didn't know how a tennis ball and a public dressing-down could do all this, but at that moment I felt a breakthrough – I felt those people.

After the session I walked around the grounds. I felt very small, very shy – silent.

David came up behind me. 'Want a cigarette?'

I didn't like his brand, but I took one anyway and he lit it.

'I'm sorry about what I said back there. I hurt you, didn't I?'

I replied that he had, but that what hurt was not what he said, but that he had spoken the truth. I told him I didn't think to ask about the coffee, I had just assumed it would be okay. I didn't want to ask in case they refused. David said that he hated being told 'no' too, that it made him feel rejected. He explained that it was another of the reasons why he was blindfolded, so he would have to ask for things, and be prepared to get the answer 'no' sometimes. I asked him to tell me what the blindfold felt like. He'd thought it was going to be a piece of piss, in his own words, but it was so dark; he could hear everything that was going on so clearly, making him aware of his own self, his hunger, his need for the bathroom and his own fear. I looked at this man whose eyes were those of a twelve-year-old. I apologized and we shook hands on friendship. We walked side by side and it felt good – so very good.

Ruth and I would wake up at six in the mornings, put on our swimsuits and trot down the path to the indoor swimming pool. Every night I would sneak in and mark up the thermostat to eighty-two so, by the morning, it was like walking into a steam room. We'd giggle, our bodies covered in goose bumps from the chill morning air, the blast of the steam was like a big bathrobe being wrapped around us. Every day we swam a little further. I had an idea to make our swimming time less boring. We bought two masks and snorkels. This allowed us to swim without raising our heads above the water, and to hum as we went along. I think we sounded like two beached whales.

Sixteen laps was a quarter of a mile, and it felt so good. Whatever happened the day before was wiped clean with those swims. Afterwards we would shower, dress, grab a couple of cups of coffee and go out on to the deck to look out at the sea.

When I asked Ruth what she thought of the place she said, 'It's nice, a bit cuckoo. The people are sweet – a little retarded, but it's a nice break.'

'You don't think that you are an alcoholic, do you?'

'No, I don't.'

'Why not?' I insisted.

'I've never done those things or had those things happen to me. I had a wonderful upbringing, some of those people's lives are a lot worse. It's no wonder they drink.'

'Why do you drink?'

'Because I like it.' She made it sound so simple.

I had a counsellor I saw a couple of hours a week alone. She was an odd-looking woman. She reminded me of a cartoon figure. She was over six feet tall, had a huge pear-shaped behind, small shoulders and blonde hair, cut as if a bowl had been placed over her head. Her room was stuffed with toys, books and sugary things, like a frilly lamp, a pastel-shaded rug and pink cushions. It felt claustrophobic, giving a false sense of security. It was in this room that my innermost secrets were prised out of me. Here I spoke too much, gave too much away.

I'd been at The Friary for three weeks; I expected Kenneth to come soon to visit me. I was asked how I felt about it. I was a little apprehensive, a little scared. I could have had a pass for the day to go out. I wasn't sure, I didn't know what we would do. How on earth was I to know? The fear made me feel sick. In the end I decided that we would stay at The Friary, have lunch and spend the afternoon together there.

Kenneth's secretary, Brenda, had flown in twice before to get me to sign forms – court forms, lawyers' forms, so many forms placed down in front of me. My mind was so jumbled, so scared, I did everything they asked of me, grateful I hadn't been abandoned. My worst fear was one of abandonment. Brenda had smiled, held my hand and told me that all people wanted was for me to get better and to hurry back. She told me everything was being taken care of. Tusk Force was doing well, everyone sent their love. The dogs and cats were well and Madeline was looking after the house. The bathroom was nearly finished. All I had to do was to get well. I cried and told her how grateful I was, apologizing for all the work everyone was having to do. She reassured me and told me that was what everyone was there for. She told me that I was loved by everyone, they just wanted me to get better.

I had always been in control of my affairs; it felt so odd to be so powerless, having to rely on everyone, being so far away without any contact. It all felt unreal. The court case for the taxi incident was being put forward so that I could continue my treatment, and in about a month I would be home. A month – it seemed like a lifetime.

I waited alone at the entrance. Kenneth turned up and my heart pounded. He came towards me, held out his arms and I walked into them. I wanted to feel safe – but I didn't. We walked over to the dock and sat down.

Kenneth turned to me. 'Do you remember that night?'

My back stiffened. 'Not really.'

'Do you want me to fill you in?'

'No.'

'You need to hear it, Peanut.'

'Okay,' though my mind was resisting the information it was about to receive.

'After the interview you caused a huge scene. Do you remember?'

'No,' I replied, not wanting to hear any more.

He continued. 'Katie stopped you. She poured you into the front of a minicab and you drove towards home. Just as you were coming into South London, you dropped the bottle of champagne you were carrying on the floor of the taxi, and lost control. You were shouting and raving. You got into an argument with the driver. You tried to pull out his radio, kicked his dashboard, you punched the windscreen and cracked it. The driver took you to Brixton police station where they booked you. Don't you remember anything?'

I remember Frances coming to get me out. Frances was my best friend, with whom I had been in treatment in 1989. She told the police she'd never seen me drunk, which was true.

'They thought you were on drugs. They say you were acting crazy. Why did you do it?'

I looked at him and was too overwhelmed to answer, even if I knew the answer, which I didn't.

'You told them that they were messing with the wrong woman. You mentioned my name over and over again, saying I would fire them. The press somehow got the story. We've had to put injunctions out against all the newspapers. The press have been crawling all over my family, the people I work with. They've gone to your family, school friends, your model agency. You can't imagine the devastation and chaos you caused.'

No words came, I could say nothing, I could only stare at my hands.

'You've hurt me and my wife.'

Wife – my head snapped up.

'I've told her everything.'

I wanted to slap him. His wife – I had believed that he and his wife were separated.

'I thought you were separated.'

I couldn't take any more. I told him I felt ill and needed to lie down. He told me he'd see me the following week.

I lay on my bed, my mind going over everything he'd said. Oh God. Why, why did I hurt so many people? One day, one day out of my life – the devastation and the destruction. I wanted to die. Why didn't I have the guts? Why couldn't I just die? I hadn't known just how low a human being's feelings could go. Now I knew hell; I'd visited it. I knew what hell was, I was in hell, a hell that I believed I was responsible for.

Blaming oneself out of all proportion, as I have done, is self-defeating. The emotion is a powerful one, and only treatment put that blame into proportion. I now know I am NOT to blame for being an alcoholic. But I will only have myself to blame if, as a recovering alcoholic and addict, I relapse. For I now have the skills, tools and knowledge that I didn't have before. I alone am responsible for my recovery and the quality of my own life.

Ruth came into the room. She sat on my bed and stroked my hair. 'Oh, my darlin', you've so much to learn. Your life is like an open sore. You invite people to wiggle their finger in it.'

I cried and cried for what seemed like hours. Half the time I walked around in a daze. I honestly believe it was depression, and this depression was a mechanism of self-protection. All of me had so much to take in, I felt like a war victim, shell-shocked, too numb to be confused. I became close to shut-off. My body felt icy inside; food tasted like cardboard; I didn't feel anything. Gently placed hands felt like nothing. Faces of concern were seen through glass. Words were just words, without emotion or meaning. They made me take walks, made me swim, made me draw, made me eat. For about a week I just existed, merely existed.

One day John, another patient and an ex-basketball player, walked by me in the corridor.

'Hey, Polly. When are you going to get off your Pity Pot?'

His words sunk in as I turned around and looked at him, my face full of the agony that I felt.

'Pity Pot Polly, get off your Pity Pot, or otherwise you're going to get a ring around your ass.'

I looked at him, felt a rumble in my tummy that went up to my chest and popped out of my mouth in a giggle. The giggle got louder and louder. John was laughing, too, as he opened his arms. He was six feet six inches and had huge shoulders – my head just about came to his chest. As quickly as the laughter came, so did a flood of tears. John, dear John, brought me back and I've never forgotten those words: Get off your Pity Pot, Polly.

Kenneth came again to see me; another counselling session on how I felt about this. It was his second visit so we were allowed out for the day. Apart from a few faxes from the people at Tusk Force – Kate, Andy and Kenneth's PA, Maryann, and the visits from Brenda – I hadn't had any other contact with home at this point. I was nervous, but looking forward to the visit. At eleven on Saturday morning, he arrived. I was in my room getting ready.

Ruth put her head around the door. 'He's here.'

'Do I look all right?'

'You look lovely.'

'I'm nervous, Ruth.'

'Take deep breaths, you'll be fine. Must love you lots to fly all the way from England.'

I grabbed my coat, cigarettes and a last spray of scent, and half-walked, half-trotted through the grounds to the visitor's lounge. There he was with his back towards me. I took a deep breath and walked in.

He turned around, gave one of his enigmatic smiles and opened his arms. I came in for a hug and rested my head on his chest.

'Do you want to have some lunch on the ocean front? Some seafood?'

'Sounds good.'

We walked hand in hand to the car. 'Want to drive?'

'I'd love to,' I replied. We drove in silence for a while.

'You've left quite a mess behind you. Brenda's sorting out your finances; they're in a mess.'

'Why? They weren't when I left.'

'Well, you seem to have so many accounts with varied amounts of money in them.'

'There's a system,' I said. 'There's a household account, a current account, a deposit account, tax and VAT accounts. Then there's the accounts of the film company and Tusk Force. What's the problem?'

He looked at me and laughed. 'Nothing, Peanut, you've just got an odd way with finance.'

'I want to come home, Kenneth. It was a one-day relapse. I didn't murder anyone. I know I've caused you problems, but I haven't committed a crime. This is my fourth treatment centre. I can't live my life going to treatment. I want to come home, to deal with the consequence of my relapses. Face to face with the problems I've caused.'

'Peanut, you need to stay. Everything is being taken care of.'

'Kenneth, I've been here three weeks, two more weeks and I'll be home anyway.'

'It's better you're here. Come on, let's have some lunch. You'll feel better once you have eaten.'

I felt odd. I felt like he wasn't being straight with me.

The day passed pleasantly enough; when he dropped me off, he asked me if I needed anything. We had not discussed the taxi incident; in fact, it was never mentioned between us again.

'Nothing, I just want to come home. There are campaigns I'm needed for. I can't just walk away.'

'Look, Polly, just because you're not around doesn't mean everything has stopped. They're all doing a good job. All you need to do is concentrate on your treatment. As long as you need to stay in the States, I'll look after you financially. The rest will look after itself.'

'Why can't I finish treatment in England?'

'Because you can't,' he barked.

I withdrew from him. He looked down at his lap, his hands folded.

'Look, it's been very hard for me. Can't you just for once think of others beside yourself?'

I felt awful. 'You're right. I'm sorry.'

He dropped me off outside The Friary. I walked in feeling low, depressed and trapped. I went to the patients' kitchen, isolated. As soon as someone came in I went out and looked for a quiet spot. Why couldn't I go home?

He called me from the airport. 'Look, what I haven't told you is the press have been crawling everywhere. You don't need the press all over you. You've lost your modelling contracts, your agency doesn't want you back. No one wants to know. We've had to take out injunctions against the newspapers. It's cost me a fortune. Besides this, the builders are still in the house.'

A month before, Kenneth had asked me what I wanted most. I wanted to spend time with him in my home When I bought my house, it had been split into two flats. It had a beautiful bedroom with another adjoining room that was a kitchen. It would make a beautiful bathroom, and that's what he'd done: he had organized builders through his chauffeur, and bought the most outrageous bath I'd ever seen, and a white marble fireplace and a walk-in wardrobe designed by Roger Banks from Colefax and Fowler.

Kenneth's last words made me think. 'Come on, Pol. What's a few weeks?'

'Thank you for calling me, and thank you for all that you're doing. It's just so difficult, I miss everyone so much.'

'It will be okay. Bye for now, Peanut. I'll call you in a few days.'

Feeling a bit better I went to find Ruth to fill her in.

The next few days went by uneventfully. David would be leaving; we had a little ceremony every time someone left. We all individually told the person who was leaving how much they'd changed. What we, personally, thought their trigger points were and wishing them good luck. Each patient left with The Friary medallion. David really had changed. He now understood and accepted he was an alcoholic. Before recovery, he had been ignorant of what alcoholism was, therefore he had not been responsible for his actions. Now he had the tools and education, he alone was responsible for his illness. He understood that if he didn't pick up a drink he wouldn't repeat the behaviour. For the first time since he was twelve he was sober. He knew he had a chance to make amends for the past and move on. Living, not merely existing from day to day. He now asked for help and took advice. His face had changed, and he no longer looked like a hunted animal. He wasn't defensive or sullen. He looked softer, more approachable. He'd even cut his hair. I wished it was me who was leaving. Little did I know what tomorrow would bring.

I was having my usual blood pressure check when one of the nurses came in. 'Your counsellor wants to see you after breakfast.' I thought it was strange, I wasn't supposed to see her for a few days. I walked down the lawn to the deck which jutted out to sea for about fifty yards. When I was halfway down, I looked back. The mist was so thick that I couldn't see the lawn or building, and when I looked out to sea I couldn't see the end of the jetty. I stood there and listened – nothing. Even the water wasn't lapping as it normally did. The gulls that usually screamed and called to each other were silent. I drew on my cigarette and exhaled; the smoke was lost in the fog. This was exactly how I felt – a nothingness. I didn't feel anything. I wanted to stay here, to slide down on to the deck and let the mist blanket me in.

The meditation bell pulled me out of it. I looked up – there was no use staying, I'd be found in a short while, and then go through the whole bloody rigmarole of: Why wasn't I doing what I was supposed to do? I slowly walked back up the deck. It was only when I was crossing the lawn that I realized I'd forgotten I was supposed to see my counsellor. I made my way over to her office.

'Yes, Polly, I need some time with you this morning.'

I sat down and watched her switch on her answerphone.

'Polly, in a few minutes all the counsellors will come, we have something to discuss with you.'

My stomach did a somersault. I sat there while they came in one by one, until five counsellors sat in her small sugar-candy office.

'How are you this morning?' This came from a face that smiled too wide.

Jesus – what's coming? Dear God – what was up?

'I'd feel a whole lot better if you told me what this meeting is all about.'

'Polly, we hear from Kenneth you want to go home.'

'Yes, I do. I've been here for three weeks. A month is about the usual, isn't it?'

'Well, that's for patients on insurance. You're lucky because Kenneth's paying, you can stay six weeks. In fact, we'd like you to stay for eight weeks.'

My stomach lurched. Eight weeks! 'Why?' knowing my voice held panic, wishing I could cover my terror.

'We feel, given the circumstances under which you left England, there'd be too much pressure for you to handle. After speaking with Kenneth, we feel that it would be best for you to stay. You said you'd never gone to any lengths before, well, that is what's being asked of you now.'

Oh, this isn't fucking fair, my mind screamed.

'Also, unless you follow the treatment programme that's been given you, you would have to consider whether Kenneth will fund your charity or pay for your stay here.'

I looked at them in disbelief.

'You need to go to any lengths. We all feel that would be the best for you. What do you think?'

I got up. 'I need some air, I'll let you know.'

I somehow got up and headed for the door. Black spots jumped in front of my eyes, my hand couldn't find the door handle, my eyes couldn't focus. Once outside, I headed for the road, a quiet country road that ran along beside the sea's edge. I couldn't breathe. I felt my chest had shrunk. If I didn't follow their suggestion, Kenneth would stop funding the administration costs of the charity. That would be the end of it. The charity would fall, with all the work and effort put in by me and my staff. The people in Africa, they were relying on me too. The elephants – the elephants . . . I couldn't let them down. I began to run, faster and faster, my feet pounding on the paved road. I listened, I heard their voices mocking me from the concrete: *They're going to break you. They've got you for the first time in your life. You're cornered.* The harder I ran, the louder the voices. Panting and sobbing, my mind raced to find a way out. There wasn't one, and my heart felt it was going to explode. I wanted to die – I was dying. Me, myself and I died on that run; a part of me, the part of me that protected me, was slowly dying.

I sat down on the side of the road, hidden by trees, and cried like I'd never cried before. All I could say, over and over again, was – NO.

It was late afternoon by the time they found me. I walked into treatment, white-faced, in shock and had to be led away. I was put to bed. Ruth came to me and asked me what was wrong. I couldn't speak, couldn't open my mouth. I'd gone deep inside myself. I lay there and left the room and went back inside my head – back to South Africa where I found my Nanny. I lay there all night, with Ruth holding me while she stroked me.

The next morning I was called back to my counsellor's office.

'Have you come to a decision?'

David's face flew in front of mine. 'There's no decision. Tusk Force will continue. If you've come to a deal with Kenneth, there's no contest. Tusk Force wins.'

'What does that mean?'

'What the fuck do you think that means?' I screamed at her. 'It means I agree. I'll do whatever you say. You hold all the cards.'

'Polly, you have the choice not to do any of this.'

'Bullshit. Look, you've asked me to think it over and I have and given you my answer. Can I go now?'

'Not with that attitude. If you don't change your attitude and embrace this decision you've made, you will be asked to leave.'

Dear God, they're killing me. I hung my head and wept like a child – no grace, no pride, no dignity. My filly had been brought in, broken and sold. I felt as if I had been sold, by life or by my disease or both. I looked at my counsellor.

'Do you want a hug?' she asked.

I just walked out, back to my room. Then his words hit me from the call a few nights before: You've lost your modelling contracts. They just don't want to know. Neither do the television companies. We've had to take out injunctions against the newspapers.

I was walking around inside hell. I knew this was only the beginning of going to any lengths. They could ask anything of me. I couldn't run. It never entered my head to betray Tusk Force – that wasn't even feasible.

Again the days blurred together; again I isolated myself. They gave me time to let the information sink in. At last I hit my emotional rock bottom. The only way from here was up.

CHAPTER EIGHT

Letting Go

The next intensive therapy work was called Sculpturing. This was where they had you relive incidents in your life, as far back as childhood. Darkened rooms, music. We sat on the floor while we watched each other's nightmares or grief that hadn't been resolved. It was painful, fascinating, freeing. At times I wanted to run and bury myself, thinking that I couldn't take any more, I couldn't cry any more, I can't give any more. I spent each night crying until I fell into an exhausted sleep.

Then I woke up one morning and felt different. I'd found my little girl the day before. The little girl, the one who I'd shut out, and stopped listening to years ago. We'd done some Sculpture work. They'd asked me who in the group reminded me of my mother, my sisters and my brothers. Then they asked those people to come forward and proceeded to stick my family's names on the relevant patients. On went the music, down went the lights.

'Tell your mother how it felt growing up.'

At first I felt stupid, melodramatic. I giggled, feeling this to be *so* American that any moment ET would walk in the door on the arm of Spielberg.

As I began to speak, I felt the past come up and hit me and I stood in front of this patient who had 'Mummy' pinned to her right breast and poured out my heart, telling her how lost, lonely, scared and unwanted I felt, that I only wanted to be a good girl, for her to love me. Each and every member of my family was spoken to by me. By the time I'd finished, I felt about four years old. I had crawled on to pillows on the floor and sobbed like a little girl. I'd never planned to go along with their ideas, I'd never planned to do that work, to expose myself. If I had known what was going to happen, I would never have done it. But I did do it, and at the end I felt different, I felt safe, safe and gentle, I felt what was called – peace. For a few hours afterwards I'd lain on my bed, absorbing this foreign feeling of peace. Little did I know I was healing my past, embracing it, understanding it, and slowly learning to forgive it. My work had begun.

As much as I was against the idea of my mother coming into treatment, I understood that if she was willing it would help enormously. A call was made and she kindly agreed. I was very nervous at the prospect of her coming and what would be dragged up, what coals we would both be dragged over.

In the couple of days it took my mother to fly out to the States, I found myself with time for reflection. I felt apprehensive at the thought of seeing my mother again, especially under these circumstances. I found myself withdrawing from the day-to-day activities of treatment, thinking back on other mothers I'd known. Were my expectations of my own mother realistic?

It seemed I was drawn towards men whose mothers either had problems or had worked through problems. Tom's mother, who had recognized my alcoholism nine years previously, had subconsciously had an effect on me. Although I had not taken her advice at the time, one of my most treasured possessions was the little wooden tobacco box that she had sent me soon after my flight to New York. It contained two pebbles from the lake beach, a corn stalk, feathers from the hens and a photo of herself, Tom and Tom's sister stuck inside the lid. Even though I had not seen her since I ran away, Anna's teaching and love had not been wasted on me. What she taught me had helped, and is still helping, me to find myself along my way. She also taught me that you can still hold love dearly in your heart for someone, even though it has been years since contact, touch, sight or sound has passed between you.

*

My mother's arrival caused quite a stir. She arrived, having flown straight from Africa, thin as a rake, brown as a berry and hyper due to nerves. The administrators showed her to her room and told her she'd be sharing. My mother's reaction was to feel that somehow she'd been tricked into treatment.

'I'm not a bloody patient, love, my daughter is.'

'Yes, correct. But all family members will be doing extensive emotional work, and we've found it best not to isolate people. A lot of emotions come up and feelings that can be pretty powerful.'

Finally she allowed herself to settle in.

It was so good to see her. She looked so small and vulnerable with all the weight she'd lost, yet she was the life and soul of treatment. She loved meeting everyone and soon got the hang of speaking quite openly about her feelings and emotions. There were conflicts between us that here we might understand better – might be able to resolve.

We had the first of several meetings with my counsellor.

'Today I'd like to do a few exercises that will show you both how well or not you communicate with each other.'

Mummy looked at the surgery's pastel carpet and I looked at the top of her head.

'Sheila, I would like you to tell Polly something important, something you think she needs to hear.'

Here it comes, I thought, feeling trapped and apprehensive, wondering what would come from her mouth.

'Polly, I feel you blame me for what has happened to you.'

The counsellor looked at my mother. 'Have you finished?'

'Yes.'

'Right. Polly, what did your mother say to you?'

'Mummy's wishing me not to get heavy with her.'

'That's not what she said.'

'That's what she meant.'

'No, I didn't,' said my mother.

'Polly, can you repeat what your mother said?'

'Yes.'

'What was it?'

' "I feel you blame me for what's happened to you," ' I repeated my mother's words.

'You see, it's quite peculiar, Polly. You're able to tell me word for word what Sheila has told you, yet whilst listening to that, the interpretation YOU hear is "Don't get heavy".'

Then the counsellor asked me to say something important to my mother.

'Mummy, I'm upset because you always forgot my birth date and gave me my presents two days early. That always made me feel as if I wasn't important enough to you.'

'Sheila, what is Paula saying to you?'

'Polly thinks I don't care for her,' came the reply. Then she realized she had done the same as I had.

My mother and I looked at each other in surprise; interested and forgetting our nerves we listened to what the counsellor was telling us.

'Dysfunctional families communicate badly. We act out with each other rather than state our own feelings. We expect family members to be mind readers or act as victims, doormats. Rarely do we state our needs clearly – perhaps we're afraid we won't be heard, perhaps we have stated our needs in the past and have been punished for it. Once a family is aware it has been damaged, or is damaging the relationship in the family dynamics, generally members want to undo the work and learn to communicate in a more healthy way.'

My mother and I did more of these exercises. Each time, I would hear a second voice that was unspoken and yet chose to ignore it, just focusing on what Mummy had to say. At the end we were both very moved and had a good cry. For the first time in many years Mummy and I really listened to each other. Powerful work indeed.

Now that small but powerful work had been done, trust slowly built up between us. The work that lay ahead was unknown, so everyone in treatment lived in the moment, otherwise we wouldn't be present to do whatever project we were on, if our heads were constantly trying to work out what was coming next.

More Sculpturing work. There were about eighteen family members and nine patients and we were all put in a room and sat on cushions.

'Today we are going to do some really important work.'

There were two counsellors. They walked over to the windows and drew the curtains and switched on a tape machine.

'Old wounds need to heal before we're able to move on. Who's ready to do some work?'

Trust Mummy. I didn't need to look up to know her hand was up. I cringed and tried to disappear into the foliage on my cushion.

'Sheila. Excellent. Come over here.'

She stood up and walked over.

'You and Polly are pretty close but at the same time there are a lot of power struggles and conflicts. We're going to work towards the roots of those. Polly, why don't you come and join us?'

The music started to play gently in the background. Lulling me into a sense of – oh, this is okay, this is gentle.

'I'd like you both to kneel down in front of each other.'

We did, looking at each other, wondering what was next, aware that over twenty-five people were watching our every move. Three cushions on top of each other were placed in front of us. A baton covered in foam was then placed in my hands.

'Polly, you are very angry with your mother.'

'No, I'm not.'

'Not at this precise moment, but you do have a lot of anger towards her. Don't you?'

'Yes, I suppose I do. I feel over-responsible for her.'

'Why? Put both hands on the baton and thump the cushions as you say why.'

'I really don't want to do this in front of all these people.'

'Polly, trust the process. Let yourself go and focus on your mother.'

I tried to call up a memory of a time when I had really wanted her support and had not got it. One incident sprang to mind. When in South Africa with Johnny, my stepfather, we had a roast dinner every Sunday. We all had to sit in regimental fashion, each of us in our set place, I to Johnny's left at one end of the table, with my mother at the other end. The table was always fully laid with three sets of cutlery. I mention this because at times, even to this day, due to those tense meals, I can forget which knife and fork to use. We always ate in silence, often too scared to say anything, confused because both our parents were unpredictable drinkers, and so many lunches had been awful. If I dropped my fork or spilt my peas, Johnny's hand would come down, and slam my face into my plate. My head would literally bounce up, my face full of food. I was so frightened, so humiliated, I wanted to crawl into a hole. Four tense little faces stared back at me: I would take my napkin, wipe my face, and sit waiting for the meal to end, not daring to move, not daring to cry. One lunch time when Johnny had bounced my face into the plate yet again, Mummy screamed, stretched over, and bounced my face back into my plate.

'Do you realize how ridiculous this is? Why don't we all just try to kill her off?' she screamed at him. She then jumped up from her chair, which crashed to the floor, and ran out into the garden where she lay in one of the kennels, crying her heart out. I remained seated in my chair, blood and food on my face, feeling that I was about to suffocate. I felt empty, abandoned.

I took a deep breath. Here goes, I thought. At first gently tapping the cushion, I began to say what it felt like always listening to the same stuff for over eighteen years about her wanting to sell the house and not doing so. Not knowing what to do with her life. Listening to how depressed she was. How much I wanted to make her happy. How angry I felt that I couldn't really enjoy my success, knowing how unhappy she was. Feeling responsible for her because of the unhappiness I had created for her when she became pregnant with me outside her marriage. Unaware that the baton now crashed down with powerful whacks against the cushion, unaware of how loud my voice was getting, only aware when I screamed at the top of my lungs, 'Get a fucking life, stop trying to live your life through me.'

I stopped, only aware of the last sentence. The room was silent, Mummy's face white and shrunken in front of me.

'Oh, Mummy.'

Just before I was able to lean forward and hug her, the counsellor's voice interrupted. 'Wait, Polly, and sit back. Polly, what would happen if you let your mother go? Let her be responsible for her own life. Let her make her own mistakes. Stop listening and advising. Just be there to love her.'

The thought horrified me. 'She'd drown, drown. I see her in the sea from my little boat and she's putting her hands out to me and you're telling me to let her go.' This image was very real to me.

'Let her go, Polly.'

I began to sob as if Mummy was truly drowning. I let her go and she disappeared under the water. I felt hysterical, I felt I was allowing her to drown, and then she bobbed back up, smiling and waving at me. The relief I felt was enormous. She was all right – would always be all right. Her life was her own. I was not responsible to save or fix her or be trapped into suggestions she wouldn't accept anyway. We were becoming unravelled. We hugged. How much love for my mother and her courage to do this work with me I had. Words cannot describe that first time in our lives together when our love felt pure, felt right.

That evening, Mummy and I talked and talked about her life, her history. I heard her, and saw her without children, without the role of mother. I saw her as the girl she was, who had struggled with the legacies passed down to her, and on to me and the rest of her offspring and partners. My love and admiration went out to her. Realizing, in my gut, that her actions had been out of the necessity to survive, without the tools, in the only way she knew how. The strong convictions, the personal beliefs that kept her going.

I saw qualities in her that before I had chosen to ignore. I felt an overwhelming sense of gratitude that this magnificent woman had given birth to me, had protected me in the only way she knew how. I now understood why she had concealed my real father's identity, as she was trying to protect me from another of her mistakes. She had also known how unhappy I was as a child, and that I would have tried to find my real father if I had known of his existence.

I knew that what we'd found through this time together would stay with us always. I'd found a friend, a mother and a person I'd barely known. Respect, admiration and a fierce sense of pride took the place of judging her. Who has the right to judge another's actions or lack of action? Who truly knows another's nightmare?

When Mummy left, knowing that each of us would deal with whatever life had thrown our way, she said, 'Polly darling, I leave you with this one message. If you live your life the way you think other people think you should live it, then you are not living your life. Blast to hell what other people think. Do what is right for you. And if you don't know what is right, then spend time reflecting on that.' With that, my mother was gone. From my thoughts and feelings – never. She would always be with me.

It's amazing how much clearer one's mind becomes when you stop being preoccupied with what others think or say of you. Instead, concentrate on how 'we' feel about the decision on hand.

My fear of life was fading. I had dealt with the biggest bogeymen of all. There would be more to come. Financial instability, celibacy, loneliness. I would experience lawyers, the tax man, the VAT man. I would face public functions, the press. I'd go on chat shows and discuss in length alcoholism and addictions without shame or guilt. I would wade through the debris of the consequences of my relapse. I would deal with the loss of my charity and film production company, and I would grieve for the friendships that had died along with my dreams for the elephants.

I would experience new feelings: dignity, graciousness and a clear conscience. A conscience that lets me know when I am doing something not quite right; it makes me feel uncomfortable. Thank God I have feelings, and now, instead of running away from them, I feel and own them, and deal with them. The more I do this, the more I trust myself.

To this day, I continue to work with my counsellor, Susie Hogarth. She shows me how far I've come. We've worked hard together. Without Susie, I don't think I'd be this far ahead, this mature, this confident or this secure. I've still got a long way to go. But today, for the first time, I feel I have a concrete foundation of self to work from.

By living in today, I let things happen, take their natural course. I go with the flow and experience life, rather than fighting or controlling it. The phone for me is a good guide. Once, if the number was engaged, I would sit and push the redial constantly, trying to get through, getting more and more frustrated; by the time I did get through, I'd let the person know just how long I'd been trying. Or I'd be curt, particularly if it was a receptionist. There were two reasons for this. One, because when I wanted to do something I wanted to do it there and then. And two, my mind was all over the place and I'd be afraid that if I stopped and did something else in the meantime, I'd lose my train of thought. Very real. Alcohol and pot give one short-term memory loss. Today I do not have short-term memory loss. Today, if the phone's engaged, I call later.

I know what you are thinking – what a cuckoo. But think about it. How many times does one push a situation, or, let's say, expend an enormous amount of energy getting cross in traffic jams? We get cross or stressed out about a situation we are totally powerless over. If you think about it, it's quite ridiculous but we do.

The group of people I found myself sharing my life with at The

Friary became my family and my friends. I began to care for them individually, souls I wouldn't normally look at twice in the streets. Jerry was a school janitor, he had a thick southern drawl and would call me 'darlin''. He would keep laps when I swam and made the best coconut cookies. He was in his sixties, had been a maintenance drunk most of his adult life. If he hadn't started gambling on top, making his life financially unmanageable, he'd have probably died without ever knowing a sober day in his life.

Sandra's self-esteem came up a little each day. Sober, she'd found herself married to a possessive, controlling sixty-year-old, thirty years her senior. Sandra was a trained nurse, and had married her patient. She realized she'd have to leave, and start up home for herself. No longer was the prospect so daunting, so overwhelming. Before she didn't even know she had the choice to start afresh, she was so beaten down by her alcoholism. The belief that she was a bad mother began to fade. Sober, she would never have ignored her children's needs. She had to get sober and face her losses before she could put things right. Her ex-husband came to treatment which was good of him, and they worked through a few things. It was hard for her to hear how she used to be. The children were scattered because he couldn't take care of them. Some were with his parents, and the oldest had gone missing. She had a long way to go but, one day at a time, she was able to see there was a life for her. That maybe one day, sober, she'd be able to reach her children, and be there for them.

On Saturdays, the patients' families and friends would come to visit. I looked at some of them and thought, My God. What have they had to face and to deal with? A lot of families were hurt, angry. They mistrusted the situation, having been told over and over again 'I won't drink', only for it to happen again. Lives had been smashed left, right and centre. After a few visits they would work with the counsellors, and spouses and friends gained a greater understanding, and learnt to be more supportive. They had a right to their anger and mistrust. However, just like the alcoholic, they needed our understanding, a platform of knowledge to move on. After a while of watching this go on around me, I began to feel a little hope.

Barbara was a part-time counsellor whom we saw three times a week. She taught us relaxation methods with tapes and breathing exercises. She led us in discussions about taboos on females and sex; she motivated and inspired us to find and own our female power, teaching us when and how we gave it away. I enjoyed her lectures immensely and grew to like and trust her.

Although we were finding the learning curve at The Friary tough going, we did make time to have fun – it was a great way of letting off steam. John, the ex-pro basketball player, and Brett, the pro golfer, shared a room. Ruth and I would giggle like two schoolgirls in the mornings and at night. Their room was next to ours, and Ruth had told Brett that a former patient had committed suicide in his shower. It wasn't a very nice thing to do – I put it down to an over-warped sense of humour. As a result of this story, Brett would make John take his showers first.

One Saturday, whilst John and Brett were smashing golf balls off the jetty, Ruth and I sneaked into their room, unscrewed the shower head and put red jelly powder – the kind you make squash with – into it, and screwed it back on again.

When John and Brett came back, Ruth asked, 'How come John takes his shower first?'

Brett, red-faced, just looked at us.

Ruth teased him. 'Come now, Brett, you being such a big man, so tall and handsome, you couldn't possibly be scared by that lil' ol' tale I told you.'

'No, Ruth, just I'm nervous.'

'Well now, Brett, I'm counting on you to put that behind you, and shower first, or you'll make me feel bad I ever told you that story.'

'Yes, Ruth.'

John, Ruth and I sat outside on the porch opposite. We heard

Brett humming softly, heard the shower go on and then we heard a yell.

'The fucking water's red, John!'

John shot in the room and saw the last of the red squash swirl down the plug hole.

'You cut yourself shaving.'

'I haven't shaved, you damn idiot.'

A few minutes later Brett came out with a towel round his waist; John followed. In the meantime, Ruth and I sat like butter wouldn't melt in our mouths. It took all our control not to burst out laughing, giving the game away.

'Hey Brett, nice body,' said Ruth, swinging her legs back and forth. John and Brett went to the pool. I shot back in, refilled the shower head, and waited for them to return.

John went in first – we sat waiting. Would John scream too? The shower went on, not a sound. We waited for what seemed ages, then out he came. He walked up to me, and from behind his back came the jelly packet. Damn, I'd left it in his room. He picked me up effortlessly and walked towards the pool.

'Don't you dare,' I yelled. 'Pick on Ruth, it was her idea. You pig, put me down.'

He did – straight into the pool. That little incident had us grounded for a week and no television, but just to have seen John and Brett's faces was worth it.

Ruth was a hard nut to crack. Her age and upbringing was used as a shield. Every time we got to her she'd snap it back up into place.

'Ruth, are you telling us you're a social drinker?'

'Yes.'

'Ruth, do social drinkers slip into comas?'

'Ah, come on, so I got my insulin measurements wrong.'

'Ruth, you're an acute diabetic. If you weren't addicted to booze, you'd give it up. Your daughter says when you drink you become argumentative, forgetful, bitchy, loud and boring.'

'Janice is sensitive, she gets embarrassed easily.'

'Ruth, what will it take to show you you have an illness?'

'Nothing, not a damned thing. My parents were wonderful. I haven't had the things happen to me that some of these people have been through. I had a happy marriage.'

'Then how come you got divorced?'

'Was it my fault he fell for a younger woman?'

'Ruth, come on.'

We tried everything. I loved her so much and so much wanted for her to get well. If the truth be known, Ruth didn't know who she was. She'd drunk socially at first, the butterfly of the ball. She had an affinity with men and could keep up with their drinking. Society back then in New Orleans required you to drink. Life was a social round of cocktails, parties, picnics, concerts, shooting parties – all requiring drink. If you didn't, you were boring. As I said, Ruth was a beauty. I can imagine she drove the young men wild. She had three children and a very wealthy husband. She also had money of her own. Sadly, by the time she married she was already relying on the booze, and wouldn't dream of going to a party, to be the life of it as her reputation required, unless she'd had a couple of shots of vodka.

Communication broke down in her marriage, and the less attention her favourite love gave her, the more her self-esteem went down. Over the years accidents happened, like driving her car off a bridge when she was drunk, and getting her insulin levels wrong. Her husband divorced her, which crushed and humiliated her. Dealing with society, back then, as a divorcée was agony. Family friends struggled: whether to invite her or not to social functions. No, she didn't want to have to face that when her long-standing friend, the bottle, made her feel better.

I found myself relaxing and trusting the process of treatment. Patients came and left and with them, their families. It wasn't until Ruth said she only had a week left to go that I realized I had been at The Friary for eight weeks. I thought about what I had learnt, what I'd been through, and how much I'd let go of to arrive at this point.

Ruth interrupted my thought process. 'Pol, want some pop-corn?' In she came with a huge bowl filled to the brim. We sat on the bed and munched.

'You going to the AA meeting tonight, Ruth?'

'Don't think so.'

'Ruth, don't you want to say goodbye to the people at the meeting? You won't be seeing them again.'

'What, those retards? No, thank you.'

I looked at her and saw that she'd been crying. 'Ruth, what is it?'

Her shoulders slumped and her mouth twisted open; all her hurt rose up and betrayed her. Ruth hated for anyone to see her cry. 'I hurt so bad. What's the use of digging up all that stuff? Nothing's going to change what happened – nothing. I'll go back to New Orleans doing what I always did. Things go on. What's the use?'

She was serious, she couldn't get in touch and let it go. She had been at The Friary for five weeks, and still she couldn't break through. All I could do was hug her and stroke her hair whilst she cried her heart out. She wouldn't betray her mother and father by talking about them, other than to say they were wonderful. I lay her down, pulled the bedcovers over her and sat with her until she fell asleep. I then walked out under the stars, listened to the crickets and felt a surge of gratitude. I could heal my past and move on, I wouldn't be stuck at sixty, too set in my ways, too shocked and confused. I had a whole life ahead of me. It was the first intimation that I *could* change.

I felt great tenderness towards all the women in the world who were too scared, too confused, and too stuck in their own grief and denial. Who would lead them out of it? Who would show them the way? What would motivate them to change? I thought of Diego's mother, drinking every night and sleeping till noon, still sitting in Marbella, stuck in her grief. Although she had been the one to send me on my way to my first real job in Madrid, she was incapable of motivating herself in the same way. She had become, as many people do, comforted by the familiar, not wanting to take any risks. She had married Diego's father at eighteen. She moved to France, broke both her ankles in a horrific skiing accident and lost the ability to walk properly and to dance, both passions of hers. When Diego fell off his motorbike and ended up in a wheelchair, she felt enormous guilt that his accident had mirrored hers. She never got over it, never received any counselling or help and just lived with her grief and guilt, numbed by alcohol. At night, alone, she would play Tahitian songs on her guitar, never knowing if she was grieving for her own lost dreams, or her son's. The two had become enmeshed.

I had always been ruled by my behaviour, I had never been able to control it. Every time something bad happened, whether it was my fault or not, I started to become more secretive and less communicative. Alcohol and drugs had been the perfect aids to this behaviour. My actions always seemed to show the opposite of what I was feeling and of course this alienated me from people, especially those I loved. I had become a master of masks, sadly inconsistent. But now, at The Friary, I was beginning to find the tools that could remedy this and that night, for the first time, I felt a layer of my mask slipping away.

When I awoke in the morning, Ruth was in the bathroom putting on some lipstick. 'You cut my hair lopsided.'

'I did not, your head's not on straight.'

I heard her chuckle. 'Going to miss you, Polnut.'

'Going to miss you, too, old fart.'

With that a wet flannel flew through the air and wrapped itself around my head.

We laughed, got ready and headed for the coffee.

CHAPTER NINE

Abandonment

'Oh, Polly, I'm glad I found you. Your counsellor wants to see you.'

Once again my stomach somersaulted. I walked very slowly to her office, opened the door and sat down.

'We'd like you to think about going to another treatment centre in New Jersey.'

'Why?'

'We feel you need more time away from your environment.'

'I've been away for two months. Look, I appreciate all that you are doing for me, really I do, and I've learnt so much.'

'Polly' – she took my hands – 'would you really be able to cope? Kenneth won't stand by you or your charity if you don't follow suggestions.'

'You mean Kenneth knows what's being asked of me?'

'Yes, he does, and he's willing to finance everything. I know you can't see it, but you're lucky to get this opportunity.'

I looked right at her, right into her eyes. 'How long?'

'One year.'

'Do you really believe that's what I need?'

She looked down and looked back up again. 'It's a group decision.'

'Did you all come to the same conclusion? Did you vote for it?'

She looked at me again. 'Bruni felt you needed it too.'

'Was it also your decision?'

'Not entirely. I'd prefer to see you go to a halfway house and after a while work part-time.'

'For how long?'

'A few months.'

'Why can't I do that in England, in my own country?'

'Because you're too well known. Here you can focus on treatment, there it would be more difficult.'

'And more real, that's where I live and ultimately need to be.'

She ignored the last statement. 'There's a place for you in New Jersey. We'd like you to go. There are a few rules: no smoking – no jeans or trousers – no leaving the ranch for one year – no phone calls – no letters in the first six months.'

'Absolutely no way, I absolutely will not go.'

'There are other places.' She had in reserve five other places. I bet they knew I wouldn't go to New Jersey, and would bale out at that point. My self-esteem was higher, I felt more for myself and felt stronger.

'I understand. There's a place in Colorado called Spring View. Here, perhaps you would like to see the video and there's a brochure. Have a look and we could talk more about it tomorrow.'

I walked out of the office. This time the terror wasn't overwhelming me as it had done before. There was a change in me, an acceptance. I went to the television room and put the cassette in the machine. Snow-peaked Rockies, clear blue skies, piano music, credits. By a log fire on the floor sat two women who talked openly about their alcoholism, their treatment and recovery at Spring View. They talked about what Spring View had to offer. Outward-bound courses up in the great Rockies, cross-country skiing, horseback riding, releasing the past through art and expression. A Red Indian counsellor taught spiritualism. A team of women set up to help women. The video finally came to an end. I flicked through the brochure and saw smiling, laughing faces. As I had given myself no option to break my promise to Tusk Force, I made up my mind. I would go.

My leaving day arrived, bags packed, phone calls made, addresses swapped. The ceremony over, I walked out of The Friary. Kenneth was waiting for me at the end of the drive. I'd had to make my own phone call to Spring View. They accepted me. The deposit of twenty thousand dollars, Kenneth paid.

I'd been called Polly Vaughn for eight weeks.

Arriving at Spring View was a shock, to say the least. We drove around the block to make sure we were at the correct place. It was, much to my dismay.

'Kenneth, it looks horrible, nothing like it did on the video.'

He agreed. A bleak, prefabricated bungalow stared back at us. 'Come on, Peanut, if it's absolutely ghastly, call me in a few days, and we'll find somewhere else.'

I looked down into my lap. Did he care?

He took my hand and raised it to his lips. 'Come on, be a brave girl.'

That small gesture gave me the little bit of hope I needed, hope that somehow it would work out.

'Kenneth. What about us? Is there an "us"?'

'As long as you want a friend, I am one.'

He leaned over and kissed the tip of my nose.

'You're cold, sweetheart.' He took off his scarf, wrapped it gently around me and buttoned up my coat to the chin. 'Ready to face the enemy? Come on, then.'

The walk up to the front door of that building was one of the longest I can remember. Looking back I didn't feel right, I couldn't put my finger on it but somehow I felt a great sense of abandonment. The door sprang open just as we got to it. A girl with huge brown eyes, wild, gaudy hair, legs that went to her armpits and a cracking figure appeared. She was extremely manic. 'Hi, come in, welcome. Let me take those for you, you can hang your coat there, you must be cold, cold, cold. Would you like coffee? Of course you would. Will that be two? Good, I'll go and get some.'

Kenneth and I just stood and stared. With eyes that grew even bigger, she gave a huge smile, spun on her heel and half ran, half jogged down the corridor. We looked at each other.

'Some live wire,' commented Kenneth.

'A patient, I hope,' I replied.

A calmer, older woman came over to us. 'Are you Polly Vaughn?'

'Yes, and this is my friend Kenneth.'

'Are you a relative?'

'No,' replied Kenneth. 'Just a friend.'

'Well, thank you for dropping her off. Will you stay for coffee?'

'No thanks, I've got to get back. Peanut, call me in a few days.'

It was 8 December 1991.

With that, he left. I watched him walk down the path; he got into the car, and without waving or looking back, he was gone. I had an overwhelming premonition that this was to be the last time I'd ever see him.

'Let me show you to your room. You're sharing with Sherry, she's about your age, and this is her sixth treatment centre.'

'How many girls are there?' I asked.

'Oh, about nineteen.'

'How many bedrooms?'

'Nine.'

The floors vibrated as we walked. The atmosphere was hot and airless. Strip lighting gave an impersonal feel to the place. She opened a flimsy door leading to the toilets and showers.

'No bath?'

'No bath, that's right.'

God, how I longed for a long soak in a bath. Unfortunately for the next eight weeks, it was not to be.

She opened another door. 'Well, here we are.'

I looked in. The room was tiny, with two beds on either side. She opened an even smaller door leading to a minuscule shower and sink. The shower head was dripping, the water bouncing noisily on the plastic base.

'That will need fixing,' I said, 'the drip, drip, drip will drive me mad.'

She replied that the janitor would be coming the following week.

Underneath the sink was a cupboard. When I opened its doors I found two inches of water in the bottom.

'That too.'

'Uh huh,' she replied. 'No hanging or sticking things on the wall. Lights out at eleven sharp. Up at six-thirty. Walk before breakfast. You may go out alone after two weeks. You'll soon get used to the routine.'

I sat down on the bed and looked up. She was leaving.

'Excuse me,' I said. 'Either that shower and sink are fixed now, or you will please call me a taxi. Your choice.'

She looked at me, picked up the phone and called the Head of Treatment.

'I know my limits, I won't be able to sleep. I'm sorry if I appear rude. I'm overwhelmed and very angry. This is not the place on the video. Would you please explain that to me?'

'That was shot in the mountains on location two years ago. We never said it was Spring View. Why don't you give it a few days? I'll see the shower head's fixed immediately. Have you eaten?'

'No.'

'Well, let me call the kitchen. Would you like some soup and crackers? You can make yourself some tea or coffee if you like.'

'Thank you.'

I walked into the kitchen. Decaf, that's all I could find. Then I saw the notice: Caffeinated Coffee Forbidden at Spring View.

Fuckadoodledoo.

The nervous girl who had greeted me on my arrival was called Sherry – it was she with whom I was to share a room. She never stopped talking, and was seriously mentally damaged. Her thoughts bounced from one subject to another continuously. In fact, it was quite scary. It wasn't long before our dislike for each other became apparent. I got up early every morning, and went for a walk in temperatures below zero. Coming from Florida, the contrast at first was quite a shock. It got light around eight-thirty; some of the sunrises were spectacular. Most of the time I was too depressed to notice.

The actual town of Florence is tucked snugly between the Rocky Mountains of Colorado. Fields and meadows of dry, blond, brittle grasses with tall, ancient firs, their tops burnt by pollution. Even here Mother Nature is under attack. Old, battered four-wheel drives creaked and rattled past me on long walks. I could hear them coming from way off as their engines vibrated and their suspensions bounced off the rocks. The trees were sleepy, waiting patiently for spring as they dried against the ice. It was hard to believe that in a few months they would come to life. Small, fragile buds peeked through, tightly wrapped against themselves, waiting for a warm day signalling them to unfold in their greenness.

POPULATION 2,000 – a sign informed me on the outskirts of the town. Where? is my first thought as I looked at the handful of small houses scattered widely. Telltale signs of chimney smoke floated up to the sky. Winter mountain air is still, light and cold. The humidity of Florida became a distant memory.

I spent as much time as possible outside. I always have. I need to be. It's as necessary to me as water is to a fish.

It didn't take long to discover that out of the two months I would be there, only three days would be spent in the Rockies, doing outward-bound trips. No horse riding, no skiing. It was also a primary treatment centre, not what I thought it would be at all.

Primary treatment is condensed and one looks at the behaviour. The work is done in a group and is called therapy, mirroring each other, helping each other get a better perspective of ourselves. I wasn't aware how my behaviour affected others. It does and I needed to recognize that. Sometimes you are disgusted and don't want to accept certain aspects of yourself.

With the help of the group, you can begin to tackle and change the behaviour.

Halfway house is a safe place before going back into the full swing of life – a protected environment. There's still group therapy once a day. It still has the routines of treatment. The difference is you are able to work part time to deal with issues that may be too overwhelming if you went back home. For instance, if a woman's husband is blaming and not being supportive, the pressure at home may be too great. Of course the roles go both ways. So the halfway house helps build self-esteem, gives breathing space, on-going counselling and a chance to meet in a safe place to discuss any drawbacks in a relationship.

The time I was to spend at Spring View – another primary treatment centre – was difficult for me after The Friary. I didn't find the staff friendly; the food was terrible. It was brought over from a state nursing home on a trolley. By the time it arrived, it was cold. I have always enjoyed food, it means a lot to me. Sleeping in the same room as Sherry was, literally, a nightmare. A state law, and insurance regulations, meant that the night nurse checked us every hour, shining her flashlight on our faces to see if we were still alive. I was told I'd get used to that, too. I never did.

After a few days I called Kenneth. I got through to Maryann who worked for Kenneth in New York.

'Maryann, it's Polly. Would you ask Kenneth to call me? Thanks.'

Normally Kenneth would call me back within minutes. One hour went by and then another. I called again.

'Maryann, he hasn't called.'

'Oh, hasn't he? I'll let him know you called again.'

He didn't. I lay awake all night.

I called again in the morning, and he called me back at eleven.

'Kenneth, I have to leave here. It's not a good place, maybe –'

He shut me off. 'You're bloody staying, you don't know how

much trouble you've caused. Focus on what you have to focus on.'

'Kenneth, you don't understand.'

'Oh, I do. You always want everything to be perfect. Well, life isn't.'

'Kenneth, that's not true.'

I heard him take a deep breath. 'Give it until just before Christmas. If you really can't stand it, call me.' Click.

I sat on the floor with the dialling tone growling. Dear God, I thought. I called The Friary. 'There's not a lot we can do, Polly, I'm sorry. Call Kenneth before Christmas and talk to him about it.'

Those were the longest two weeks of my life. Finally the twenty-fourth arrived, and I contacted Maryann again. Kenneth shouted down the phone at me and told me not to push it, that I was ungrateful and selfish. He slammed the phone down. Little did I know it was to be the last time I'd hear or speak to him – ever again.

I had been abandoned.

In my schooldays I had learned about children's cruelty to each other.

I now remembered the first time I found out that adults were capable of the same behaviour. I had been moved down to a special group of seven for English. The thickos again. An enormous rush of humiliation overwhelmed me, and the only way I had known how to fight back was with anger.

The bell had gone for classes, and I dragged my satchel along the floor behind me. They had converted a large storage room that still retained the title written upon the door for all to see. Yep – store the thickos away, get them out of the classroom, and squash them out of sight into storage. Tears welled up in my eyes, but somewhere deep in my brain I heard a voice from the past.

'She's a gifted child, an enormous imagination, talented, a delight to teach.' That's what my teacher in South Africa had said.

I stood outside the door, swatted away my hot angry tears, squared my shoulders, and yet again braced myself to face someone new who would have heard all about me by then. As I opened the door with a thrust, the handle left my hand, and the door ricocheted off the makeshift blackboard. Six heads snapped up from their work, and a pretty lady stepped back and gasped as a notice fell to the ground.

'Hello, you must be Paula.'

'Why must I be Paula?' I retorted, at the same time wondering to myself if they handed out photographs with the report cards now.

'Well, I know I have seven pupils, four boys and three girls, and there are only two girls here.'

I looked long and hard at her, weighing up whether she was being sarcastic. I saw she was smiling and had nice eyes. She asked me to pick up the notice from the floor. I reached down to pick it up, and as I hung it back on the door I slowly read its message.

ASK A QUESTION AND FEEL A FOOL FOR A MOMENT
DON'T ASK THE QUESTION AND REMAIN A FOOL FOR EVER

I knew what a fool felt like, and it was that horrible feeling of not being good enough, a feeling that lurked around waiting to attach itself to me at any available opportunity. I looked at her, she winked and smiled. She said she had saved me a seat by the window, as she imagined I must love being outside. How did she know? She'd saved *me* a seat by the window. I smiled shyly back and quietly sat down. She had a lovely voice, it was soft and light, and she was always smiling. Most of us in her class were dyslexic, but in those days England was way behind the States with this vital news. She had been trained – unlike our own teachers – to look out for it.

She won us over in a very short time. How I loved her and her lessons – they were gay and fun, full of imagination. Sometimes we laughed so hard a teacher would put her head around the door, thinking to catch us mucking around on our own. Mrs

Adams would reassure the inquiring face that all was well and thank the person for their concern. She was our special teacher; she was our friend. She showed us that we weren't stupid, that being in her class was because we were special, and therefore we needed special time set aside for us. She gave me and the other children our dignity back; in return, we worked so hard, harder than any of us had ever worked before. Little by little the classroom numbers were allocated back into the mainstream. In six months she brought me not just to the standard required, but to the top of the class, for English.

My turn came to leave her. She pulled me aside and gently spoke to me. 'You're ready, you've done so well. It's no use pretending that you are slow, Paula – you're not. Stop fighting the world, little one – join in. You'll see it's easy if you try.'

I asked her if I could stay, she told me I couldn't, that I needed to join the others. She hugged me, and I sobbed into her blouse. Sobbed for all the goodbyes, for all the lack of understanding I had received since leaving South Africa, sobbed because she had saved me, and was now pushing me through the door. I felt like a baby bird – pink, without feathers. They'd eat me up again and hurt me, but I told her none of this; I just held on and cried.

Walking down the long, dark, green corridor, I dragged my feet. A door banged, I heard a voice calling.

'Girl, girl. You there! Why aren't you in class?'

'Mrs Adams held me back, sir.'

'Where should you be?'

'In Form A for English, sir.'

His eyebrows shot up. 'Are you sure?'

'Yes, sir. Here, look.' I showed him my transfer papers.

'Mmm,' he said. 'Most odd. Well, off you go. What are you doing just standing there?'

Talking to you, I thought. What else? There it was again; that angry feeling, the one that always made me want to piss in my pants and scream in frustration. How dare adults treat kids like that? What gives them that right?

Outside yet another classroom I stood with my hand on the

door handle. Mrs Adams said I could do it; she said it would be easy; she said I must listen. I knocked, went in without looking and turned to close the door. Slowly I turned back and thirty-four faces stared back at me. Some began to giggle. One boy who I particularly disliked said, 'Ooh, sir, one of the thickos has escaped from the storage room.'

The classroom erupted into giggles, my face grew hot and red.

'Quiet,' the master bellowed. 'Come here, girl.'

I walked down through the line of desks, and stood before him.

'You have a reputation, young lady, of being a disruptive in-fluence in classes. I've read your report card and, quite frankly, I don't want you in my class, but I don't seem to have any choice. You will sit right in front of me where I can keep an eye on you.'

I hated him. I'd show him.

It was the end-of-term tests. He walked up and down the line of desks, dramatically slapping down each test form, all the while shouting at us, saying how important these marks were, that there would be dire consequences if anyone failed, that his reputation as an English teacher would not allow us to make fools of him. Even the cockiest of pupils now sat in silence with tight faces. I stared long and hard out of the window. Suddenly his hand, like a vice, gripped my neck, squeezing it painfully, directing my head towards my desk.

'That's where you'll be looking, there and only there, for the next two hours. If I see you lift your head, I will assume you are cheating and, if you cheat, you will be expelled.'

My head felt as if all my blood was trying to escape into it. I truly thought it would burst. For a long time I just stared at an inkwell – lost, gone from the classroom up into my head where I hid in its rooms, rooms filled with safety where they couldn't reach me. Someone behind me dropped their pen, and it broke the spell.

I picked up my pen and looked at the test paper for the first time. I knew the answers. I stared in amazement – I *knew* the answers, I knew all of them! My pen flew over the paper. For the first time in my short life I knew what it felt like to get it right, to understand. No longer were the letters jumping off the paper, no longer did it look like Japanese to me. For the next forty-five minutes I sat with my eyes glued to the paper because I didn't want him to think that I was cheating, and because I was beside myself with a feeling of pure joy – I belong here, I got this right, this is easy. Oh joy, bloody joy! I was going to work hard from now on, I may even like this class, and like this teacher. Suddenly his big hand snatched my paper off the desk, and off he went stomping up and down the line of desks.

When the results of the test paper were announced I discovered that my paper had been mixed up with someone else's, and the mark I achieved was 'Failed'. This mistake was never corrected and it was deemed that my level of English was still poor, that I was to go down a year. I was crushed; I felt all the light go out of my body; I grew so very small. Why had this happened? Mrs Adams was so very good, I knew she was good. She had loved us, she had made us feel special. She left the school, her teaching methods rejected by the system. In my young mind, I realized that adults can even make adults go away, that adults can make you disappear.

In my gut, I knew I'd had problems with Kenneth even before the relapse. I wasn't in love with him. I thought I could grow to love him. It seemed wrong and uncomfortable that he had wanted to keep our friendship a secret. He had begun to take more and more control. I had my fairy-tale idea of what our relationship could be. It's one thing to build castles in the air, but it's another thing to live in them, and that's what I did.

I was very depressed after that phone call. I walked around dazed and lost. The group asked me more and more difficult questions. Who was I? Why did I have a false name? When I replied, to protect myself and someone else, it didn't satisfy them.

Christmas at Spring View was empty, transparent, with painful reminders that we were not with the family or loved ones. Christmas, for me personally, is a time I dread. Christmas cards received from those you only hear from once a year: year to year passes without a word, then plop goes the letter as it hits the mat. Christmas is lost to me, it belongs in the past. I would cheerfully cancel Christmas whenever possible. I'd been told to go with the flow, what flow? I just don't like Christmas, what it's become and what it's becoming.

Here were all sorts of women, with different problems, thrown together: eating disorders (anorexia and bulimia), sexual abuse, co-dependency, drug and alcohol addiction. Addictions all come under one heading, yet they divided us up. Foodies on one side, alkies and druggies on the other. I felt uncomfortable with this. I heard girls with eating disorders chucking up in the loo, a recognizable sign of relapse – the equivalent of my walking out, buying a bottle of booze and drinking it. Yet they weren't asked to leave. In treatment one agrees to commit oneself to complete abstinence from one's addiction. I could see this was regularly being broken, and couldn't understand why there were no consequences to their actions. If you're in treatment, and continue to stay active in your addiction, it means you're not ready.

I believe, and have seen enough proof, that success in treatment has to come from the self – a burning desire to stop. Without that, rarely have I seen someone recover. I have my own experience of this; that's why I kept relapsing after periods of sobriety. The first time I was in treatment, after my problems in New York came to a head, I could see the reasons behind stopping taking drugs. I could clearly see that cocaine would kill me slowly; I could see the scars on my bank balance; I saw the loss of work created by the habit. When they told me to stay away from all mood-altering chemicals, I could see why. But when they told me I was an alcoholic, my first thought was that I couldn't be, I was too young. The concept of being an alcoholic just wasn't real, therefore I knew I would drink again. It's easy to go to India for three months and say 'I didn't smoke grass, therefore I'm not an addict', if you know you will smoke again in England. So I let go of cocaine, knowing I would still have alcohol. I once stayed sober for a whole year, and then relapsed. In Spring View I could see the reason why.

The honesty of The Friary amongst the patients was not to be found at Spring View. I never once felt safe and secure. People lying in group, watching counsellors have favourite patients – it felt false, therefore I had little encouragement to take the risks that were needed to open up.

Julie was a girl who'd married into a rich, horse-breeding family in Kentucky. Her husband was younger than her by a few years, rich, spoilt and very demanding. There used to be long and painful phone calls and, as the telephone was in the hallway, it was impossible not to hear what was being said.

'I'm doing the best I can, Ray . . . No, I can't come home yet . . . Look, I'm not running away, I'm trying to get well . . . Ray, please stop; look, why don't you get some help from your sister to run the office . . . Ray, I feel guilty enough . . . Of course I love you. Look, please . . .'

Often he would slam the phone down and Julie would go to her room and cry her heart out. On one of these occasions I walked in and sat down on the end of her bed.

'Want to talk?'

'Why doesn't he understand, Polly? What's the matter with him? He thinks I'm hiding in here; he says he feels like I've abandoned him. We both agreed I needed help. Now I'm here, he just makes me feel so guilty, like maybe there isn't anything wrong, maybe I'm just, just . . .'

'Julie, listen. You've got to stop being his victim. Stop justifying yourself. Stand up for yourself and tell him your needs; like you need to be here right now, doing what you are doing – for you.'

'Yes, I know. I'm just so scared. He says if I don't go home soon he'll file for divorce. He'll say I walked out, abandoned him and the family business. He says I won't be entitled to anything.'

'Julie, these are all threats, and also, have you thought that unless he changes his attitude, how on earth do you think you'll manage when you do finally go home? A part of the reason for you being here is to learn to stand on your own two feet. If he continues with this attitude towards you, how will you cope? How will you remain sober? Would you want this kind of life? Always being a victim, always having threats over your head when you do something he doesn't agree with?'

Julie looked at me. 'How do you know all this stuff?'

I looked down. 'Well, I was married once to someone I loved very much; he couldn't accept I was an alcoholic, he used to say it was all in my head. He used to get so hurt and frustrated when I drank, saying I threw his love for me in his face. When I finally did go and get some help, he told me that if I went into treatment he'd leave me.'

'Did he?'

'Not straight away. After being in treatment for eight weeks, they'd convinced me not to make any major decisions for a year, that I needed to form a support network, which I did. I went to AA and NA, every day, making sobriety my priority over my marriage, my work and my family. He didn't like that and wanted to move away. Looking back, I think he was very hurt and angry.'

I now had Julie's full attention. 'So what happened?'

'After a huge fight he left and fought me every step of the way through the divorce. Finally I called his lawyer and said it was ridiculous. He was fighting for a house that wasn't his – we'd been married only a year and a half – none of the goods inside and neither of the two cars I owned were his and that he had abandoned me in early recovery. That's the last time I heard from his lawyers. I was divorced in a year, but I was sober, and stayed sober through it.'

'How did you manage?'

'A day at a time. Sometimes it was hell; I wanted to die; I

honestly believed I'd never fall in love again. I was twenty-six years old before I fell in love with anyone, so it hit me hard. I was so young in my emotions, I hadn't grown up at all: every time I had a problem I fixed it with a drink or a drug. Therefore I never knew how to get through anything, especially relationships. Counsellors advise that if you are not in a relationship when you first recover, stay away from them for a year or two. It takes that long to find our feet and find out who we are.'

I looked at Julie, who had the face of a child – her legs hugged up to her chin, blue eyes staring out of thick, black lashes, her dark hair framing her face like a china doll. Girlie, sweet, adorable: that had been how she had operated, but none of those qualities would help her right now. She needed to feel appropriate anger in order to move her, to push her out of the door so she could grow up and take control and responsibility for herself.

It's partly acceptable for a male to be an alcoholic. Certain comments feature strongly, such as: 'Oh, he's always enjoyed his drinking'; 'but it's the pressure of work'; 'he seemed to hold it all together until *she* walked out.'

Alcoholism is so difficult to detect. Psychiatrists and doctors will all say how difficult it is to diagnose. Yet a woman is supposed to know her husband is an alcoholic and somehow it's her fault if she can't stop him drinking. Why does he drink in the first place? Why is drink the first thing he turns to if he's not happy? If she were a good wife, he wouldn't drink. Again she is blamed. For years she may have put up with abusive behaviour, even if it is just verbal. Alcoholics, when drinking, often are blaming, angry, self-pitying, selfish, sneaky; they have mood swings, use emotional blackmail.

A woman who has lived with this for years also becomes emotionally unwell. Self-esteem, dreams, promises, are all shattered repeatedly. Yet, somehow, all the blame is put neatly upon her. So, to support her husband she has to climb a mountain of shame. For years she struggles, juggles and uses innovative ideas to keep the family together. She tries desperately not to deprive her children of their father. Then she finally manages to get him help only to find herself being told she needs to go to Al-Anon or that perhaps she's co-dependent and is in some way enjoying her suffering.

It is only recently that treatment centres have realized the need for a family programme. So much damage has been done. Betrayal and hurt need to be cleared. Resentments that burn to the core need to be aired. Whole families do recover. But this myth that women should have more knowledge than psychiatrists, doctors or therapists needs to be challenged. An alcoholic male or female is solely responsible for their illness. Nobody pours the booze down their throat, or stands with a gun to their heads. Once we know we have an illness we are responsible for our recovery, not the spouse, or the children, or the job, or the pressures of life. We must take full responsibility if we are to recover and have any sort of quality life.

I knew my talk with Julie had moved her. 'Want a cup of the disgusting decaf, or want to break the rules and go to get a cappuccino over the road, like everyone else does?'

She smiled at me. 'You're so strong, Polly.'

'Oh yeah, so strong. Strong and stupid. Aren't you forgetting, I'm here too? I haven't got it all right. I do know that I want to this time, whatever it takes. Whatever. You know, Julie, I meant what I said. I haven't got it all sussed – some people are brilliant at seeing other people's problems and not their own. I guess that's how treatment works; we all help each other get a better perspective of ourselves.'

'You're not happy here, are you, Pol?'

I looked out of the window, but tears betrayed me. 'No, I'm not, I just don't feel safe any more. This place doesn't seem right, doesn't ring true. Is it helping you, Julie?'

'Yeah, I guess. So what you said back there, about being Ray's victim – you're right, you know. I'm scared he'll dump and divorce me. I worked so hard to become part of that family. I love the life I have, horse shows, social events; it's what I dreamed of as a little girl.'

'So why do you drink?'

'I never felt I was enough. I felt I had to prove myself all the time. Ray became more and more demanding. His sister didn't like me very much, and I found myself competing with her. At social gatherings with all the family, I could always count on her to show me up. The humiliation I felt at times was awful, a drink made me feel better. At first Ray didn't notice. Getting up each day with a hangover and feeling anxious was horrendous. During the week I'd work in the office, he was always shouting at me over the smallest mistakes I made. So I started taking a glass of wine at lunch and then, after a while, I was drinking the whole bottle during the day; it kept the hurt and inadequacy I felt away.

'Away from Ray I used to get so angry with him, feeling full of resentment, but I couldn't talk to him about it. I spent a fortune on underwear, trying to find ways to please him. He wanted to make love and I didn't, but I did to keep the peace, to try and win him round. That was awful, too, not wanting the man you married to make love to you. And again I couldn't say no. I felt exhausted and stressed most of the time. Then family and friends began to notice. I couldn't stand it. I had wanted the perfect marriage. I didn't want anyone else to see what was going on – keeping up the pretence was a living nightmare.

'Then one day, just before coming here, I blew. I didn't go to work. I told Ray I had a migraine, which was true. We had a fight and he called me a lazy slut, slamming the door after him. I just lay there, sobbing. I was tired, beaten down, I felt so hopeless. I can remember taking double the quantity of my migraine medication and going to the drinks cabinet, pouring out a bourbon and swallowing down the pills and drink together. By the time he came back I'd wrecked the place, smashing all our crockery which was a wedding present from his family. In fact, I smashed up just about everything.'

A giggle escaped her lips. I smiled back, knowing how that felt. Rage, lashing back, being pushed to the brink. She stopped and stirred her coffee absentmindedly.

'Go on,' I said.

'Oh . . . oh yes, he came home. I let him have it. I cursed and screamed what an asshole he was, how sick I was at the sight of him. He made a move to walk over to me and I threw a vase at his face, Polly. He was so shocked. He said I was mad. Oh, poor Ray. I told him that we'd been living a lie, that I was unhappy, that I hated working for him and his family. I resented not being paid, I resented him never having time for me. He was so con-fused, and I understood why. I never said no, always said "Yes, sweetie" with a smile: because if Julie was a good, good girl, he'd love me, but if Julie was horrid, I felt he would leave me. I'm gutless, aren't I?'

'No. "People-pleaser", I think it's called. Co-dependency: always putting others before you, something like that.'

Julie looked at me. 'How do I stop being Ray's victim?'

'By owning your side to all of this. By being honest with yourself and Ray. Why don't you ask for a family visit and tell him all of this stuff? Do you honestly think you can go back to all of that and stay sober?'

'No, not any more.'

'Then you have to be prepared to lose everything to get your-self back. You need to go to any lengths. Does that make sense to you?'

Julie looked down at her wedding band, twisting it. Her hair hanging forward, coming over her face. My mind went back to The Friary and I heard Bruni's voice saying 'you need to go to any lengths'.

'I loved him so much.' Tears streamed down Julie's face. 'I think I still do.'

'Then tell him. Put yourself first. It's the only way.'

'You're a good friend, Polly.'

'Guess what, Julie?'

'What?'

'I'm in exactly the same boat. I have to confront that in my life, too. That's why I'm here, I guess.

'The one thing I didn't seem to get before in recovery, at a gut level, was self-esteem. I felt that when I came out of treatment, I had to be one hundred per cent well immediately and pick up my life where I'd left off. Rushing to get everything back in order. Wanting people to believe in me again. I put so much pressure on myself to manage and cope. So this time I'm taking a good look at this thing called co-dependency.'

We went back to the treatment centre. I'd made a friend and felt much better. In the early hours of the morning, Julie was taken to hospital with a series of migraine clusters. They gave her an injection to relieve the pressure, but for the next week she went back four times. She'd never had them so bad but, despite them, she faced her problems with Ray; putting her foot down, and getting the support from the group and the counsellor.

Ray came to treatment and listened to what she had to say. Treatment suggested she go on from Spring View to a halfway house. They explained to her that she needed to build her self-esteem, to discover a higher regard for herself.

When she came out of her initial family meeting, her face had changed. She looked lighter, younger, her eyes shining and excited.

'Polly, oh, Polly, Ray's going to get help too.'

'That's fantastic, Julie.'

'He understands, he really understands. He started talking about the pressure to be perfect for his father, and that he didn't feel good enough, either. That's why he bullied me.'

I went to my room and lay on my bed, thinking over what Julie had said. It had helped me enormously when my mother came to treatment in 1989, and again at The Friary for that one weekend. She herself was now in recovery. Was it all about understanding? God, how I wished Kenneth would contact me. Did he love me? Did I love him? Did he use me? Was I using him? Did I have any choices? I could leave Spring View, go home and get control over my life again. Was I strong enough to do so? Would I follow the patterns of before: trying to fix things quickly again and not taking care of myself? Was I fooling myself? I couldn't think clearly, but for months now I had been in treatment. What was best for me? Did I know what was best for me? I'd lost the confidence I needed to answer that.

There's enough research to prove that behaviour is a legacy we pass on from generation to generation. It is known that eighty per cent of battered women's children witness or hear their mothers being physically abused, and that these children repeat the behaviour as adults. It has been proven that when this behaviour is arrested and the abuser is given therapy he rarely re-offends. The victims are nine times out of ten women. When she is educated, rarely does she go back into further abusive behaviour. She learns the telltale signs.

But the abusive man is put away in prison. He has to practically beat a woman to death before this action takes place. He does his time with no counselling, no therapy, leaves prison and re-offends. Therefore, children of alcoholic parents learn behaviour patterns; who are their role models? Who can they trust? Eighty per cent of domestic violence is alcohol-related, and it is well documented that most children from this kind of background either become abusers, or abuse themselves. So this damaging behaviour is taught. Monkey do what monkey see.

Over the years in recovery I have watched people struggle and grow. The procedure is almost always painful. Who wants to admit complete failure as a human? *But* – we soon learn that we are not bad people. We knew our behaviour wasn't right, and couldn't stop. Once we knew we could take responsibility, we had the ability to respond.

We do need our treatment centres that are under threat. We need to write and read books about it. This is not a self-help book – I'm not qualified to write it. What I have is personal experience which I wish to share.

Julie left one week later, and I felt very lonely. I hadn't really connected with anyone else at Spring View. It was really strange, quiet; the energy level was low in the house. I would take one of the bikes, and go for long rides, alone. A river ran along the edge of town, I would ride down the ridge and walk along the river bank, looking at the large chunks of ice floating on its surface. It reminded me of recovery: chip, chip away at my wall, finding out who I was and how I ticked.

Blue, winter skies, grass like blond hair encased in ice, waiting to thaw out, waiting for spring. Wondering where I'd be then? What was waiting for me? A day at a time, I needed to keep things at bay. I couldn't plan. I wasn't making the decisions – Kenneth was. If he cared, why wasn't he here? Why didn't he come to visit? I needed to know. I half ran up to the bike, dragged it back up the ridge and rode back to treatment. I sat in the porch area where we could smoke and got out my writing paper.

> Dear Kenneth
> There are a number of facts I need to know so I may make some decisions, along with my counsellor, to see where I go next.
>   What is the state of my finances?
>   When is my court case?
>   What is my position at Tusk Force – has it changed, is it likely to do so?
>   What is happening to my home, my dogs, my cats? Is my housekeeper still there?

. . . and so on.

I put the letter in an envelope, addressed it, got the bike back out, went into the town and dropped the letter off in the mail chute. Done. Now I felt better than I had for ages. I had done something when I'd been told to sit and wait. I had sat and waited, and it wasn't doing me any good anymore. I needed to know the answers.

To take action, a decision and then let go of the results is very freeing. To try to control the outcome leads to frustration and disenchantment. On a couple of occasions I have empowered myself by taking a decision when, even though I know I may not get the end result I want, I need to let go of my expectations.

It took Kenneth two weeks to answer, and his reply came through a third party. Jeremy Vaughn would come out and update me. I was angry and hurt. I had thought Kenneth would contact me, but at last someone from the outside world was coming to visit. Jeremy was on the board of trustees of Tusk Force.

I lost my temper with Sherry and we had a huge argument. We couldn't stand the sight of each other. To be honest, I was terrified of her. She talked of wanting to cut herself up, jumping out of windows. That, and the combination of her speediness, exhausted me. I just couldn't keep up with her mood swings. What I didn't know at the time was that I was very co-dependent myself, and felt a failure that my long soothing chats with her didn't fix her, or make her feel better. When she kept repeating her behaviour, I subconsciously felt she devalued my advice. What a lot I had to learn, and it seemed that each lesson came with a barrel-load of pain.

The treatment centre sent me to see a psychiatrist. He wanted to put me on the drug, Prozac, because I was depressed. I refused. Of course I was depressed, but it was an appropriate depression – I was without friends, family and support network. I was in a foreign place with not the nicest of people. I didn't know when I would see my home again or if I'd been abandoned. Only a regular cheque to pay my fees showed me that I wasn't.

'Wouldn't you be bloody depressed?' I asked the psychiatrist. 'Think about it. I need to get through this depression without a crutch, that's why I'm bloody well here.'

'We can make it part of your programme; if you refuse, you're the one holding up your treatment.'

'Threats and blackmail won't work. I will leave if this is forced upon me. How much do you get paid to put us on Prozac? This drug is highly controversial, with impending court cases in the US. Isn't this the perfect environment to observe its use?'

He looked at me and half smiled. 'Must be difficult for you, all this. You're very astute, aren't you?'

I left his office, furious. Although I had heard of other patients in treatment taking Prozac, I wanted to go through my depression, which I believed was a natural part of my recovery, without the use of any substances.

We are told in treatment we need to take care, that it is, in fact, vital that we do not take alcohol in any form, or any mood-altering chemicals during our ongoing recovery. This means a continuing vigilance and awareness of any 'medicinal' preparations that are given to us, or those we purchase across a counter.

At first I thought this was excessive. It wasn't until I'd accepted recovery, that I realized just how dangerous it was not to be aware of everything I take. Today, I believe, without doubt, that any amount of alcohol or mood-altering drugs can trigger off a relapse.

A few Christmases ago, I ate Christmas pudding without thinking about it. The following day I felt an enormous craving for a drink and a joint. My behaviour was off the wall – jumpy, nervous, short tempered. I couldn't understand it, and called a friend of mine who belonged to the fellowship. She asked me what I'd eaten and I told her. It was only when she told me that the Christmas pudding had contained brandy and a cherry liqueur that I realized what an idiot I'd been not to have twigged. I, personally, needed that experience to understand how powerful alcohol is, even in tiny amounts. The thought that I might relapse by taking alcohol unwittingly has made me more vigilant as to what I eat and drink now, and I will continue to be so in the future.

Today I know, if I have a headache, that it is safe for me to take an anti-inflammatory, such as Nurofen. If I have a cold, I call my doctor, who is also a recovering alcoholic and addict, and ask what I'm able to take. I do not medicate myself.

My dentist is also aware of my illness. On the medical questionnaires I have to fill out, where it asks for any allergies, I

COSMOPOLITAN

January 1988 • £1

Men who hate women and the women who love them

What would you do with a big bust?

Get in the money with our financial health plan

Living and loving in 1988
- It's better with a younger man
- No sex please we're ecstatic
- Black and white's all right

RECHARGE! 10 pages of mind and body boosters to make you look and feel terrific

Domestic violence
Why the police don't give a damn

Who'll be big in '88? We've lined up the names you'll all be talking about

Married and hiding my drinking from my husband

Kevin Costner in Mexico 1989
just before I went back into
treatment

Aged twenty-five, a
New York photo
session the day after a
coke binge

Not even at the top of
my career did it feel
enough

Sober, sad and missing
Danny after the divorce

THE BURBERRY LOO

During my best financial year between leaving Danny
and starting Tusk Force.

WOMAN'S JOURNAL

SEPTEMBER 1990 £1.35

THE 40 MOST INFLUENTIAL WOMEN IN BRITAIN
WHO ARE THEY?

HEART DISEASE
ARE YOU AT RISK?

COLOURFUL BEAUTY
SHADES OF AUTUMN

HARDY AMIES
AT HOME

GIVE PEACE A CHANCE
EXCLUSIVE INTERVIEW WITH THE DALAI LAMA

PARIS, MILAN, LONDON, NEW YORK
STYLE REPORT

Sober at the beginning of Tusk Force

Tusk Force up and running

My Ark award, one of only four in
the world

Sober and fighting back,
fighting fit

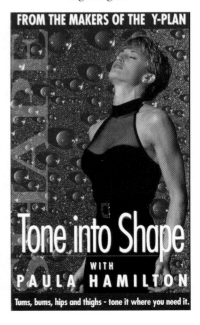

Tich at home on a lazy Sunday

Mummy, happy and relaxed,
summer 1995

On set with Natassja Kinski shooting *The Ring*. Dreams do come true

Hamilton and Hurley,
summer 1995

Summer 1995, happy on
holiday, my past behind
me now

reply yes, to alcohol and drugs. I also write 'Do not administer anything without my consent'. Of course, I am not going to have a tooth pulled without some form of analgesia, so, if any drug is needed, I ask a friend to accompany me. I also have to take into consideration what I will be doing the next day, as the analgesics affect me quite badly. I can get argumentative, weepy, and self-pitying, therefore I take the necessary precautions.

If one hasn't touched drugs or alcohol for a number of months or years, even the smallest amount makes itself known. We become acutely sensitive. Owing to my awareness, I have discovered many products that contain alcohol. Most mouth-washes contain up to twenty-five per cent alcohol. Right up until the late 1950s, baby's Gripe Water had a percentage of al-cohol in the product, which is mind-blowing when one thinks of it today, especially considering the fact that alcoholism and ad-diction are possibly hereditary.

I recently bought some homeopathic Royal Jelly. I snapped open the capsule and threw it back. Thirty per cent of it was brandy, used to preserve the medicine. It was such a shock, I can tell you. I can also tell you I craved a drink all day long and had at least three arguments that day. It might sound strange to some readers, but with my hand on my heart, I can say that any amount of alcohol or mood-altering medication, for someone who is in recovery, is quite lethal. Many an alcoholic or addict has innocently relapsed this way.

I have five years of recovery behind me. Today, if I relapse, I would lose all that clean time, and tomorrow I would be back at one day sober again. I don't feel, personally, that I have another recovery in me.

I lost it in group therapy that day. There was a counsellor who made it very plain she didn't like me, and I felt picked upon in group. So I confronted her, and vented my grievances about the treatment centre: the lies, the relapses, the bitchiness. They were stunned into silence.

'I want recovery. I want to change. I want to find out what makes me tick. I don't give a shit whether you're envious or jealous of me. That's your problem. We need each other to find out who we are.'

With that I got up and walked out, an action which was itself completely forbidden. I went to my room and packed all my bric-à-brac and books into a box. The Head of Treatment came in.

'What's going on, Polly?'

'What's going on is this place. It doesn't feel safe; the patients all split up into cliquey little groups. People are allowed to isolate themselves. Unacceptable behaviour isn't confronted. I don't trust this and I don't feel safe. Why is it that you don't contact my counsellor who's looked after me for four years, and ask her if I need Prozac? Or even what she thinks? Who the hell do you think you all are, playing God with us? No, I don't trust this place or you or your staff.'

She smiled a condescending smile and left me. I was tempted to walk out there and then, but I had to stay.

For nearly six weeks I endured being ostracized by the group. When I put my food tray down at a table, they got up and sat elsewhere. It was pathetic, and at first it angered me, then it hurt me and finally depressed me. In the meantime, I saw the Assistant Director of Treatment and asked how could they allow a community to behave like this? They knew I was in a hell of a lot of emotional pain. Why didn't they hold a meeting and patch this up? It was supposed to be one big, happy family. He looked at me and said that I'd brought something to his attention that he hadn't been aware of. I looked at him and thought, What's the bloody use?

Jeremy came in February. He brought devastating news.

'They're asking you to resign from the charity.'

'Why?' I wailed.

'You bring bad publicity. They've had to deal with the newspapers saying that the administration and account records were wrong. (This wasn't true, and they had to publish an apology.) Kenneth feels, as administrator guardian, it would be best that you resign. There's been such a fuss, it's best you don't come back until they collect the outstanding money from the charity events.'

'When will that be?'

'July. I need three months to collect the funds. If there was a further investigation by the newspapers, it may create bad press around it and many, many charities rely on this money.'

More guilt, more shame. 'What about my court case?'

'They can push that to July. Polly, you are very thin.'

The Director interrupted. 'Yes, Polly's been working very hard.'

'You want me to stay here another five months? No one has ever stayed that long, for God's sake.'

'You would go to a halfway house, Polly.'

'What about my finances?'

'You've almost come to the bottom of the barrel. I don't know any details, Polly. I'm just passing on messages.'

'Jeremy, you were chosen by me to be a trustee, a position of trust. What the hell is going on? Are you working for Kenneth or for me?'

'For Kenneth, actually. Working for him in Aruba on the treatment centre he's setting up.'

I looked at him and it dawned on me slowly. My God, the man standing in front of me had changed sides.

'Pay you well, does he?' Knowing Jeremy had been broke, knowing he had a son for whom he had to pay school fees. Jeremy couldn't look me in the eye.

'Jeremy, I need to know what the hell's going on. Please,' I begged him.

'If Kenneth said he'll look after your finances, then you only have one choice – to trust him. You're powerless to do anything else. I'll be off then.'

I just sat there, watching as he left.

I walked outside. Jeremy was someone I'd trusted, how could he turn against me like this? I'd chosen him to be a trustee of my charity, and now he believed Kenneth rather than me.

'You'll need a coat,' the nurse shouted after me. I didn't bother to turn, I just walked. I looked at the mountains, looked at the crisp, cool, blue sky. The dried grasses encased in ice crunched under my feet. My breath billowed out and hung in the air. I walked down the lane towards the veal farm. White plastic bubbles were scattered in a field, surrounded by barbed wire. I walked over the field, sat down on some straw next to one of the bubbles and looked inside. There, curled up asleep, was a small calf. I could hear the cows mooing mournfully from a field beyond.

The calf awoke and stared at me with huge, brown, inquisitive eyes. He licked his nose, and I watched as the tip of his tongue disappeared into each nostril. It brought a twitch to my lips – not a smile, but almost. That little calf could only see out of the same small hole through which I was staring in. I put my hand inside; he sniffed my fingers, gently opened his mouth and sucked hard on two of them. His eyes never left mine. That feeling of warmth, trust and the need for company, from something so new and innocent, stirred something deep inside of me. I gave him a last rub on his head, got up and walked back to Spring View.

I knew now I had to get away from Spring View. I went straight to my room, got my suitcase out from under the bed, and threw my belongings into it. In no time at all I was packed. My bric-à-brac was already packed – they hadn't even noticed. My mind was blank, no thoughts came in or out. I moved automatically.

I walked over to the mirror and looked at my face. My reflection stared back, weak, scared, a victim's face. I thought I was gently tapping my head on the wall; it wasn't until I heard a noise at the door that I realized I'd banged my head repeatedly until it was black and blue. I believe I shocked myself into snapping out of my depression. I needed to get away from this place and these people. A nurse had witnessed everything from the door and had done nothing about it.

I went to reception. 'Please order me a cab.'

'Polly, your forehead. What happened?'

'Please order me a cab.'

'Does your counsellor know?'

Through clenched teeth I replied, 'No, now are you going to call me a taxi or not?'

She picked up the phone and spoke to the director. I spun on my heel, went down the hallway to the patient's phone, got out the telephone directory and ordered my own cab. Why hadn't I done that before? Looking back, whilst making that phone call to leave, I realized that when I put my foot down and refused Prozac in the psychiatrist's office, I was assertive, even if it meant I would have to leave treatment. Prozac was not a solution, it only prolonged the problem. It was the beginning of taking back control of my life.

CHAPTER TEN

Fighting Back

I knew that Jeremy was staying in a hotel near Spring View. I called my sponsor, Brenda, who met me at the hotel. I'd met Brenda at an AA meeting. Most evenings I and other patients would go to either NA or AA meetings. The bus would take us to the various little towns scattered amongst the Rockies. It was these outside meetings that kept me sane.

It was at one of these meetings that Brenda and I met. I listened to her speak. She was a nurse, divorced and eight years clean. I identified strongly with her and found myself comforted just seeing her. The AA programme suggests that you start looking for a sponsor as soon as you come into treatment. Brenda agreed to sponsor me and we began to meet once a week. Sponsors guide you through the twelve steps and are there for you. It's a one-to-one relationship.

Brenda had a fiery, strawberry-blonde mane, wore Levis and drove a truck. She loved the outdoors and often at night we would get a blanket and lay it on the lawn outside the treatment centre, talk and watch the stars shoot across the wide open skies.

I loved her story, her strength, experience and hopes. She was in her early forties, tall and fit. It was hard to believe that when she came into treatment she weighed only seven and a half stone. I will always be grateful to her for pulling me through those hard lonely times at Spring View.

We sat in the lobby of the hotel, discussing what my next move would be. It was decided that I would send the personal effects I had gathered in the States and didn't need back to the

UK, so I could travel lightly as I wasn't sure where I would be staying. Brenda and I went and knocked on the door of Jeremy's room. He opened it.

'Hi, Jeremy, I've left Spring View. Want to talk about it?'

I knew he was amazed at the sight of me standing in the doorway, I watched his facial muscles move as this bit of information sunk in.

I introduced him to Brenda.

'Hi, I've heard a lot about you.'

Clearing his throat, he said, 'Why did you leave, Polly?'

'Oh, give me a break, Jeremy. It's pretty obvious except you choose not to see it. Spring View was a shithole. I could have gone totally insane in there, and no one would have given a toss, because no one was listening to me. I told Kenneth from day one I wasn't happy there. Look, even you said how thin I was.

'And another thing, what's all this about my finances, and why do you want me to step down from Tusk Force? I mean, what the hell's been going on?'

'I don't really know.'

'You were my trustee and friend.'

'Look, Polly, you caused such a mess with . . .'

'Bullshit, Jeremy. I had a one-day relapse that put me in the cells of Brixton for drunk and disorderly conduct, I had an argument with a taxi driver. I didn't murder anyone, maim anyone. I had a breakdown. Here I am, sitting like an idiot in a treatment centre that is detrimental to my health, is not where I want to be, because that's what seems necessary. If I don't begin to stand on my own two feet now, I feel I never will.'

I felt so angry, betrayed and hurt.

'I don't have any money left and, as you have asked me to step down from the charity, I don't have anything left to lose. There is nothing to control me with any more,' I challenged him.

His expression had softened while this was going on. Brenda just sat and listened.

'Look, Polly,' Jeremy replied. 'I'm sorry. If Kenneth said he'd deal with the finances while you needed to be here in the States, then that's what he'll do.'

'Damn right. I only agreed to come here on that basis, and to protect Tusk Force. There's nothing wrong with the treatment centres in England.'

'What are you going to do?'

'If my credit cards are still good, I'll catch a plane this afternoon.'

'Will you be all right?'

'Do you care, do you really care?'

He looked away. 'Of course I care, Polly, we all do.'

'Bullshit.'

I left the hotel room with Brenda, who took me to UPS Parcels and we shipped back boxes of books and personal effects. She then took me to the airport. I felt sick to my stomach. I knew Jeremy was in a difficult position. Kenneth paid him a salary, which at the age of sixty he needed. Jeremy was also in recovery. I had trusted him implicitly, and now I couldn't get a straight answer from him. I hugged Brenda goodbye; she'd been a rock to me at Spring View.

Thank God I had met her. She had taken me under her wing, had taken me to AA meetings outside of treatment, had kept me sane. I could talk to her about anything. I told her who I was, told her about Kenneth and what had happened.

It was Brenda who had kept saying 'It was your choice, Polly, you accepted him into your life, you attract that stuff, and you are here to find out why.'

What she was doing was saying the same thing I had said to Julie. We had a choice: to be or not be someone's or everyone's victim or scapegoat. I used to get cross with her when she said this, not wanting to own up to it, finding excuses. But Brenda was warm, loving and very mischievous. It was difficult being cross with her for long. I knew she was on my side and wanted the best for me, and therefore slowly, bit by bit, the information she fed me took root. It wasn't until months later that I felt her words work at gut level and I was able to take the action needed.

I flew to Georgia where I was met by Joe. I was standing at the carousel waiting for my luggage, feeling drained. Joe came up behind me and gave me a huge hug. I turned into his arms and felt the warmth from him, and promptly burst into tears.

'There, there, flower, it's going to be all right. You're safe.' He passed me his hanky and I blew loudly into it.

'Keep it,' he said and I laughed despite myself.

Joe was gay, tall, dark and very handsome, looking like an exotic American Indian. I'd met Joe at The Friary – he was also an alcoholic. He'd been in a relationship for eighteen years, but his lover, to whom he had been faithful, hadn't returned the favour. Over the years this had robbed Joe of his self-confidence and much of his esteem. He'd done everything he could to keep the lid on his emotions by drinking, and slowly he'd drunk more and more, until finally reaching rock bottom. Luckily for him, his friends intervened and had helped him to help himself by suggesting treatment. He'd done very well at The Friary, realizing he'd made it so easy for his partner throughout their relationship, never complaining or making a scene, letting each betrayal float by, drinking away his rage and hurt until he'd made himself ill, both mentally and physically.

'Come, the fires are lit, the cats are sleeping curled up in my armchair, there's food in the oven and a warm bed. After a long, hot soak in the bath you'll feel better.'

I looked up at him, grateful for his kindness. We had driven from the airport to his house in silence, but I was too emotionally exhausted to sleep.

'Sweetpea.'

'Mmm,' I replied.

'I don't think much of your new make-up.'

I looked at him, puzzled.

'Your forehead is blue.'

'I know, I thumped it against a wall until I woke up.'

'Wouldn't an alarm clock have been better?'

I smiled, letting my head roll against the headrest. 'Probably,' I replied drowsily as I closed my eyes. 'No more talk, Joe, tomorrow; tomorrow I'll tell you everything.'

Joe was as good as his word – the fire crackled, the cats slept, the bath, after five months of showers, was delicious. I soaked for over an hour, just topping it up with hot water. I wanted to stay there forever. A big, fluffy bathrobe, lotions and smellies had been left out for me. I scrubbed and washed until I was pink and squeaky clean. I dried and creamed my body and slipped into the warm robe, feeling so much better. I sat down in Joe's kitchen, smells wafting from the oven.

'Joe, smells yummy, what is it?'

'Cottage pie.'

'Ah, Joe, you remembered my favourite.'

He dropped a large portion on to my plate. I hadn't had the dish for so long; comfort food, I call it.

'Joe, it's delicious, thank you, I'm really touched you've gone to all this trouble.'

'No trouble, darlin', just a bit of love for my friend.'

I reached across the table.

'I love you, Joe, thank you.'

He wrinkled his nose. 'I'm a man's man, sweetheart, don't you get no funny ideas.'

I made a face back at him.

'And,' he continued, 'I firmly suggest you finish eating and go to bed. Nancy is coming tomorrow.'

'Who's Nancy?'

'A dear friend who is picking you up at eleven-thirty tomorrow morning, to take you to a women's meeting.' He had thought of everything. 'Thought you might need one.'

'I do, Joe darling. Tell me about Nancy.'

'Tomorrow. Right now you need to eat and go to bed.'

Joe tucked me in and I lay back, feather pillows and linen sheets, the ceiling fan blowing gently down on me.

'Sleep well, little bird.'

'You too, Joebird.'

'Thank you.'

He switched off the light and I fell asleep almost immediately.

I woke to the smell of bacon and Joe singing in the kitchen. I looked out of the window: clear blue skies, sunshine streaming in as I pulled back the curtains to reveal the garden below. In the centre was a bird table covered with blue tits, a robin perched on a gardening fork, squirrels running and lying amongst the thick branches of pecan trees. I opened the window and breathed deeply. Fresh moist air, bird sounds. I allowed myself to really see and feel, didn't hurry the feeling, just let myself be.

'Good morning, sunshine, thought you might like your famous fix – strong coffee.'

Joe held out a steaming mug, I took it and smiled.

'Sleep well?'

'Like a baby.'

'Good. Now, how about a hearty Georgia breakfast? The works: sausages, grits and gravy, bacon and eggs, sunny-side up.'

'Lead me to it, maestro.'

Sitting in Joe's kitchen, I filled him in on the homesick few months I had spent at Spring View.

'Oh, you poor baby, what a horror story. What happens now?'

'I'm not sure, Joe. I think I've got to take the next few days a moment at a time, or I'm going to feel overwhelmed. First, I'm looking forward to meeting Nancy and going to this women's meeting. Then, this afternoon I thought I'd rake some leaves. Your garden is beautiful.'

'Thank you, flower. You have a think. You are welcome to stay for as long as you want.'

As long as I kept calm and sorted things out, one at a time, I'd feel safe.

I met Nancy; she was steady and calming. She understood how fragile I was feeling, even how the noise of the traffic affected me. Walking into the meeting was an experience in itself. Eight women sat around, smoking, talking and sipping coffee. The meeting was held in a community centre, the floors wooden, the chairs made for schoolrooms, the walls lurid with collages and drawings. I went over to have a look. 'My Elephant' by Tania, aged four years, was made out of egg cartons. My heart gave a jerk. It reminded me of a little girl in England who had worked so hard for Tusk Force: collecting money, sweets, organizing events with her money. I felt I'd let so many people down, including children. When would this feeling of guilt stop?

The meeting was small and cosy. It felt safe to share, so I told them how and why I had left treatment. I shared the emotions rather than the details, kept it to the minimum. I'd been given a British bulldog mug. I sat with my coffee, listening to the meeting. I realized I hadn't craved a drink since walking into The Friary. Then, suddenly, I knew for the first time what it meant to be an alcoholic, and how vulnerable I could make myself if I didn't accept this programme fully. It was a very humbling experience.

At The Friary I had intellectually accepted that I was an alcoholic, but this was the first time I had really thought of myself as one. It hit me with such a force that I realized that, more than anything else, I wanted sobriety. I knew that if I went to meetings regularly, got a sponsor, worked the programme set out for me, and others like me, integrated that programme into my daily life, then I could and would stay sober. I knew, to do so, meant I had to make my recovery the most important thing in my life, on a daily basis. That's what I've tried to do ever since.

Everything I have today I owe to all the alcoholics I've met, who have stayed sober through the fellowship. By following their example, I remain sober. I also owe what I've achieved to one other person. I owe it to me – the woman I've finally found within myself. Today I've learned how to live with her, love her, cherish her, respect her and, above all, want her sobriety. Today, I don't simply exist, or survive, I live life.

'One day at a time' is an AA principle, and one of the most

valuable sayings I know. If you have one foot in yesterday and one foot into tomorrow, then you're not living today, not present. Today I can quieten my overactive mind, though I do have a tendency to worry. I think – what can I do today about it? Then I try to do whatever I've decided and if it doesn't work out, whatever it is, I've learned to let it go. This is not always possible and I then find myself becoming obsessive about things that are not in my control. It's hard to pull back and realize I've spent nearly an entire day or weeks thinking about things that are not in my control. It gets to the point where I become anxious, nervy, then I realize: Hey, stop. Just for today do the best you can.

I had made one decision: to go back to Pensacola and stay with friends whom I met in treatment. I couldn't go back to England right then; I was not yet brave enough. In the past I would have rushed back to deal with everything all at once and put too much pressure on myself. Now I instinctively knew I must stay there until I felt more centred, and I wouldn't feel that until I'd had some answers. It seemed that any time I asked a question, there wasn't a straight answer.

Nancy dropped me off at Joe's – he was out. I felt physically drained, dreadful; it felt like a hangover. I crept into bed fully clothed and slept for a few hours. I woke to find Joe stroking my head.

'What's the matter, little one?'

'I feel horrible, Joe, like I've got a hangover.'

'Been drinking?'

'Don't be silly, of course not. I just feel so physically awful.'

'Well, you've been through a lot. You are mentally exhausted. Why don't you make a decision not to make any decisions for a week, allow yourself to regain your strength and make some plans for yourself? While your head clears there's plenty I can keep you busy with here. You know I'm selling up, so you can help me pack. I would be very grateful.'

'Oh, poor Joe.' I had completely forgotten he had his own problems too. Joe was going to Australia where he had been offered a place at a university to study for a PhD in agriculture – something he loved to do and at forty-five years old, a dream come true. Also, for the first time in twenty years, he was single, plus on top of everything, he had to sell the possessions he'd collected during the years of his relationship. Joe was very house proud and a wizard in the garden. To leave all this behind, and start again all the way across the other side of the world, sober, was a huge step for him.

'Are you scared, Joe?'

'Shitting myself. But look at the opportunity I have. One day at a time I can deal with it. If I start projecting, I find myself feeling almost paralysed with fear. All sorts of thoughts come into my head, like "You idiot, Joe, why do you think you can make this course in Australia?" I think of my ex and wonder if I should try to win him back. All these thoughts sap my energy, so I just put one foot in front of the other. I go to a meeting every day. Stick close to people who are working hard on changing their lives, who make sobriety their priority, and day by day I come closer to being the person I always knew I could be.

'What sort of person do you think is the real you, Polly, or how do you see yourself? What are the qualities you most admire in others?'

'I want to be trusted, Joe, I want to be needed, I want integrity, honesty, graciousness. I want the courage to stay on this path. I want to be free of material wants, and want to stop trying to impress people. I want to stop feeling inferior. More than anything I want to have peace of mind and be happy. I always seem to think: if I had more money, or when I become an actress, or when I have a baby, I'll be happy. Now I think I'm slowly understanding the saying that people, places, power, property, prestige don't fix feelings.'

'Easier said than done,' Joe mimicked the preamble in AA. 'Seems like a tall order, but don't forget, poppet, Rome wasn't built in a day, and we don't have to do things all at once. How about a cup of English tea?'

'Joe, I'd rather have coffee.'

'You and your coffee, Polly. Why do you drink so much?'

'Because I'm an addict, you twit.'

Joe chased me into the kitchen.

We sat in silence for a few minutes.

'Polly.'

'Mmm.'

'How come Kenneth's got such power over you, do you know why?'

'I think so,' I said automatically, feeling uncomfortable.

'Well, can you talk about it?'

'It's a funny tale, really. Do you want it from the beginning? It will take a while if I fill you in with everything.'

'Okay, why don't we sit by the fire, take a pot of coffee, cigarettes, and talk. Don't start with once upon a time.'

I smiled a mischievous smile. What Joe was saying was, don't buy into the fantasies of what happened.

'Yes, mother,' I replied, and explained to him how I had met Kenneth, to give him some idea of the pressure I was under at the time.

'I made a public promise that I would personally cover all the administration costs of Tusk Force until we found an administrator guardian. I had done so from 1989 to 1991. The drain on my income had exhausted it. I was living from day to day: modelling jobs paid for salaries, communication costs, flights to Africa. As I was working full time on the charity, I would sometimes cut back on work so that I could continue on projects. I'd put an SOS out in the newspapers; many of them gave me articles on frivolous stuff like what I liked and didn't like, where I ate – but they mentioned the charity. Anyway, the next day I was at the Savoy Hotel, at a public dinner, when a man came and asked me for a dance, and offered me two hundred pounds. I thought he had mistaken me for a call girl or something. I must have given him a dirty look because he explained I'd misunderstood him. The money he was offering was for Tusk Force. I was immediately flattered and danced with him.'

'Polly,' Joe interrupted, 'are you really going to drag this one out?'

'Might do,' I replied, throwing a cushion at him. 'Anyway, now where was I?'

'Polly, the edited version!'

So I told him how we had begun together, how Kenneth had taken over the running of the charity, how he had offered to pay the wages of my staff – and how we had become dependent on him. I hadn't realized at the time, but not only had I put myself into another co-dependent relationship, but this time all my staff had had to come with me. Then I spoke for the first time about the incident that had taken me to Brixton police station. It was the first time I had really relived my memory of the events; previously I had let everyone else tell what I had done.

'The morning of the day I relapsed, I kept thinking about having a drink to relieve the pressure and anxiety I felt. I didn't, and went into a morning meeting. When I came out, the thought popped into my head again. I was terribly confused because everything I wanted, had ever wanted, was happening around me and yet I couldn't feel any of it. My head asked me why didn't I just commit suicide, then all this nightmare would be over. Drink – I had to have a drink. Gone was my sanity to choose otherwise. I'd pushed myself so far outside of myself, I couldn't stop and think.

'I was meeting the director of a shop, Terence Bramble, who had asked me to design the Christmas table at Thomas Goode. We ate oysters and I was quite innocently asked if I wanted some champagne. I'd had three in all by the time my secretary, Kate, arrived late. Can you imagine? I hadn't drunk for nearly a year. Kate's face dropped, I told her it was okay and offered her a glass. She couldn't say anything in front of Terence but glared at me across the table. We carried on with the meeting. At about three in the afternoon we left, and went to a pub, where, despite Kate's protests, I ordered an Irish coffee. By the time the interview for the new manager of Tusk Force began, I was really low. I think I felt bought, or I'd sold out on myself. Kenneth wanted me to take a step back, but I didn't want to stop. I loved what I was doing; it had all just got out of hand.

'I drove to the dinner and met our potential employee. I don't remember much after that. A taxi was called, Kate and I got in and headed towards home. Once we got to Brixton, a fight started between the driver and me. Apparently I was sitting in the front, drunk, with a bottle of champagne that slipped out of my hands and fizzed all over the carpet. The driver started to shout at me and I kicked his dashboard, punched his window, cracked it with Kenneth's ring and ended up in Brixton police station.'

I looked at Joe.

'Darling Pol, you still haven't answered my question. Why did you give this man so much control over you?'

'Because he was willing to give me his time, his money and he believed in me. I felt I owed him the world back. I wanted to believe in fairy tales. He'd talked of us marrying, of being together and I so wanted that. I wanted to be in love, I thought I could grow to love him. But the more he tried, and successfully controlled me, the less feeling I had for him and myself.'

'Go on.'

'It seems, in the police station, I told them who I was with and that they should all be fired. Press, radio and television cameras invaded my lawn and shouted at me to come out.'

'What did you do?'

'Called Kenneth, who called Jeremy. They got me out of the country and to The Friary. That's where the deal was made. I had to do what was asked of me, which was to stay in the States until told otherwise.

'So here I sit, not knowing what the hell to do. Do I have any money left? I haven't dared call friends or family. I haven't felt I can fight back in case he cuts off the finances to the charity. Is he doing his best for me? I don't know, Joe, and I'm too damned scared to make a move.'

'He has power of attorney over you, your affairs and finances? You're afraid that if you make the wrong move he'll cut everything off. So every day you wake up to the fact that someone is controlling you.'

I hugged my knees to my chin. The afternoon had turned to twilight. Joe reached over and threw another log on the fire, which heaved and cracked.

'That's about the long and short of it. I don't know if I'll work again. If I go back, I know my agency have fired me. I don't know if I'll ever work in TV again. I don't know what to do. I have no confidence, I feel like the shell of the person I used to be, a person who is waiting to have my insides given back to me. How that will happen, I have no idea.'

'Just don't pick up a drink, my darling, and all will be revealed.' Joe came over and hugged me. 'I love you, brave girl.'

'I love you too, Joe.'

That night I thought of my options. I was still very much in denial about my situation with Kenneth and couldn't face the reality of it all. I knew I had to go somewhere, somewhere I felt safe until I could work out the jumble in my head. To do that I needed support from people who knew me. I had decided I would go back to Pensacola; there I had friends, ex-patients from The Friary, a set of counsellors who knew me, there I would get the support I needed.

Joe and I packed, and made the six-hour drive to Pensacola. I'd called John, who had shared a room with Brett at The Friary. He'd been wonderful.

'Course you can come and stay. I've got a beach house, darlin', we hardly use it, go there and stay for as long as you like.'

He told me where to find the keys and gave me a number of a real estate agent who was also in recovery. 'He'll find you a place, he's an honest guy, you'll like him. In a few days I'll come out with my wife and son. We'll have a barbecue, how does that sound?'

'John, thank you.'

I felt I was being handed from angel to angel, the support and care I was receiving was something I'd never felt, never allowed myself to feel. I'd rarely asked for help before, for fear of rejection, feeling I didn't deserve it. Yet, when I held my hand out and asked for help, I received it tenfold.

John was true to his word. The house on the beach was beautiful, peaceful, the beach littered with palms, the sand, white and fine. Joe helped me bring in my suitcases, stayed and had coffee on the wooden deck and we sat in silence watching the sun go down.

'I'd better get back, little girl, I've got a long drive ahead of me.'

'Thank you so much, Joe, I will never forget what you've done for me. Who knows, maybe one day I'll write a book about all of this.'

'It wouldn't surprise me. If you do, send me a copy.'

I hugged him goodbye. I didn't know when I'd see him again. In a week he'd be on his way to Australia.

'Hey, hon, don't forget – don't pick up a drink, no matter what, and take it one day at a time.'

He saluted me, got into his car and drove off. I watched him until he disappeared into the darkness. I climbed the stairs back up to the house and walked inside.

Now what?

John had come to the house and left food and coffee. I prepared a meal, lit a fire, and ate in front of the TV. I felt alone, so alone – my food caught in my throat and a wave of emotion took over. I curled into a ball and sobs racked their way through me. I wanted so much to be home in England. It felt like I was caught in a nightmare, month after month, waiting for it all to be over. It was not over by far. It would take years to get out of it and if I'd known all that then, I don't think I would have survived it.

Little by little I faced my fears. I met up with ex-patients, and I soon realized it was up to me to go to AA meetings. It would be up to me to grow and change. But still, somewhere in the back of my mind, I'd thought Kenneth would come and rescue me, take me home.

The house I found was on the beach, miles from anywhere. I rented a Mustang and cleared this all through Jeremy. For a while I felt okay and I took long walks along the beach, swam and even organized piano lessons, but as always, my mind was plagued with unanswered questions.

Jeremy called a couple of times a week, but no real information came back. It was decided that I would stay in the States until June when I would go to England for four days to appear in court for my case concerning the taxi incident. The days turned into weeks, the weeks into months and I lived a very simple life. But always lying underneath were the questions: what will happen, what life will I have?

I hardly saw John or his family, and the few people I did know at The Friary were getting on with the rest of their lives, working, raising families. Outside the meetings I led an isolated life. I started to feel very ill, each day hoping it would go away. It didn't and in the end I went to a doctor who referred me to a specialist. I described how I was feeling. He performed a lot of test and I waited for the results, imagining the worst. When I went back the doctor told me I had to go to the Oshner Clinic in New Orleans. I had a very high white-cell count and low-grade fever and that was sometimes connected to cancer and forms of leukaemia. I felt the blood drain from my face.

He saw my reaction. 'It could be a number of things, but this clinic is the best at being able to diagnose illnesses of this type.'

I left the office, got into my car and drove home. I felt shocked – I'd never been ill in my life, except for my illness with alcohol and drugs. I called Jeremy in a panic.

'Calm down, of course you must go.'

'Please, let Kenneth know, please ask him to call me.'

I sat and waited by the phone for a week. He didn't call, but Jeremy did.

'Kenneth asked me how much the treatment will cost.'

Jeremy spent the next fifteen minutes telling me how much I should be grateful to have friends like Kenneth to help me; and that I should work on my anger with him.

I put the phone down and contemplated killing myself. My life was so empty, so used up. What stopped me was my arrogance and my false sense of pride. I didn't want to leave behind me bad memories for the people who loved me, my family and friends. No matter how I did this, I was not going to bail out. It couldn't stay this way for ever. I had to get honest with myself. I had to face this monster and ride it out all the way.

I walked the beach up and down, miles and miles of the same scene, same sand. My mind was numb, I was caught in a time warp; not being able to break through, to feel and see. I was in a similar situation to Julie: fear of abandonment that was so acute it paralysed me, and now I had to face an illness of another kind, knowing I was ill, but not knowing the cause.

I walked back to the house. The phone was ringing.

'Polly, it's Jeremy. The court case has been set. You're going to need to fly back for three days.'

'When?'

'In about a week.'

My mind raced. 'Will Kenneth be there?'

'No!'

'I see. I want to see my family. Where will I stay?'

'Polly, you just need to know that your flight is booked for the twelfth of June and your return flight is on the sixteenth.'

'Jeremy, I'm not flying alone. I want Barbara, a counsellor from The Friary to travel with me. You know her, she says she knows you. I don't feel safe enough to come on my own.'

'I'll talk to Kenneth about it.'

I put the phone down. I was going home. My God, I was going home. I sat back on the sofa and howled like a baby.

CHAPTER ELEVEN

Surrender To Win

One week later I was packed and met Barbara at the airport. 'Okay, flower?'

'Don't feel like a flower, more like a wet weed.'

She laughed. 'Put yourself in the hands of your higher power, Polly. All this is part of our recovery – it's up to you how you choose to handle it. For many years, while we were drinking, we didn't know how to handle situations and feelings, and we'd have a drink, thinking this would either change the situation by numbing it, or make it go away. You're dealing with it sober. You're feeling your feelings, you're dealing with it as an adult.'

'Then how come I feel about twelve years old, scared and bewildered?'

'Where's your faith, Polly? Your faith will pull you through. God didn't save you from drowning so he could beat you up on the beach.'

I laughed, despite myself.

We travelled business class. Barbara was genuinely excited – she hadn't been to England before and was very much looking forward to it. We talked of recovery and how differently we handled things sober.

'It's a shame this man has so much power over you, but you're powerless over him, over people, places, things. We think we can control others, but we can't always, and to do so only causes us harm.' Barbara paused.

'Go on,' I told her.

'Well, think about it, Kenneth may be in control of your

finances and your life back in England, but he can't control your mind or how you handle it. That's up to you.'

'I'm totally obsessed by all of this, Barbara. Every day waking up, wondering what's going to happen. It makes every day a nightmare. Questions running inside my head, banging into each other, thoughts that flash by, unfinished. I used to have a life, you know. Before that one-day relapse, I used to know why I got up in the morning; I had a schedule, people wanted me, work came in, bills were paid, I accomplished things.'

'But were you happy?'

I thought for a moment. 'No, I wasn't. I didn't feel I was doing enough; nothing was enough, the work, the charity. No, I was tired, short-tempered with people. I would go nuts if mistakes were made, I'd become a tyrant. I would say to the trustees and employees that I didn't give a shit if they didn't like me, that I didn't want a fan club, that if they didn't like it they could leave.'

'How did that make you feel, Polly?'

'Awful. I wanted to be admired, to be liked. I wanted to make people feel good about the work we were doing. Instead I did the opposite. It was a very lonely feeling; I couldn't understand that either. I had accomplished so much, yet didn't see it. I only saw what more I had to accomplish. Never celebrating, not stopping to smile and congratulate people. Just pushed them harder and harder, ignoring how unhappy and tired I was, and not understanding why. I was sober then, but my thoughts weren't. Then it all caught up with me.'

Although I had been sober through the experiences I had just described to Barbara, I had now learned enough to realize that I had let work take over from alcohol. Workaholics suffer similar behaviour to alcoholics: unless they are working, preoccupied with work or busy in some way, they find themselves feeling depressed and redundant, not needed by anyone. Workaholics escape into their work for decades, not maturing through difficulties in their intimate or domestic lives. They are 'too busy' working to deal with emotions, therefore their maturity is stunted. How many women or men do you know who are brilliant in the working environment, yet are lousy at dealing with domestic situations, cannot express their emotions and find it difficult to communicate? Anything we use in excess which takes us away from our feelings will eventually cripple us emotionally and spiritually. And although workaholics do not suffer the obvious health risks of alcohol or drugs, physical stress can lead to problems, such as heart attacks, not eating properly and so on.

'You're very hard on yourself, Polly, you know that. You need to start feeling tender for that little girl.'

I wasn't so little, I was twenty-nine years old.

'Polly, your emotions were that of, say, someone about fifteen or sixteen years old. You may have looked grown up, but addicts, alcoholics don't grow up when they either keep turning to the bottle, or when they put down their drug of choice and pick up work, or become obsessed with anything outside themselves. Growing up stops and you live life with immaturity. Recovery is growing up, maturing, realizing how we affect others and how others affect us. That hurts sometimes, I can remember. If I had a feeling, I'd have a drink because I couldn't cope with those feelings.'

'Barbara, how long is it since you had a drink?'

'Over a decade, Polly, and life still hurts sometimes, but every time I handle a new situation sober, and ask for help to get me through it, I feel a little more confident, I gain a little more trust in myself. I feel good, so after a while I can go with the punches life throws at us. I do it with the support and love this fellowship gives us. It's only when I try to go it alone, that all the pride, ego and self-righteousness come back.

'Both alcoholism and addiction are a three-headed monster. It's physical, psychological and spiritual. Alcoholism affects one physically, accidents happen, as do general wear and tear on the body. Mentally it tells us we don't have a problem when we do. Spiritually we are bankrupted; feel empty, worthless, hopeless. Most alcoholics come into AA when they have emotionally reached rock bottom. Non-alcoholics commit suicide – alcoholics commit suicide a little each day.

'If we recognize the three-headed monster, we become balanced in our thoughts and actions. Until we accept that in our guts, we'll always be struggling. There's only one way not to go backwards and fall into the same traps, and that is to go forwards. To do this, we have to accept that we need guidance, and then accept the guidance we need – something addicts and alcoholics find almost impossible. So, when we do begin to recover, we're like a miracle.'

I held out my hand and she squeezed it. 'Thank you, Barbara.'

'Successful recovery means looking after all three elements: physical, psychological and spiritual, on a daily basis. That takes hard work. We're not looking for perfection, Polly, we're looking for balance.

'It sounds so simple and it is. We make it difficult, but what needs to come first is our recovery: not our family, our work, our dreams, or our relationships. Our recovery has to be our primary purpose in life. The rest will follow, not the other way round.'

The plane landed at Heathrow airport. We were met by Kenneth's security men. We were taken to a car and I asked the men sitting in front where were we going.

'To a hotel in Richmond.'

The drive into Richmond was short, the traffic not too heavy. I looked at the man who had spoken to me and saw he had a mobile phone in his hand.

'May I use your phone to call my mother?' I asked.

'Do you mind waiting until you get to the hotel?'

'No, no, not at all.'

I looked at Barbara. She smiled and patted my hand.

We pulled up outside a hotel on the outskirts of Richmond Park, overlooking the town and the Thames below. We went to our rooms to freshen up. I picked up the phone to call my mother; the line was dead. I lay down on the bed and drifted into a deep sleep.

I woke to the sound of banging on my door. Groggily I got up and opened it.

It was Barbara. She was laden down with a tea tray. 'How about a little, traditional English tea?'

She looked rested, happy and flushed. Her eyes were shining and twinkling. 'Well, when you were napping I thought as it was such a beautiful day I'd go out and explore. Anyway, I go out into the garden, and there's this small gate in the wall. I open it, and like some little kid, I skip off down the lane. Next thing I know, there's these three guys in suits asking me where I'm going. They used my name, so I turned round and said, who's asking?'

I smiled. Barbara was ballsy and didn't put up with any crap.

'So go on,' I said, completely spellbound.

'They told me they were here to look after you, and we're not allowed to leave the hotel alone. So I say, well, well, now that's interesting; why's that? They say they're just following orders. So I came back, ordered the tea, and here I sit talking to you about it.'

'Barbara, they're Kenneth's security men. I guess they're expecting the worst with this court case; they're just being cautious.'

'Jesus, Polly, you know when you told us in treatment about Kenneth, I thought you were kind of glamorizing your story.'

'Barbara, you mean you didn't believe me?'

'Well, come on, Polly, alcoholics and addicts lie, mix fiction with truth and vice versa.'

'Well, now what do you think?'

'I believe you.' She burst out laughing.

'Barbara, do me a favour. Ask one of them to come up here and fill us in on the schedule for the time we are here while I get dressed.'

'No sweat.'

After she left, I giggled. Barbara was full of life; ten years clean, a good-looking woman with style and a wicked sense of humour. She was loving, bold and was making a great recovery. Barbara was a chronic alcoholic, who ten years ago had lost everything. Today she was a counsellor and a wonderful mother. She brought love and sunshine with her. Her humour was such that there were rarely moments without laughter when you spent time in her company. She was a small woman, but one didn't see her as small. In fact, she didn't look American, more Irish. She certainly had the gift of the gab.

Whilst thinking all this, I dressed. There was a knock on my door and there was Barbara with one of the men who had driven us from the airport. He looked uncomfortable.

'What's your name?'

'Ray.'

'How many security people are there?'

'Five, including the driver.'

'Why so many?'

'Just following orders.'

'I see. I didn't order it and I'd like to know who did?'

'Perhaps you would like to take that up with Brenda Grimethorp.'

'In two days I have a court case. I'd like to know the schedule so that I can make plans around it.'

'Such as?' he replied.

'Such as seeing some friends and my family.'

'I see. Well, if you give me a list of names and addresses I'll contact them for you.'

'May I make a suggestion? You ask the hotel to open up the lines and I will call my friends and family myself. I'm going to see if my mother and a few friends can come here for supper.'

He looked even more uncomfortable.

'I'm not a prisoner, am I?' I asked, innocently.

'No, of course not.'

'Then my request wouldn't be asking too much, would it?'

'Well . . . er . . . I suppose not.'

'When will I see Mr Oliver, the lawyer who has been appointed to my case?'

'Tomorrow morning.'

'Right, so would you mind opening the lines and I can start calling?'

He left the room.

Barbara congratulated me. 'Well done, Polly, you took back a little control then.'

'Barbara, the awful part is, I don't know whether to be flattered or not. Is Kenneth protecting me with his men, or is Kenneth distancing himself further, yet still controlling me?'

'That's for you to work out.'

I called my girlfriend, Fee. I was so excited that I would be seeing her after all these months. I called Mummy and a few other close friends: Roger, Ian, Carolyn. They were all coming for supper the night after the court case.

Later that night, I sat by the open window. It was June, and the night hot and balmy. Tomorrow I would stand in court, in front of the press, in front of a judge, for an offence I couldn't remember. I had been in what they call a black out. I didn't remember a thing. I didn't know what to expect. No one had told me what the charges were. Tomorrow, before the court case, I would meet my lawyer. I couldn't sleep so I padded downstairs at about two in the morning, and asked the hotel for a snack and hot milk with honey. I went back upstairs, got into bed and lulled myself to sleep with the song my African nannies used to sing to me. I always found it a comfort when my mind was being overloaded with fear.

The next day was spent with the lawyers. Michael Oliver wore a grandiose suit with an air of self-importance. He had a habit of looking down his nose whenever he spoke. He came in, flanked by two other men in suits.

'What's the charge? I'm completely in the dark about it.'

He raised a bushy eyebrow at me. 'Well, I'm hoping for a conditional discharge and a fine.'

'Mr Oliver, who are these men?'

'They are your counsel.'

'I see. So should I be concerned, if I need such an array of men for this case? It must be very costly.'

'I've been appointed to deal with this case –' and he proceeded to call me Polly, a pet name for family and friends, 'and I will do what I feel is appropriate. Mr Oakhouse has been most generous with his help in this matter.'

I got up. 'Well, thank you for coming, I'll see you in court.'

I met security outside. We drove in silence. At Camberwell magistrate's court the security men told me they would be in the court's enclosed garage, and after the case I'd be taken up in a special lift that would bring me back to the enclosed garage.

'Expecting fuss?'

'Yes, lots. So keep your eyes open.'

We parked inside the court building; there were no press in sight. My hands began to sweat and my legs wobbled. I began to feel queasy.

A police officer led the way through a maze of corridors, then into a huge panelled room. There was a large desk with a plaque and a coat of arms on my left, a wall of benches filled with journalists and to my right a few people were scattered. I was led to a little box. Mr Oliver stood at the front and I noticed the two other suits were absent. The judge came in.

'All rise,' a voice called.

The judge sat down.

'Be seated.'

In my hands was my Friary medallion; I looked down at it. I was wearing a cream jacket and trousers, plain and simple. The intention was not to wear something that would look innocent; I had just dressed in a summer suit – it was either that or jeans.

I looked up – Mr Oliver was talking. I had blanked most of what was being said.

'She has to return to the States to continue with her recovery.

Also, she is awaiting diagnosis of an illness and she has an appointment for further tests at the Oshner Clinic, in New Orleans. This clinic deals with cancer and leukaemia.'

'I hope the fucking bitch dies!' came a harsh whisper from my right.

I was shocked and looked over to a couple who glared at me. I was later told that it was the taxi driver, who had lost his job through the incident. He'd been working for a car service for celebrities and VIPs. The policy of the company was to dump difficult passengers, and if there was a problem, to deal with it quietly. He had broken his contract by going to the press with the story, lost his job, couldn't get rehired and had decided to sue me for loss of earnings. The case had been dismissed. He had been paid six hundred pounds for his cracked windscreen and champagne-stained carpet a few days after the incident.

I got a conditional discharge and a fine of one hundred and fifty pounds. I was led out of the court, up in the elevator to the car and then the garage doors were opened. Suddenly a sea of press surged towards the car. My heart thumped and the car pushed through as the flash bulbs fired and as we sped round the corner they gave chase, on motor bikes and in cars. After a few miles' detour, we got back en route for Richmond.

That evening a picture of me, white, frightened and tense, appeared in the papers. Mummy had been brought to the hotel by security. We hugged each other and cried. I'd missed her so much.

'Why all this fuss over a conditional discharge and a one-hundred-and-fifty-pound fine?'

'I don't know, Mummy, I really don't know. I only know that Kenneth doesn't need any adverse publicity at the moment. It's the last year that he's running the charity events. I think he believes he'll have a better chance to get through if I'm out of the picture, which hurts so much that I try to find ways to justify his behaviour. Looking back, I can see we're quite alike: it's called tunnel vision. Only seeing the goal, but not the views on either side of the journey.'

'Polly, do you honestly think you should put this man's dreams and happiness before your own?'

'Mummy, you stayed in a destructive, unhappy marriage that very nearly destroyed you, which has had a long-lasting effect on us children. Didn't you used to say that you stayed together for the sake of us? Somewhere we're programmed to stand by, cope with, put up with, hang in there, for better or worse. It's really tough, though. My head can see what is happening, but somehow I still can't say – no more, this has to stop. I'm still praying he'll come and make everything right. I feel if I rock the boat now, he could break me. There's fight in my passiveness, it's a waiting game.'

'Darling, how come you understand all this and you still put up with it all?'

'Because it's so complicated, but at the same time so simple. I understand I've made a deal – I'm trying to stick to it the best I can. Otherwise he can say I broke the deal and he can wash his hands of me. Everything I've ever owned is in his hands, I'm too scared to lose the lot.'

Leaving my mother and friends was hard, not knowing truly when I would see them again. Barbara was wonderful, keeping up our spirits, but knowing I had the Oshner Clinic to face left me drained of energy, as if to keep me prepared for what lay ahead. Barbara gave me one parting shot before we separated.

'Polly, there's so much to let go of. Deal with your health first, take it step by step. It took years to create this mess; you are not going to work through it all in one night. You're doing okay, honestly you are. A lot of people would have just cracked up – you haven't. You've leant on the support and you've picked up the tools of recovery. You've listened, you've changed a lot of your behaviour and ways of dealing with issues. Take it one thing at a time. When are you leaving for New Orleans?'

'In a couple of days. I'm going to stay with Ruth.'

'Polly, I hear Ruth's drinking again. I strongly suggest you go visit her, but don't stay if she's not well. You don't need that right now. You need peace and quiet.'

I looked at Barbara – she really cared about me. I hugged her again and felt a tightness in my chest.

'Do you think it's cancer, Babs?'

'If it is, you have something like a ninety-five per cent success rate; as an alcoholic you have only a four per cent chance of out-living your alcoholism. You're a fighter, Polly – whatever you've got, you won't take it lying down. That much I know.' Her words meant so much to me and gave me comfort.

On the drive back, the Florida sunshine began to fade. There were long shadows on the deserted road. The beach looked comforting, welcoming. My neighbour had looked after my plants, and as I walked up to the deck of the house, the smell of jasmine filled the air. I breathed deeply. I looked out over the beach to the sea. Slipping off my shoes, I walked down towards the water, kicking the sand gently as I went. The sky now pink, the water's gentle movement reflected the colour of the sunset, giving a mauve hue to its surface.

A fin broke the surface of the water, then another. The dolphins were swimming back up the coast; nearly every day recently I'd seen them. Without thinking, I took off my clothes, walked naked into the sea and began to swim towards the dolphins. About twenty feet out I remembered the Florida ocean was filled with sharks at this time of the year. I felt fear begin to mount inside me. I wanted to continue swimming, to reach the dolphins, but the fear niggling in my gut told me to return to the shore. I did, and began to sense I was being followed. Something brushed against my foot; instantly I spun round, tucking myself into a ball. Fear coated itself over my body. Pushing my hands through the water to hold myself up, I couldn't see anything. The sky was now black, the only light I could see on the beach came from my house. I felt a disturbance in the water to my left. To my horror, a fin broke the surface a few feet away. My mouth wide open in horror, a frozen scream was caught in my throat. A dolphin, two feet away, lifted its head, rolled on to its side, and looked at me. A smiling dolphin, opening and closing its mouth. I let out a cry of joy, still scared but elated. It was a feeling of pure ecstasy. I reached out to touch the dolphin's body; it disappeared under the water only to resurface behind me, and bumped me in the back. One final look, eye to eye, and then the dolphin sank back into the dark water and was gone. As long as I live I will never forget the feelings of this experience. I knew I was going to recover; I knew, somehow, I was going to be all right.

I had learned that whatever terrors, like my imaginary shark, lay before me, by taking a calmer look, they could turn out to be positive steps to my recovery.

I awoke early the following day, my mind going back over the trip to England; the fears, the hopes, the false expectations that Kenneth would turn up unexpectedly, like Hitchcock appearing in a cameo role in one of his own films. Only this time it was Kenneth: the producer, the director, the script writer, the editor – controlling, manipulating. Myself: the actress – compliant, desperate for his approval, acting out his script, playing out a role. Yet, unwittingly, Kenneth's script had led me to the tools that would now enable me to abandon this role and go on to direct and star in my own life. I would write my own script, edit out everything that distorted the picture and ultimately give the performance of a lifetime. But, for the first time, a performance in the open, without masks.

I recalled the words of the taxi driver: 'I hope the fucking bitch dies.'

I had no memory of what had happened in the cab, only what people had told me. I must have blanked out the details of what happened as I found the whole episode a nightmare. When Kenneth told me about it in treatment, it was as if I were hearing it all for the first time. I'd been out of control, not responsible for my actions. Yet the taxi driver hated me, as if everything that happened was a deliberate act on my part.

Pulling back the covers, I looked down at my brown body; it looked healthy, no bumps, no rashes, no marks – nothing that indicated how ill I felt. It would have been easier to accept if something was visible. I was ill, my symptoms real, but they were a manifestation of the stress brought about by my addictions. The tests done by the Oshner Clinic would not reveal cancer. What they would reveal was that my body itself was warning me, telling me, it was under enormous physical and emotional pressure. That I needed to listen to it, take heed of its warnings in order to recover.

We assume we know our own bodies well, and we also assume that our physicians are going to know everything. This isn't always true. We have to be very aware of this. So many innocent people find themselves in treatment due to doctors handing out prescriptions, willy-nilly.

For example: a businessman goes to the general practitioner's surgery, complaining of stress in his work. The doctor listens and says, 'Well, Pete, you do sound like you have a hell of a lot on your plate. Do you relax?'

Pete replies, 'Relax, I haven't time to breathe. I feel so damned tired, worn out and anxious. I'm not sleeping.'

So the good old doctor gives him sleeping pills or anti-depressants. Even though these pills are recommended for a short time only, the doctor willingly administers them over a longer time-scale. Sleeping pills, anti-depressants, slimming pills – they are all addictive if taken over a prolonged period of time. The body will begin to need them. The doctor then becomes a perfectly legal drug pusher.

Strong words, you might say. I know many people who have had this experience. It can be destructive and sad. Perhaps Pete needed help, more than a pill. In fact, a pill was the last thing he needed – a crutch to be able to work harder, the very reason he became stressed in the first place.

Perhaps doctors' medical education should teach them more practical and simple solutions that would save the NHS millions of pounds. I was given relaxation tapes on how to unwind, how to let go for a while. What a revelation it was. You see, most of us don't know how to relax. The faster life goes, the less we witness and participate in this thing called relaxation. To be able to relax without feeling we should be doing something constructive, without feeling guilty! Besides all this, how the hell do we relax when we've got so much to do?

The body is similar to a machine. If you don't look after it, and you don't listen to its needs, it's going to break down. Then we take it to the doctor and say, 'Hey, I'm broken, fix it please.'

Have you ever owned a really old car? Mine is twenty-three years old. I have to listen to it carefully. It hasn't got one of those dashboards that look like the cockpit of a Boeing. It doesn't flash lights at me when it needs something. When I feel the brakes have gone mushy, I have to top up the brake fluid. Once I didn't do it as soon as I felt it; the next day, merrily driving through Knightsbridge, my brakes failed, and I went into the back of a brand new Mercedes.

Her tyres are a little bigger than she actually needs, which means she goes out of alignment quite often. I can tell because when I drive her on the motorway, at over sixty miles an hour, she begins to shudder. She makes all sorts of noises. I listen for changes and hear them. You see, I never got around to putting in a radio, so I listen to her engine. She has a nice smell – engine oil, a little waft of petrol whenever I fill her up. My dog muddies her seats, but that's okay. They're only covered in cheap cloth.

People often ask me, 'Hey, why do you drive that old heap?'

I'll tell you why. I like her. She needs TLC. She groans when I push her too hard, reminding me to slow down. If I had some fast new car with a big stereo, I wouldn't listen to it – maybe. Who knows? For now she suits me just fine.

I believe, with more education, learning to encourage ourselves to slow down, to listen, we'll all suffer less from stress-related illnesses. The list is endless: coronary artery disease, immunosuppressant illnesses, hypertension, cancers. The list is endless. It's common knowledge that these illnesses, or how we survive them, are linked to stress.

As long as we ignore our bodies, ignore the warning signals they are putting out, we are acting irresponsibly to ourselves and our loved ones. Those of you who have experienced a loved one who has been struck down by illness will know how much strain it puts on family life. Alcohol, medications – legal and illegal – are not always the answer. In fact, in many cases they prolong the suffering.

I am one of the 'lucky' ones. I am on the road of recovery. It is long and arduous, but it is a road I am prepared to take. It is down to me to stay on it, or fall by the wayside. I have a daily reprieve that is contingent upon the maintenance of both my spiritual and physical condition.

That's all I've got – today.

I have to nurture myself, take care of my needs, just as I would a garden: letting the plants and flowers within it blossom and take root, cutting out and holding back the weeds that threaten to choke and overrun it, in order to survive.

I was to stay with Ruth as she lived near the Oshner Clinic. The morning of my departure, padding down the short hall into the den, the room bright with early morning sunshine, the sea calm and flat, like an upturned mirror, the flowers I had planted swayed gently. I opened the door, and the rush of hot air that whipped around my body, combined with the sensation of cool air on my back, was delicious. I had my usual fix of strong coffee and cigarettes, taking them outside and sitting on the deck.

Monpierre swayed back and forth. Monpierre was the name I'd given to a thirty-five-foot palm tree I had planted. I'd been driving back from Pensacola town centre, when I saw this truck with about six palm trees, fully grown, lying on their sides, their heads blowing in the breeze as they trailed behind. I'd peeped my horn, signalling to the driver to pull over. I asked him where I could purchase one, and how much. He said I could have one for one hundred dollars, plus planting. There and then I bought Monpierre, and the driver followed me to the beach house and planted the tree about fifteen feet away. He told me not to release the strings holding the palm leaves together for at least three months, because it needed the protection until it had recovered from the shock of being transplanted.

My beach had previously had no palms, now it did. Every day it drank about fifty gallons of water. I left a hose pipe on all day at a dribble. The tree had a sixty per cent chance of taking root. It had been there nearly as long as I had and we were both still surviving.

I was now ready for my trip to New Orleans. I was excited at the prospect of seeing Ruth, and silently prayed she'd be sober. I needed her, and drunk she'd be of no help.

I had no problems finding her home, and peeped the horn on arrival. Ruth came out. 'Well, well, well; so the little girl's found her feet, you rascal.'

She opened her arms and I hugged her, subconsciously sniffing her breath. No booze, she was sober.

'Heard you were back on the hooch.'

'Nah, bunch of redneck gossips. Sober as a judge – well, today anyway.' She laughed, 'Come on, Inspector Clouseau, stop eyeballing me, get your stuff, unpack, clean up. We're going out for supper, Japanese Sushi. We have some of the best restaurants in the county.'

Ruth led the way to the guest house, a beautiful, white-painted bungalow. A courtyard between it and the house was filled with giant firs, Spanish tiles, flowers, wooden garden furniture, chimes that sung and danced in the breeze, and her dog Pip, who looked like a black, silky seal.

'Ruth, it's beautiful. Did you do all this yourself?'

'Yep, had a little help from my son and I've got someone to come in and tend this little patch of dirt from time to time.

What the heck, it's not what I'm used to, but on the money I got from Blake, the old snake in the grass, I'm lucky to have this.'

I don't think a day had gone by when she hadn't mentioned Blake, her ex-husband. It was as if, while she kept talking about him, he'd still be around. This had gone on for twenty years.

'Do you still love Blake, Ruth?'

'Gad, Polly, you don't hold back, just steam right on in.'

'Sorry, Ruth,' I said with a giggle.

'This isn't treatment, you know, ease up on your questions.'

'Do you?' I persisted.

She looked me in the eye. 'Yep, now go get ready.'

Putting my bags down I looked around my little room. Cool tiles, warm textiles from India, the bed covered with cloths from Peru, cool palms reaching the ceiling, and the walls covered with family photographs, mainly in black and white. Shadows from the shutters zig-zagged across the walls, giving the room an African appearance. Colonial wicker furniture, old English lamps, garden roses with huge blooms in pastel colours filled the room with the scent of home. Robes from far off, distant lands, hung on the bathroom door. Taking off my clothes I slipped into the shower, dousing myself with cold water, lots of it. I need water: to be near it or under it always refreshes me. Scenes flittered through my head of the dream I've always carried with me. One day I would restore a house, colonial and sited on a deserted plantation, filled with children and horses – one day – please God, one day.

'Hurry up, this ain't no beauty contest,' Ruth hollered from the deck where she was standing.

'No contest, you old fart,' came my reply.

I came out wearing white jeans, T-shirt and sandals. Plain and simple, knowing this was how I looked best.

'Let's go. Hasn't your hair grown. Want me to cut it?' she asked me with mischief in her eyes. 'When I got back from treatment, Raoul, my hairdresser, asked if they'd shaved my head to give me a frontal lobotomy.'

'Oh, come on, Ruth, I didn't cut it that badly.'

She put her head at an angle. 'Oh, no. If I stayed like this it was fine. Went round with a crick in my neck for weeks.'

She grabbed my hand, her voice gruff with emotion. 'I'm glad you're here, missed you. No one here cares whether I drink or not; all southern smiles, treat me as if I have lice or something. I can tell they're looking at me as if to say – poor old, lonely woman, she's an alcoholic, you know.'

'Oh, Ruth, who cares? Fuck them, fuck their ignorance and their pettiness. It's your life, you've just got to stop caring about what people think of you. What you think of you, that's what's important.'

She looked out of her rheumy eyes that were slowly filling with tears.

'I adore you, Ruth, you're a wonderful person. I understand more than you think. Whatever is it that is blocking you from being able to see that? I've got a block, too, which keeps me trapped in my situation with Oakhouse.'

'You mean Oaklouse.'

I giggled. 'Very witty, Ruth. The funny thing is that it fits.'

From that day on, that was Kenneth's new pet name: OAKLOUSE.

Staying with Ruth wasn't all fun at times. She'd get quite cantankerous and moody; a few sly, sarcastic comments would come from her lips and hurt my feelings. I knew what was going on – she felt bad about herself and envied the very thing she said she despised: recovery.

'Are you going to the Oshner Clinic or not?'

'Yes, Ruth, I'm going today at two-thirty. I'm so scared I could crawl into your dog's basket and stay there.'

She looked at me. 'Good place for you.'

That did it. 'Ruth, get off the bloody wood, we need the cross. You've sat on your pity pot for long enough. All you're going to do is get a ring around your ass.'

That woke her up. She rose to her full height of five feet three inches, puffed out her bosom and looked at me with all the indignation she could muster.

As quick as that came, it went, leaving her looking ten years older. 'I want a drink, I want a bloody drink.'

I walked over to her and put my arms around her. 'Ruth, if you keep giving in to that craving, if you keep relapsing, you're never going to know what it feels like to go through that craving without drinking. Why don't you come to a meeting with me?'

'Why don't you go hang yourself?' And with that she shuffled to her bedroom and banged the door after her.

I picked up my keys and bag and went to the car. The heat hit me as I left the house, sapping my energy. By the time I sat in the car and turned the air conditioning on, I was dripping with sweat. Was it the heat, or was it the fear?

The Oshner Clinic, huge, impersonal, filled with rooms and rooms of equipment and people. Blank it, Pol, just register and get on with it. I spent two days there and had every test imaginable done. I have a phobia about needles but I came out looking like a pin cushion.

I had to wait ten days for the results – ten days with Ruth. Well, at least I had my meetings. So every day I went to AA, listened, identified, shared. I found I could become detached from Ruth with love. So her words were hard, yet they didn't penetrate me, didn't hurt me. No longer did I take it personally.

Ruth was tormented; she was caught in a disease that tells us we don't have a problem. That disease is denial. Denial is NOT a river in Egypt.

When, in treatment in 1986, they said to me, 'Your denial system is so strong,' I heard them saying, 'You're lying to us.' When they said, 'Polly, you are denying the seriousness of this', I heard, 'Polly, you are not taking this seriously.' I was told to remember what DENIAL stood for: 'Don't Even Notice I Am Lying.' The behaviour of lying, of putting on a 'mask', is so strong that the alcoholic or addict begin to lie to themselves as well, in public.

Denial is, in most cases, stronger than alcoholism or addiction. That is why the 'behaviour' aspect of this illness needs to be addressed, and dealt with, before recovery can begin. This applies to all types of addictions: alcoholism, legal and illegal drugs, eating disorders, the workaholic, the co-dependent. With alcoholism, in particular, the truth becomes separated from the belief. For example, a man went to a pub, saying he'd be home at 9.00 p.m., but he failed to get home till midnight. The next day he will believe that he meant it to happen that way. He rationalizes things to himself in a different way to the non-alcoholic.

Yet the mask of denial can be worn by everyone. We all wear masks to keep up appearances – for example, a smiling face to hide nervousness, an aggressive approach to hide fear and so on. It isolates us and is a good tool to keep others out. We're sometimes afraid to show what's behind our masks for fear of rejection, or not getting the desired response. The difference begins when the addict feels that they have so much more to hide than everyone else, and they find that they can no longer remove the mask. And, like alcohol, or drugs, or work, they find that they have come to depend on their mask as well, and it is now even more difficult to break out of the vicious circle they have entered.

Over the years, I have watched and experienced denial in myself, and others. It's cunning, powerful and baffling. It can trip you up when you least expect it. I've seen the most intelligent of people do the most stupid things, to the point one looks on with displeasure. For example, there is the man who stopped drinking after a few close calls (to the point where his heart nearly gave up) in order to sober up. The struggle to stay clean for the first thirty days is nicknamed 'Thirty days and a thousand nights'. This man gets a cold, and adds brandy to his milk. This will be okay, he justifies it in his mind. Only he finds himself, for the next couple of days, back on the booze, full of remorse and not understanding how it could have happened.

I have learned the hard way. Knowledge and intellect have not kept me sober. It has been action, a gut-level acceptance without question. It's one foot in front of the other, living one day at a time. It's listening to others, following examples. To do this, one has to get humble. To get humble means one has to listen, to learn to trust. Here I baulked many times. My trust level was non-existent. That is where I learned the saying, 'Fake it to make it.' I had to listen to the voice inside me saying, Look where your best thinking got you – drunk.

When you look at the obstacles that one needs to get over in order to recover, it's a bloody miracle that one does. I knew Ruth would have to face this denial before she could go any further.

My ten-day sentence up, I returned to the Oshner Clinic and went for my appointment with the consultant. My palms were sweating. Was it leukaemia, cancer?

'Miss Vaughn, you have acute, post-traumatic stress syndrome. Your symptoms are psychosomatic, created by self.'

My mind wanted to scream back, You're saying I'm doing this to myself? Instead, I asked him to clarify what he'd said.

'You're making yourself ill. Whatever is going on in your life right now, you have to let go of it emotionally, or you'll continue to create this illness in yourself.'

I felt angry and humiliated. Not by the doctor, but by myself. I had now reached rock bottom with my health. I had to fight back. The time had come to go home and face whatever it was I was so afraid of.

I walked out of that clinic with a cloud over my head. By the time I reached my car, my mind was made up. I was going home, whatever the consequences of breaking a verbal contract. I had to play it straight. By that, I mean I could no longer allow myself to be manipulated by myself.

That evening, from Ruth's home, I called Jeremy Vaughn.

'Jeremy, I'm coming home. I need to and I want to. I don't care what you think. I'm doing what I need to for myself . . . Yes, you're right, I'm being bloody selfish . . . You're only saying

I'm selfish because I'm not doing what you and Kenneth want me to do . . . Listen, Jeremy, I'm a recovering alcoholic and the word selfish means "self first" to me . . . Call it jargon if you like, but that's what I'm going to be from now on – selfish, because if I'm not, I'm not going to make it.'

We said our goodbyes, Jeremy furious and flustered; myself, calm and almost at peace.

Ruth came out of her bedroom.

'Peanut, didn't hear you come in. So, did you get the results?'

'Apparently I'm making myself ill with worry.'

'Good grief. What did I tell you?'

I looked at her and winked.

'What's so funny?'

'Ruth, I love you very much and I'm going home.'

'What, back to Pensacola?'

'No, back to London.'

'Attagirl.' She came over and gave me a hug. 'You go home and give 'em hell.'

Back in Pensacola I went straight to the house and punched the answerphone.

Jeremy's voice came over, terse and business-like. 'Polly, call me back. Brenda and I will be over on the fourteenth of August.'

I immediately called him back.

'Polly, you're really pushing it. Why are you doing this?'

'Jeremy, I'm not a child. I'm over ten months sober and old enough not to have to explain my actions to you. I've stayed here for as long as I'm prepared to. I'd rather have a meeting face to face with Kenneth, but if he's unable to do that, I'd appreciate Brenda coming over. I'm sure, after handling my finances and home for the past ten months, there are a few things to go through.'

I felt cold and distant, refusing to allow my emotions to get the better of me and saying in my head, Feelings aren't facts.

Jeremy interrupted me. 'I'd like Bruni to be there.'

'Jeremy, I left The Friary seven months ago. What's this got to do with Bruni?'

'Well, he's been out a few times to see us.'

'What? Counsellors aren't supposed to mix socially with family members or partners.'

'It wasn't social, it was business.'

'That figures.' I felt my face grow hot. 'Are you telling me Bruni's been giving Kenneth reports on me?'

'He's kept Kenneth up to date on your developments.'

'Do you realize that I signed a confidentiality form with him?'

'Don't get technical, Polly. He's just trying to help.'

'Bullshit. What he's trying to do is sell out on me and line his own pocket.'

I wanted to throw the phone across the room, smash it into little pieces. Christ, I felt so betrayed. It took all my willpower to continue with the conversation.

'Bruni will not attend the meeting. I will see you on the fourteenth. In the meantime, Jeremy, I suggest if there are any loose ends to tie up, then tie them, because I plan to leave on the twenty-first of August. Goodbye.'

My rage bounced around inside my head and then the floodgates opened and I howled on my knees like an animal.

The next day I called Bruni. He confirmed he'd discussed my progress and had been to Aruba. I told him point-blank that I was going to sue him for breach of contract and slammed the phone down.

I then began to call lawyers. After briefly discussing it on the phone and then giving Bruni's name, I found that all three law firms would be unable to represent me as he, and The Friary, were clients. I had to let it go. But the fact that my spirit was back gave me all the confidence I needed to pack and prepare for my return home.

Brenda and Jeremy arrived on the fourteenth. We met at a hotel. I was nervous – the moment had come to end the charade.

'Good to see you, Polly,' said Brenda.

I looked at her and thought, Bullshit, lady. Let's face it, you work for Kenneth and I'm a thorn in his side.

'Here are all your files and documents.'

I interrupted her. 'How's Kenneth? Why doesn't he want me to see him? Why won't he accept my calls? Why are you here and not him?'

'What do you expect from him, Polly?'

'A little decency. We had a relationship.'

'No, you didn't. He's bought *me* a few clothes – that doesn't mean I've had a *relationship* with him.'

I looked at Brenda, stunned. So that was the game. We were all going to pretend that Kenneth and I hadn't been friends. God, I felt sick.

Brenda's words came through a fog and hit me hard. 'You don't have any money left.'

'What? What the hell are you telling me? I had over one hundred thousand in the bank.'

'You did, but treatment, flight, court cases, they were all expensive.'

'Jesus, Kenneth said he'd look after all that.' I looked over at Jeremy who sat back, not saying anything. He wouldn't look me in the eye. 'Jeremy, for God's sake. Are you just going to sit there?'

He shrugged his shoulders in a non-committal way. 'You owe taxes, lawyer's bills, et cetera.'

The humiliation, the anger and contempt I felt for the two people in the room, and for Kenneth sitting on his fat safe ass in Aruba, made dark spots dance before my eyes.

'By the way, we lost your passport, so I suggest you do something about it if you wish to fly back home.'

I could not believe I was now without even a passport. I remembered the scrap book I'd kept of all the places we'd visited. Finally able to find my voice I heard myself saying, 'You tell him that, if he wants me to stay in the States, it will cost him five hundred thousand dollars and for that he has two years, then I return.'

Brenda laughed. 'Don't be ridiculous.'

'Just tell him,' I screamed at her. 'That's what you are, aren't you, just a fucking messenger?'

The atmosphere hung heavy and airless, each of us waiting for the other to make their move.

'Your rent hasn't been paid for the beach house or the car.'

'Then deal with it or I'll call the press back home quicker than you can get a flight out.'

I stood up. 'Jeremy, what you've done is unforgivable. It makes me sick to think I trusted you. It makes me sicker to think that you are handling Tusk Force and everything else that was set up.'

I picked up my files and walked out into the blazing heat of the Florida sun. Taking a deep breath, I promptly threw up over the side of the balcony. I watched my lunch fall four floors and splatter on to the windscreen of the car Jeremy and Brenda had hired.

The extent of my feelings left me numb. I'd been used, tossed aside for someone else's gain. I had fooled myself I was cared for, fooled myself completely, only now realizing the full extent of the consequences, the damage. Through a one-day relapse ten months ago, I'd lost all my achievements. The charity, my life savings, my reputation, work. It had cost me dearly. I lay on my bed and swam down deep into grief and self-pity. It really was a horror story. How and why had I allowed this to happen to myself?

I began to focus on preparing to leave for England. Forcing my mind to stay on one track, I called the lawyer who had handled my court case, Michael Oliver. I told him everything.

'Polly, I'm really very sorry. I'm not quite sure what I can do. Kenneth has run up quite a large bill with us. If he doesn't pay, we'll sue him.'

I was sure he would. Kenneth didn't like to leave messes. I told

Michael Oliver I'd be home in a week. Putting the phone down, I began to feel sick again. Why had he done this? Why?

I went to my regular AA meetings, and shared my emotions minus the details. I'd become an expert. There was a time when I would have shared inappropriately, not knowing any better. Now I could share how I felt. I heard myself whining in my own ears. Heard myself loud and clear: VICTIM. I was continuing to be a victim. Somehow I needed to take responsibility, and move out of this negative hole.

It was all right if I was doing something, packing or some other chore. As soon as I had free time on my hands I felt myself go numb and started to stare into space, not wanting to move, not wanting to accept my predicament. Finally, parcels packed and sent, passport in order and tickets bought, I sat on the deck for the last time. Today I would fly back – to what, I had no idea.

The taxi beeped its horn. I picked up my suitcases and walked down the steps. I climbed up the palm tree with the bread knife tucked in my back pocket, sliced through the strings holding the leaves and released their bondage. I slid down, stepped back and watched the tree unfold. I saluted my palm tree and wished it good luck, and I swear it saluted me back. I'd left a huge notice pinned to its trunk.

HI – MY NAME'S MONPIERRE
I NEED FIFTY GALLONS OF WATER A DAY
FOR THE NEXT SIX MONTHS PLEASE

I wondered if the next occupants would bother. I hoped so.

It was six-thirty London time. The plan was for me to take a taxi to Frances's house. She was the friend who had helped me through the court case. When I got through passport control and customs, there she stood. I could have wept with relief. We hugged and I cried, 'Frances, thank you so much for coming.'

Frances was such a good friend. We'd met in treatment in 1989. She was now studying to be an architect. Frances was one of the miracles. She came to treatment dying, weighing less than seven and a half stone, with sores and ulcers on her body from the use of heroin and needles. Today she is four years' clean, with a degree. Her son Brian, whom she had when she was sixteen, is so proud of her. She inspired me. When she came into recovery she had big debts and no job prospects. She found, through a lot or hard work, an architectural course and began to study. It took her two years to complete it. Today she is in the Yemen, studying mud buildings and structures.

It never fails to amaze me. Most alcoholics and addicts who clean up and change their behaviour become productive people, talented and dedicated.

Sitting in Frances's home, I felt far from talented or productive. Breakfast was delicious and the idea of her futon upstairs sounded wonderful.

'Go up and sleep for a few hours, and then we'll talk.' I did just that.

What woke me were the wonderful aromas of lunch. Frances had spent many years in Egypt and had learned to cook their succulent dishes. Herbs and spices assaulted my nostrils.

I stumbled down the stairs, groggy and disoriented. She looked at me. 'I can see you're in desperate need of a strong espresso.' I smiled sheepishly and sat on her modest sofa.

'After this mouth-watering lamb stew and couscous, we're going to the women's pond in Hampstead.'

I didn't argue. The stew and coffee hit the right spot.

'Ready?'

'As I'll ever be.'

So off we went with swimming costumes and a bottle of water.

Lying by the pond surrounded only by women, I felt their gentleness; it was moving. Treating me like a child, Frances spread out the towels and motioned me to sit down.

'Beautiful, isn't it? No children, no dogs, just women.'

I looked and listened. Gentle . . . it felt so gentle.

'Pol, darling, I'll go with you to your house. Once you're through the door, the heebee-jeebees will leave you. It's a fear we build up. I promise you, trust me, huh.'

I looked over at her and smiled. 'Can we go to a meeting tonight?'

'Which, AA or NA?'

'Whatever, just a little meeting though.'

And that's what we did.

The first week passed in a blur of women's meetings and visits to the pond in Hampstead. Frances's gentleness and simplicity carried me back to normality.

I'd called Tusk Force when I arrived in England. Katie had told me that it was better if we didn't have any contact – a clean break. I found it incomprehensible that all this could be happening.

The day came to see my home again. I was still full of fears. When I entered my house I had a shock. The life had been snuffed out of it. All my plants had died. It smelt damp and looked cold and unloved. Before I left I had a full-time house-keeper, flowers and plants in every room and it was always cosy and inviting. Now, the bathroom was still half-finished and the loo had leaked, causing damp. I felt overwhelmed. How was I going to afford anything? I had no money left, no work, no agent.

You bastard, Kenneth, I thought.

The doorbell rang. I went downstairs and opened the door. 'Miss Hamilton?'

'Yes?'

'I'm here to serve you with a bankruptcy order. Will you sign here?'

I must have looked a simpleton – my mouth hung open. I took the pen and signed his paper. He handed me an envelope and walked away. I closed the front door and looked at the papers. Campbell Hooper. They were my lawyers Kenneth had used whilst I was away.

I immediately went to the phone and called them. 'Michael Oliver, please.'

A few minutes later he came on the line.

'Michael, what the hell's going on? I've just been served with a bankruptcy order by your firm.'

'That's right. It would appear that whilst you were in treatment in the States, you signed power of attorney over to Kenneth Oakhouse.'

'I don't remember doing that.'

'Well, you did. We have your signature.'

'So what does that mean?'

'Well, it means that on your behalf he instructed us to work for you which means . . .'

I interrupted him. 'You're telling me this 25-thousand-pound bill is mine?'

'Correct.'

'What does it mean?'

'It means you either pay or we'll bankrupt you. I'm under instructions, Paula, that's all I can tell you.'

My God, due to the circumstances, I seemed to be cornered at every turn.

A meeting – I needed a meeting. I walked outside and realized for the first time that my car was gone. VW had taken it while I was away. I rang them and they said that the executives who arranged it had been moved overseas, that there was nothing they could do. But there had been a mistake – the car was mine.

I called a cab and went to a meeting in Chelsea. Familiar faces came up to me – welcoming me back, reassuring me, telling me to take it one day at a time, to go to meetings and not to pick up a drink, telling me that things would slowly work out. As I looked around at their faces I realized that many of them had been through far worse than me. I needed to follow their example, their light of hope.

Meeting after meeting, day after day, went by.

Bailiffs knocked at my door. Various bills hadn't been paid.

Another bankruptcy order, this time from the tax man for backdated VAT. You name it, it all avalanched in the first two weeks of my arrival home. I called my old accountant, Shabia. He told me he had been informed not to continue with my account, that I'd be living in the United States. I listened, shocked and appalled at the extent of financial damage that had been done. Why had the world been so vindictive? It made me feel ashamed of myself in some way, that somehow I deserved this kind of treatment. It started to crush any sense of self-worth that had been there.

People, friends, family, even strangers would look at me as if to say 'What did you do that made him behave this way towards you?' I would try to think of reasons to justify his behaviour. I felt how I imagine women feel who have been battered physically, abused or raped. Always the questions: 'Why did you stay with him? What did you do to provoke him?' No woman deserves to be physically and mentally abused. No woman should need to justify any man's behaviour.

I had involved myself with a man who was capable of behaving like a monster. He did not have monster tattooed on his forehead or act like a control freak. Had I been more mature, I would have seen the telltale signs earlier on in the relationship. Except then, I didn't want to see it. I had glossed over the faults, believed with my eyes and my heart, not my brain. I had also used Kenneth, his power and the support he offered, and I'd done it greedily.

Now I was paying for it: the consequences were ugly and tough. And today I thank God, because the lessons I learned then will stay with me until the day I die. So Kenneth had underestimated me. Good rules out bad. I'd allowed myself to be used, allowed myself, through my own wild dreams for Tusk Force, to let it happen. I had been given a ring and on it I'd had engraved a bumble bee. When bumble bees sting they die. Though wanting to avenge what Kenneth had done, I would have to sting: to sting meant to die a little. I put my faith in the maxim: 'If you interfere with someone else's destiny, you will never reach your own.'

The press had put investigative journalists on to Kenneth and me. It sounded like a good story. They knew we had been friends, yet they couldn't get the dirt. Kenneth had enough people in high places to make it difficult for the papers. I was offered big money for my story – it would have been a juicy one for the press. I have never taken them up on it.

So, the first few months were spent keeping my head above water, keeping my sobriety my priority even though I wanted to fight back, but at the same time knowing the old way didn't work for me.

Who would have thought that Paula Hamilton would set the alarm clock for 3 a.m., get up, dress in old clothes and hunt down car-boot sales? At these sales I bought dog and cat food at knockdown prices, plus dented food cans for myself. Who would have thought that, after phoning VW and getting nowhere with them, I would buy a 23-year-old orange Mini for two hundred and fifty pounds? I would take up my fight with VW later. I had my priorities in life, and I had to keep a low press profile or I'd never manage to get myself work. But I still needed to pay my bills, and I even asked a friend if I could help out in his restaurant. He replied with a categoric 'no', pointing out that, if a customer recognized me, it would soon get out, doing my image no good at all.

The betrayal I felt from my charity was enormous, sometimes overwhelming me and depressing me to the point where I'd find myself sitting in a chair in my drawing-room in front of a winter fire all day long, only coming to when the last embers had died and the room had gone cold.

Susie, my counsellor, told me kindly to let it go and make each thought, each action, manoeuvre me towards recovery.

I couldn't look at an elephant in any shape or form. If they appeared on the TV I'd turn it over – that also went for books, magazines, newspapers. I wouldn't allow my mind to wander, thinking of projects we'd started and implemented, wondering if we'd accomplished them successfully or not.

When I called the charity and asked for my day-to-day log books and diaries in which I'd recorded every phone call, meeting and outcome, they told me they'd been lost when the charity moved. I felt as if someone had wiped away the last three years, stolen them from me. The pain in my soul was excruciating. I had to grieve, had to let it go. I had to accept that Tusk Force was still up and running, and being successful, without me.

I felt that the one thing that I was truly proud of in my life had just disappeared. Journalists continued to ask me about the charity and elephants and each time I would say that I'd set it up and put it on its feet, that that had been my aim. Not entirely true. I believe today that if I had not relapsed and had a healthy recovery, I would still be working with the elephants and the ecosystem of Africa. The main reason I haven't gone back into this kind of charity work is that I've been afraid of my passion, my passion to help, change, make a difference. I'm too afraid of losing myself again. I now know that this tendency is a part of my nature.

For the first time as I write these words, I know deep inside me I will work again, using my energies on the environment, children, animals, doing exactly what, I'm not sure. Enthusiasm runs deep in me. It's something I cannot and do not want to squash. Enthusiasm is infectious, it's as contagious as measles. Without enthusiasm we'd all die of boredom and dead brains. It takes a rebel to yell: don't conform, don't get scared, don't turn away from the environmental issues because you feel overwhelmed or that you don't have the power to make a difference. When one sticks one's neck out and fights, it's a natural reaction to scorn the one that rocks the boat. But, as I said, enthusiasm is infectious. Keep banging the drum.

Through this very difficult time I phoned Terence Bramble, who had witnessed my relapse. I had wanted to apologize for my behaviour almost a year later. He answered on my third ring.

'Bramble.'

'Terence?'

'Yes.'

'Hi, do you remember me, Paula Hamilton?'

'Good God, yes. How are you?'

'I'm well. I just called to say how sorry I am for what happened at lunch on the 22nd October.'

'Good heavens, you don't need to apologize. You were lovely.'

After putting the phone down I felt much better. One, I'd found out that, contrary to what I'd thought, because it was what I'd been told, I hadn't been drunk at lunch with Terence. Two, that he was supportive and kind, and I was in desperate need of a few good friends. Terence became a very good friend when he found out the mess Oakhouse had left me with. He took me to one of his solicitors, who began to unravel what would prove to be an extremely complex case.

One day at the solicitors, after going through the case for the umpteenth time, I said, 'So it seems I've signed power of attorney over to Kenneth and that they have my signature on the relevant document. One, I don't remember signing it and two, under the Florida State laws, treatment centres come under the Mental Hospital Act. Therefore, how can something so relevant and important hold up if I'm supposed to be mental? Can it not be questioned that I wasn't in my right mind when it was signed?'

This argument went back and forth. I found it all so frustrating. I had my own set of competent lawyers who had looked after my family for over forty years. Why couldn't they deal with my situation now?

The other question that plagued me was the taxi-driver incident on the night of the relapse. Why had I been allowed into the front seat, drunk, with a bottle of alcohol that was open? Apparently I was drinking it blatantly. Why hadn't that come up in the court case? Was it legal to be drunk and drinking alcohol in a moving car? The case went on while the fees went up and up. I was getting nowhere with Terence's solicitors. In fact, their bill nearly matched Campbell Hooper's. Money I thought I had was no longer there, leaving me penniless. There was nothing I could do, except to surrender in order to win.

So, in the end, I had to strike a deal with Campbell Hooper to pay back so much per month, allowing them entry into my accounts every quarter to see if I could afford to pay more. I made a similar deal to pay Terence's solicitors. I could not afford to take Kenneth, and Campbell Hooper, to court. That would have been the only way. The frustration was unbelievable, the law stood on his side.

I guess what saved the day financially was Roderick Gilchrist, Deputy Editor of the *Mail on Sunday*. He had been very supportive of Tusk Force. He called to say he'd like to do a cover story on my comeback for *You* magazine, and would pay a good fee – ten thousand pounds, in fact.

I told him outright I wouldn't discuss Oakhouse at all but would give an open honest interview. It amazes me how Hugh Grant can be caught with a prostitute and come home a hero, while I get drunk and my world tumbles around my ears. Michael Barrymore allows press into his treatment centre and receives similar press adulation. The same old story. Women are not allowed to be dishonest. Women are shamed if they create a drunken scene. Little boys have the same behaviour and excuse after excuse is made. How they're under a lot of stress, et cetera, et cetera.

Yet, by being up front and honest in that article, I received some very supportive letters. One of them from Anton Mosimann, who invited me to lunch, and what a treat it was. Once a month I would visit him in his kitchens and we would laugh and joke together. He was profound and supportive. I would drop in from time to time for a coffee and a chat. His restaurant became my haven from the pace of the outside world. It was during this period of positive press coverage that I decided to go back to modelling. After a tentative start, pounding the pavements with my portfolio tucked under my arm, I joined IMG, Lauren Ashton's model agency, when they called me after I parted company with Storm.

IMG would send me on auditions where I found myself standing in stairwells with seventeen year olds, waiting to be seen for jobs that I'd stopped doing ten years earlier. Clients would recognize me and become embarrassed at seeing me line up with the others to wait.

'Why didn't IMG say you were coming?' they'd ask.

'I guess they thought you wouldn't see me considering all the bad press I've had. I guess they thought if you saw me face to face, you'd see I'm well and haven't grown two heads.'

And it was true. It had been very hard for IMG to get me work.

My manager, Ian Wilson, who has looked after me since October 1992, has worked extremely hard, and is dedicated and loyal. He has fought for my reputation, which was hanging in rags. I remember meeting him in Weybridge, in a hotel. I'd asked him for a meeting, I knew I needed a manager if I was going to try to put together a career that was shattered. He came to the meeting wearing a suit, raincoat, mobile phone in one hand and a battered attaché case in the other. He was late and I was on my third cappuccino. Needless to say, I was as nervous as a cat on coals.

I'd met him briefly in 1991 when John Fashanu and I presented *Good Sport*. John would breeze in and out of shoot days, Ian took the slack for him. I, on the other hand, had no protection at this time. No one managed me. I did that myself. At that time I was running Tusk Force with a small tight team that relied on my public persona to highlight the charity; juggling my production company and the pre-production of the documentary, 'Mothers of Nature', modelling assignments and TV appearances.

The producers of *Good Sport* dealt directly with me; they

could call me at any time of the day or night, change schedules on me at the drop of a hat. Bedside manner was non-existent. The telephone would ring at five in the morning: 'Paula, we're rescheduling, you need to be on the set at six this evening instead of eight. Wardrobe's been changed too.' There were times when I thought I was going mad, and on a couple of occasions I think I did.

Ian Wilson understood this as I sat opposite him sipping my fourth cup of cappuccino. He kept his cards close to his chest, but over the months and years he openly admired my gall and tenacity. I didn't always get it right, but I had a bloody good go. Ian's job was to kill the negative aspects of my reputation and start building a consistently positive one. It was painstakingly slow, and although very painful, today I am grateful. It was hard work, taking patience and skill. Ian has looked after a number of celebrities who have had precarious careers at times. His management tools have been learned over the years, and rarely does he make the same mistake twice! He has a knack of turning a mistake around to favour the situation we find ourselves in.

The YMCA asked me to put my name and image on their fitness tapes. Three were made – this then enabled them to get the press publicity required to sell. The fitness video industry is tough and competitive. By using me, the guaranteed press would help to sell them. A huge publicity tour was set up and down the country. I would go on TV, radio, press and magazines, selling them. The press was guaranteed to bring up the fact I was an alcoholic, so I knew beforehand I had to be prepared to talk about it. I did and the video sold, and this meant that slowly more work began to come in. All the time I managed to keep my head above water, pay my mortgage and debts, keep my self-worth and crawl on.

Britannia, a pharmaceutical company, approached us. Would I endorse their product – Vital 3? This was an anti-oxidant product. Again a deal was struck. So now I'd gone from being bad girl, drug addict and alcoholic to fitness guru. A health book and product launch. More press, more angles on my alcoholism. Little by little the stress on this became less and less.

I must say all the while the title of 'the VW girl' was always there. I joke that they'll probably try to put it on my gravestone. Chances are, even if I became Prime Minister I'd be known as the VW girl.

Working with the press – and I do, it comes with the territory – can be heartbreaking at times and one has to grow a thick skin. Copy approval, photo approval, can be abused by the press and often is. They'll call and tell you that you have copy approval of something, ask you what you think of this and read it to you over the telephone. We discuss and adjust but when I pick up a copy of whatever publication is carrying the article, I see they've cleverly twisted the copy by punctuation, headlines, et cetera. I have little or no control over that. I'll see a good, honest piece turned into a condescending piece of trash. For peace of mind, I let it go. It's tomorrow's fish and chip paper. Feelings aren't facts. Egos, well, egos are things that stand in the way of happiness.

I must add that my family have been brilliant concerning this area. I have managed to protect them insomuch as their lives have been kept out as much as is humanly possible. They have not judged or criticized my actions concerning the press. In fact, at every opportunity, they have given me their support and open appraisal of my dilemmas.

I wish to take this opportunity to thank them for their love, patience and tolerance. Without it, I would not have been able to reach my goals, knowing always that whatever I did, they would not desert me. I couldn't ask for a more loving and supportive family. On the other hand, I do know they have suffered through the press. Reading about painful moments in my life, and at times going back into my past brings it up in their faces without them wanting it.

Clients were afraid to put my face against their products, but with hard slog and a lot of determination and dedication from myself, Ian and IMG, we slowly began to push forward.

A commercial for Walnut Whip put me back on the TV screens; positive interviews began to pop up. Ian networked his way through the reactions to pitching me for certain projects, protecting me from negative responses. When I complained that things weren't what they used to be, or weren't moving ahead quickly enough, he came down on me like a ton of bricks. 'Life owes you nothing. You threw it away; now have a little graciousness and gratitude that you're working at all.'

Ironically, a security car company asked me if I'd promote their car theft package for a press call with the police. Of course, the press covered it in every newspaper, all referring back to the taxi incident in October 1991. I blatantly flaunted the incident and somehow, by doing that, by showing that shit happens, even to the best families, I won the support of the public who generously seemed to forgive me. They reacted well to my ballsiness. No one likes a victim or a wimp and by refusing to become a victim, my shame began to melt and each day began a little easier. But I will never forget, and never want to, that very painful and confusing year of coming home and literally crawling back to stand once more on my own two feet. Slowly my image changed from wild child alcoholic to fitness, inner health and beauty guru. I owe all these tactical moves to Ian Wilson who stuck his neck out for me on more than one occasion.

All the while Terence would be there supporting and encouraging me, introducing me to two of my closest friends today, Hicky Taylor and Simon Gibbs. They are decent people who have hearts of gold, and through their love and, sometimes, guidance, have shown me, along with Terence, what true friendship can bring. Socializing without alcohol or drugs had previously escaped me. The skill to develop close friendships was absent. Perhaps the knocks I took in my younger life, when I was constantly moved around from town to town and school to school, kept this knowledge from me. I believe I thought so little of myself, I was unable to keep up first impressions. Lying came so easily. When caught out, I couldn't explain why, I didn't know myself. Today I have friendships that mean so much to me. They're close, honest and loving. My loyalties are no longer upside down and back to front.

I began to feel comfortable in my house again. All sorts of things seemed missing from my house, all remembrances from my previous life. It hadn't seemed my house anymore.

All the things that I'd put a value on had gone. My self-worth had come from my work, money and possessions. Now my 'valuables' were gone: my car, my work status. I was forced to look for self-worth elsewhere, and that elsewhere came from within me. My set of values changed. I spent time with people who cared, I spent money on what was needed, I drove a little rust-bucket of a car and I grew to love it, even though at first I didn't have a choice.

There's a saying in AA: Fake it to make it. So I'd walk down my garden path and say in a cheery voice, 'Hello, sweet little car. I wonder what's in store for us today.' It sounds nuts now, but back then it worked. And to be totally honest, after a while I truly began to grow quite fond of it. In fact, so much so, that it became a topic of conversation in my interviews. The windows rattled due to corrosion of the rubber seals over the years. I'd heard that if you poured yoghurt along them, moss grew and did the same job. It worked and this tip was passed on. I didn't have a radio so I'd sing to myself to keep up my spirits. I got a kick out of people looking in, recognizing me and smiling.

One day I opened the paper to see a full page on how the once stunning Paula Hamilton was now down and out and driving a seventeen-year-old car. In fact, the picture was quite good. What I thought was a little strange was that eighty per cent of the readers of *Today* newspaper drove old cars, and how dangerous and inconsiderate they were to put my registration plate in full view.

In meetings Ian would get upset with me. He'd say, 'Sit back, stop selling yourself, you don't have to. You're an intelligent woman and that frightens them. Let me do the talking.'

I would get furious with him. 'What the hell! Do you want me to be a sexy, bloody ice-cream?'

'Yes, if that will help you to get back on your feet.'

No compromise. He 'power-struggled' with me, for ever reminding me of who I was, and that I had to play myself down until my commodity raised itself. In other words, the more work I had under my belt, the more we had to negotiate with.

Out of the blue I got a phone call from the States – my tax man. Although I had paid the bulk of my taxes at the time, there were some outstanding dribs and drabs left over. He laid into me pretty heavily. In 1981 I owed almost two thousand dollars in back taxes. I thought it would have been handled while I was in treatment. By 1993, it had gone from just under two thousand dollars to ten thousand dollars in fines and penalties.

I calmly listened and then told the tax man I had not modelled in the States for dollars since 1989. I no longer had a work visa, and would not activate my green card until I was ready: that it would be a few years before I did, if ever. I explained that I'd spent the last year in treatment for addiction and I didn't have a bean. Nor would I frighten or pressure myself into doing work that would affect my recovery. I told him my recovery was my priority, not a tax debt that, through no fault of my own, had accumulated. He said he'd be in touch.

A few weeks later I received a phone call.

'Miss Hamilton, your tax debt has been waived. You're worth more to society sober than drunk, and we wish you the best. If you do come to the States and apply for a green card, you will find you have a clean record!'

I was so moved by that phone call. I'd been honest. What I also understood was that, in the States, the attitude towards alcoholism and recovery was very positive because of the education they received. It was very unlike our own country.

The difference between the tax man in the States and the one in England has no comparison. After being sent a bankruptcy order by the UK tax man, my accountant and manager went to see them. We explained the whole story and even showed them my accounts. I've always held a tax account and put aside my tax payments. They could clearly see from the account movements that money had been taken in my absence. They estimated I owed them a total of fifty-six thousand pounds. I explained that if they bankrupted me, I would not work because it would be picked up by the press, then potential clients would run a mile, thinking of me, and rightly so, not only as a drunk but also as a criminal and therefore irresponsible. It was pointed out to them that they would never get the money if I could not work. It just didn't make sense.

I personally know of many people in AA who have lost everything to alcohol and owe huge taxes but have had them waived. Not because we deserve a break when we clean up, but because we honestly have no way of paying vast sums of money. I also happen to know that when alcoholics and addicts clean up they become ten times more productive than when they were drinking and therefore, in the long run, are a benefit, not a hindrance, to the tax man. In California in 1992, 150,000 men and women received some form of drug or alcohol treatment, at a cost of $207 million to their companies, but the savings to state taxpayers was $1.5 billion. Treatment produces a cost-to-savings benefit of between 1:4 and 1:10 depending on the type of treatment. This is the sort of financial benefit that employers like. In the US, it is now the accepted way of dealing with addiction. Britain would do well to follow the example set in America. The treatment Paul Merson received from his club, Arsenal, and the Football Association, is a good start.

After speaking to a number of barristers and solicitors, out of interest, I found out that there are a huge percentage of women in prison for petty crimes: parking tickets, community charge, TV licences, shoplifting and taxes. Women are severely punished and rarely are the full circumstances of their situations taken into account.

Before writing this book, I am ashamed to say I had not heard of other women writers such as Naomi Wolf, Germaine Greer and Erica Jong, whose book, *Fear of 50*, seems to say a lot of what I am writing in relation to my own life and experiences.

My recovery didn't stop when I put the bottle down. My recovery has allowed me to free myself. I expect to be ostracized — if I feared that I would remain silent. Ridicule and criticism follow women in their daily lives, and as Erica Jong writes, 'It generally means we are doing something right.'

CHAPTER TWELVE

Live and Let Live

I always knew I'd do a film. I always new that a director would approach me and tell me my part was written with me in mind. I always knew I'd fall in love with the director and that's exactly how it happened.

Henry Cole was to make a film called *Mad Dogs and Englishmen*. We met by chance as he was trying to find out how to make contact with me. He was to direct a pilot for a programme called *The Restaurant Show* and I was to present it.

We met on set and there was an instant chemistry which sparked and crackled between us, so much so that it was obvious to the film crew. We were only aware of each other.

After the shoot I fled as the others sat down to a late meal. Safely in the car, driving back to my home, I allowed my mind to reflect on the evening. Henry seemed like a blonde version of my ex-husband, Danny. They had the same nose, the same hooded eyes, except Henry's were blue. They both worked in similar clothes, except for the ridiculous cowboy boots Henry had on. They were black and red with worn-down heels, and were at least a size too large. Danny and Henry even used the same type of bag to carry round all the tools of their trade.

The following day I left for St Barts, a small island in the Caribbean, to shoot a campaign. On the plane I wanted to shut out Henry and brush off the incident. I'd been down the 'Danny lookalike' road before and I wasn't going to fall for it again.

Whilst picking up my ticket, I'd noticed a beautiful half-caste man with caramel skin, dreadlocks, green piercing eyes, and a well-dressed athletic body; he was carrying an obviously heavy bag over one shoulder. I'd never experienced a one-night stand, or even had a brief fling. Why not? I thought it would be the perfect remedy for forgetting Henry.

His luggage label informed me his name was Christian. I rolled the name around my tongue, trying to taste it. Wasn't I a woman in my own right? Didn't I have choices? Did I not have a right to follow through my fantasy and experience this thing that wrongly labels a woman a slut, if I wanted to?

I stalked him through the airport, now knowing his destination. As luck would have it he picked a flight for St Barts; I sat through two legs of the long journey before I finally plucked up the courage to make my approach. We arranged to meet up on the island for a walk after my work was over. I had done it all in a reserved businesslike manner, but with a glint in my eye that Clint Eastwood would have been proud of.

St Barts was beautiful and I settled into my villa which was tucked between the beach and gentle green foliage, Film Director and Dreadlocks soon forgotten. I knew the fashion team well and the week flew by. Friday and the team's departure arrived, and I stayed on, wondering if Christian would appear. He did, although darker and less healthy than at the airport, due to the heavy sun and partying of the Caribbean.

I made him pay for his own room, which was not to his liking. We had supper under the stars, with him drinking beer and me, water. He was French, and a professional footballer to boot. The time came and we walked down the winding, seductively torch-lit pathway to his room. Closing the door, he walked over to the side of the bed and lit a candle. I began to undress and we slipped between the sheets and he kissed me.

Suddenly my mind snapped awake. 'This will harm you, don't do this!' it said.

'Shut up! I want to do this. I am a woman, not a child.' But my head would not keep quiet.

I pulled back and looked at this stranger. I realized I did not know what his reaction would be when I told him I did not want to do this – would he beat me, rape me? But he just looked at me and rolled onto his side, leaning on his elbow to let me out.

I walked away, walked down to the beach where the waves crashed onto the sand, cool and gentle under my feet. I sat there, watching the wave crests flashing silver, like fish reflecting in the moonlight. The moon looked down on me, holding me in her light until two dawns arrived: mine and Mother Nature's.

My dawn told me that I had the right to make mistakes, that I had a right to say no. I had come a long way. If this had happened sooner in my recovery, I would have shut my eyes, ears and heart and slept with this man, not knowing how much I would damage my soul. That day was the first time I had consciously protected myself and my child within. My reward was that the little girl inside me knew I had finally grown up and was now able to protect her, and myself. That dawn, I had become a woman.

As I write, many ideas and concepts that have held my world together unravel. My rigidity becomes less so. I feel safe to look at this thing called feminism.

I have a girlfriend called Carolyn, who is extremely talented in many areas, excelling herself in a few of them. We have a good friendship which is now nine years old. For many years Carolyn has placed books in front of me which I have chosen to ignore out of fear. Carolyn has poked into the spooky, dark corners concerning the role of women today.

'Polly, read Naomi Wolf.'

'Yes, okay, I will some time.' Hoping to throw her off.

'What are you scared of?'

'I'm scared I'll hate men. It's tough enough now with more and more information coming in. I run to keep it out. If I recognize it, own it, I'll have more work to do, more pain to wade through, more anger to hold back.'

'So you bury your head in the sand, hoping it will go away or doesn't exist.'

Blast you, Carolyn, I thought, blast you for bashing the doors open in my mind.

Weeks and months would pass and I'd make excuses not to see my friend. But slowly I'd miss her and yearn for her company. Only to be bombarded with new information, new concepts. I'd listen to her and I'd criticize her in my head. Out of fear? You're damned right, out of fear.

All my life I strived for male approval, to please them. My stepfather's silent disapproval of me trained me from my innocent years to seek approval and please males. Carolyn was challenging my strongest link to the victim in myself. As long as I stayed in the belief system, I would sabotage myself, keep myself down. Now Carolyn was waking me up to this. She was tireless in her efforts, and the more I let her in, the more I opened my mind. I was inspired by her. Today, Carolyn has successfully changed careers and has become a well sought-after photographer, something she'd always dreamed about. Not only had she helped me, she had also helped herself and I admired her for showing me the way through the power of her example.

Women are terrified of their anger. What will become of the world if they confront the anger? Most are afraid to leave their prisons. I have to say that Carolyn is one of the matriarchs – large, magnificent, angry. Yes, angry. What is so wrong with anger? Used appropriately, it's a fantastic tool to motivate. Anger is another word, another tool that males have robbed us of, to keep us stuck. And it has worked beautifully. We are schooled from an early age that men are right, women are wrong. Strong women only begin to be recognized in their late forties or fifties. Before that, 'God', a woman who knows her own mind is a moving target. Her courage must be true and run deep to survive the barrage of abuse she will receive. Stay in your place, don't rock the boat. She will be denounced as a radical, a lesbian, frigid, heavy. Growing up is tough enough. No wonder many females opt out, only to pick it up again in their forties. Look into the eyes of a woman who has lived life truly for herself – see the beauty in those eyes. Look at a woman who has succumbed and conformed – she has the eyes of an animal who has resigned herself to her own fate.

Living in South Africa taught me that, if you split the family, the community loses its power, its momentum. The South African government from one day to the next would suddenly decide that Zulus could not intermix in marriage. Those married were split up and sent to townships thousands of miles away. Laws would continue to change overnight. The effect was to weaken the family unit. Sadly it worked for a time. Without anger, passive acceptance naturally moves in and depletes energy and more commonly, kills all hope. Here are a few examples of squashing female anger.

1. You're getting hysterical.
2. A woman's anger turns me off.
3. You're so masculine when you get angry.
4. It's so unfeminine to be so angry.
5. You look so ugly.
6. Have you got your period?
7. You don't know what you want.

Perhaps you can add some of your own.

There is very little, if any, guidance or support for women in their twenties and thirties concerning feminism. I want my experiences, strength and hope to motivate, to awaken slumbering princesses. I was very, very angry. It's called rage; like the dancing bear who, after years, went berserk one day during her usual routine of tricks and mauled to death her trainer, who had humiliated her, abused her and made her perform for years. One cannot bury feelings; if you do, you bury them alive and they scream in your gut until they find a way to burst out.

I've always said it's easy to be a holy person on the top of a mountain, but try being that holy person in the madness of a city, town or village with all the stresses of life. Growing up is tough at the best of times, yet we're just supposed to 'know'. Know what?

After two years of being alone, sexually inactive and non-committed to a relationship with the opposite sex, I fell truly, madly, deeply in love.

Ten days into the relationship, Henry asked me to marry him and I said yes. He moved in immediately, and I experienced emotions that had me walking around feeling higher than a kite. I felt loved, cherished, adored. I was sexually desirable. It gave me so much confidence that my self-esteem and -worth blossomed. People commented on how happy, relaxed and 'soft' I looked, and I felt it.

We were both addicts, both alcoholics. We shared our stories with each other, identifying and relating, which made us feel we 'validated' each other. I now call this stage of our relationship 'the honeymoon period'.

Both of us were working towards the same goals, a film. He was directing and writing, while I was acting, and supporting him in all the ways I knew how. But it wasn't enough. I soon realized, and so did he, that it was going to take a lot of hard work on both sides to make this relationship work. He had never committed himself to a relationship before, and was honest about how he felt. This made me realize that, although I had been married, I hadn't been committed either. The reason was that at the time I had been drinking, and had been unaware of my behaviour, blind to it. So for both of us it was a first.

I went headlong into my meetings, and saw my counsellor regularly. I had a strange belief, whilst staying celibate and un-involved for those two years, that when I eventually had a rela-tionship I would have a successful one. After all, hadn't I spent all that time being a good girl, getting to know myself and my issues, my defects of character and my shortcomings?

My counsellor, Susie, was terrific. She suggested my boy-friend get a counsellor, and when I put this to him, although he hesitated, he eventually went to see one. So both of us were working things through. Or so I thought. I wanted to believe it *so* much.

Again I felt a sense of belonging when I met his parents, and soon felt very tender towards them. Their home was beautiful; the garden tiny yet tended with love, every nook and cranny filled with flowers and plants, all cultivated over the years they had lived there. Henry's bedroom in his parents' house was filled with old Etonian school photos and childhood memorabilia. It felt cosy and safe; the biscuit tin by the bed was always full, ready for nibbles late at night as we lay safely tucked under the covers, listening to his father snoring across the landing. I loved our weekend visits and would feel homesick by Wednesday back in London.

The more my partner worked on his film, the less he saw his counsellor or went to his meetings. I felt him distance himself from me more and more and it made me panic. Then he came home with the news that he wanted to delay the wedding. I felt nauseous, dizzy; I hadn't had these feelings for anyone else since Danny, and for this man they were even stronger. I had learnt to love, to care for, to respect, to admire. Yet I was (and still am) co-dependent, which means that if I don't watch out and take care, I put others' needs before my own. I can wear down my energies and health very easily, letting each day go by focusing on another's needs. I forget, or don't make time, to sit and eat properly, drink too much coffee instead, and before I know it, a snowball effect has occurred, and I spiral down to low self-worth.

I knew my relationship with this man was going to be tough, I knew our schedules at times were gruelling, so I took precautions. I hired a housekeeper, who cooked, cleaned and kept the home fires burning, candles and flowers in every room, food in the fridge, making it impossible not to feel comfortable and stress-free at home. I could control all of that, but I couldn't control my partner, I couldn't stop him from bringing home all his anxieties, fears, insecurities and problems.

My counsellor said to me one day, 'Polly, you need to step

back and look at this objectively. Don't try to advise or fix your partner's problems. He will be grateful at the time, but a few days later he'll feel inadequate.'

She was right. I wanted him to feel better, so I'd try to give him solutions and remedies, when what I should have done was just listen and give him a sympathetic sound, or an understanding look, or say something like 'Gosh, what a lot you have to deal with at work at the moment, but I trust you will manage.'

His interpretation of my efforts to help was that I didn't believe he could manage his own affairs, and that, by advising him, he thought I didn't trust him to handle his own problems. So, classically, he ended up resenting me. I felt terribly hurt by him, and felt 'dumped on', even though I was only trying to help.

So, as soon as I let myself hear Susie's words and was faced with the evidence in front of me, I began to let go. My partner would come home cross and grumpy and dump his mess all over the place. I would be attentive and listen, and after a while, when he realized I wasn't reacting, he'd stop. Then I'd say 'Would you like a cup of tea?' and smile. At first, it felt so false I must have seemed like a robot. But it worked! He started to apologize for going on.

I would request little things from him, and weigh up the responses. Susie pointed this out: 'Is he supportive?' I had to get a clear view, so without reacting to his answers, I'd log them in a diary. It was becoming painfully obvious to me that the man I loved was, at this time of his life, not able to make a commitment to our relationship, and could not be supportive.

I had to have an operation; it came out of the blue. I was devastated and scared and he said he'd go with me. The morning I had to go he said I was selfish, couldn't I go alone and didn't I know he was in pre-production for the film? I told him if he didn't come it would damage our relationship, and that this damage would be irreversible. He came but the damage was already done in my heart.

Then the film was on. Nights and days became one long

anxiety. Tension teased the air between us. On set he barely acknowledged me. I'd never made a film before – he'd never directed one. We were unable to give each other love and support, we weren't hearing each other. We both withdrew. Somewhere towards the end of the film, I sat in the back of the car with my partner in the front. His PA was driving us home. The Waterboys came on the radio, 'Whole of the Moon', and I realized it was over. My heart crumbled and the pain was excruciating. He looked back and held out his hand. As I touched it, it felt different, or perhaps I felt different.

After the film was over, I asked him to move out, hoping that the space between us, with time to rest and reflect, to get over the mad schedule of filming that had taken up every waking hour for nearly nine months, would get things back into perspective for us. But no, post production carried on. Would it sell? Would they like it? Would the backers get their money back? He had worked for this for ten years, worked against the odds of addiction, crawled out of the hole he'd dug himself into six years earlier and had achieved something. But he couldn't see it, it wasn't enough. Now he had to sell it, now they had to like it. His self-esteem hung in rags.

I, on the other hand, went for hypnotherapy. I worked on my self-esteem, on my most blazing shortcoming, abandonment. I worked my feelings through with my counsellor and my meetings. I would not allow myself, my recovery or my life to either be put on hold by this man or go down the tubes.

I started to write this book in August 1994. I went to Spain to track down Peter Viertel and talked to him. I had read his autobiography, *Dangerous Friends*, and wanted his advice. He told me to go away and write and come back and show him something. A month later I went back with *Hello!* magazine, who had asked me to support a Dog Shelter charity that had been set up in Marbella. I went and saw Peter with a chapter. He read it in silence, then looked up and said, 'You don't need me, you have a talent for writing. Go away and do it.' His words gave me the encouragement I needed. I also saw old faces like Diego and his mother, and I was able to make amends.

I was invited to dinners and parties. I hadn't gone out for nearly all of 1994 because of supporting my partner and the film we had both worked on. I went to the occasional premiere, but that was it. So the attention and the sun, and the beautiful home I'd been invited to stay in, were a great tonic, and my self-esteem and strength came back. I would not become a victim of my broken heart and broken dreams, and my partner's broken promises. However, that never stopped me loving him.

I invited my partner out to Marbella. He came and it was a wonderful reunion. He told me he knew he loved me, what an idiot he had been and how he would work on himself from now on; he still wanted to marry me. I started writing this book on the beach in Puerto Romano and he read the part about Andrew and his mother. 'You're good,' he said; he complimented my work for the first time in many months. My partner had become very threatened by my public persona; it wounded him deeply that they cut him out of the pictures printed in the newspapers, so that only his hand and wrist showed. He took it personally. I pointed out that they did the same to Hugh Grant, only show-ing Elizabeth Hurley, that Prince Charles was left in the dark for years as they kept focusing on the Princess of Wales. But he would not listen and I watched him withdraw more and more from complimenting my achievements.

He got a lot of press attention before the film, as Elizabeth Hurley was cast for the main lead. Then it went quiet for a while. When we came back from Spain, I saw my partner only on the weekends. The press heard we'd split up, and they sat outside my garden, waiting for me to come and go.

August and September passed by with us just seeing each other at weekends. I continued to work through my grief, and instead of finishing the relationship, my counsellor asked me to work through it, and not run away. If I ran, I would never learn the valuable lessons which would prevent me from repeating the same patterns over and over in any future relationships. Just the thought of this kept me hanging in there. I took it day by day, determined to be fully aware, without any denial, without any fantasy; in the past I had built castles in the sky, and tried to live in them. I had to see the relationship for what it was, not what I wanted it to be. I could easily have chosen to ignore it and allow my fear of abandonment to be so great that I could have stayed stuck, accepting the little scraps of love that came my way. I thought of Catherine, Andrew's mother, whom I had witnessed in a dependent relationship – no way! When you've grown up all your life without self-worth, it's not a natural feeling to have it. So I have to work at it every day in some small way.

One Saturday afternoon, my partner, Titch and I went into Battersea Park, armed with a picnic rug and cushions, and lay by the lake under the willows. I had said to him a few months earlier, 'When are we going to be able to enjoy our life? I just want to lie on the grass in the country with you and watch clouds. That's all. How long am I going to have to wait for that?' I'd stopped waiting. I rolled over towards him, head on my hand, looked into his eyes and said, 'You don't have any intention of marrying me, do you?'

He plucked a blade of grass, and twiddled it in his fingers while I held my breath. He looked up at me with those beautiful blue hooded eyes and said back in a whisper, 'No.'

My body jerked and before I knew what I was doing, both hands slapped across his face. 'Bastard!' I screamed. My head felt like it would explode and the slug crawled up. I felt it coming from the pit of my stomach as it bit a huge chunk out of my heart. On my knees, head bent and both arms wrapped around my belly, I cried. I was aware of his arms around me as he pulled me towards him.

'I'm so sorry, Pol, I'm just too damaged, I'm not ready, I don't even know who I am.'

I heard him and looked up. He had blood on his lip. I gently wiped it away and said, 'You will one day if you want to.'

I no longer felt the pain. I had grieved for this relationship whilst in it. At that very moment in time, I knew that, however much I wanted this, and what this man had presented to me, it was not going to happen, no matter how hard I worked, no matter how patient I was. The disappointment was overwhelming. But for the first time in my life I knew it wasn't because I was unlovable, unlikeable, defective or damaged. At last I really felt whole.

It took three more weeks before we were finally able to say goodbye to each other.

One evening, a friend asked me what my definition of love was.

I replied, 'To like the person. We need to be friends and allow each other our own space. I need to respect and admire them and vice versa. To allow myself to be nurtured and to nurture back, not to control or be controlled.'

My friend said, 'Have you ever received that?'

My heart hurt at that point and tears welled up. 'No.'

'Why not?' was the reply.

The next day I called my partner and said, 'We need to let go. I need to let go.' We spoke for forty-five minutes. I was in my car in the freezing rain on my new mobile, my first call. Afterwards, I put the phone down and howled in that car, allowing my grief to come up and wash over me, cleansing me. The rain beat against the roof of my little green Beetle. I sat there for about an hour – I wanted something, anything, but I didn't know what. I called a friend in the fellowship. The message was: 'Go to a meeting'. My energy spent, all I wanted to do was go to bed. 'Go to a meeting and share it while it's with you.'

I made a commitment to go. I drove on autopilot, and somehow made it to Fulham Road, to a little basement. I walked in, soaking wet, and listened to the speaker. My body began to unwind and relax. Here I was safe, here I was with my own kind. After the speaker finished, I spoke up.

'My name's Polly and I'm an alcoholic.' I shared about my partner, I shared my broken dreams, I shared my grief and why I had worked through it before ending that relationship, and I cried and cried. When I had finished someone handed me some tea, someone else gave me some loo paper. I felt a surge of gratitude and love.

The old Polly would never have been able to do what I had done. And what I had done had been in the name of love – the love I felt towards myself. And that feeling grew into respect for myself, the realization of the courage I'd had to have to deal with it, and the commitment to myself to recover and grow. I had had a major breakthrough.

I loved and trusted myself.

Thank you, Henry.

Today, more than a year since we split, we are friends who don't see each other; occasionally we call and share our news, wanting the best for each other.

In 1995 I was filming *The Ring* in Prague with Natassja Kinski, Michael York and Leigh Lawson. On a day off I went into town with Leigh. As we crossed the bridge in the centre of Prague, he began to whistle a tune. It stopped me in my tracks because it was the song Stephen used to whistle to me all those years ago in Japan. I had worried about Stephen ever since I found out he was drinking, and when I heard of his death, while I was in recovery in 1993, I had begun to understand what had made him turn to drink, when it seemed to be so much against what he had believed in. As long as Stephen was able to play at life he could cope. He fantasized until the fantasy became his reality. When that all changed he was unable to cope on life's terms. A big part of the disease of alcoholism is behaviour, and this eventually catches up with us.

I'm sure he could have lived his life out in comfort, style and fantasy, except his Japanese friend and financial benefactor became bored with him and, after ten years of supporting his Western playmate, dropped him just like that. In shock and disbelief, Stephen turned to the comfort alcohol can give, desperately trying to drink his way out of the waking nightmare his life in Japan had become. He had no money, no profession, no friends, nowhere to stay, no permit to live there and nothing to go back to in the States, and he was also confused, and unable to see that any of it was of his own doing. Somehow he got involved with the Japanese mafia, and lost himself completely. He was arrested for drugs and spent a few years in prison. It was all too much for Stephen. After his sentence, the Japanese deported him back to the States. He walked into a hotel in New York, booked a room and blew his brains out. Where he got the gun we'll never know. After I heard of his death, I couldn't lay him to rest; the tune that he always whistled kept going round and round in my head.

Now, Leigh explained that he had starred in the film *Tess*, and it was the song his character D'Urberville always used to whistle to Tess during the film. It dawned on me that Stephen had modelled himself on that character. I felt a great sense of peace; at last I was able to lay Stephen to rest.

I spoke to Ruth's daughter recently. Even though we went through the same intense treatment together, why did it work for me but not for her? Ruth is still drinking, but through education her family has more awareness of how to let go, how to detach from her with love and allow her to make her own way. They know that no amount of worry will change her, so the focus returns back to the individual members of the family. They do what they can for themselves, to make their predicament with their mother less all-consuming. Her daughter told me that Ruth was still killing herself slowly. Her son is living with her, and from time to time will find her crawling across the kitchen floor to the fridge. All he can do is put her back to bed, and she remembers nothing the next day. I love and adore Ruth, and always will. My friendship and love will not get her sober, and I know I have to accept her the way she is. But I can never allow myself the pleasure of her company too long – as the saying goes: if you sit in a barber's chair long enough, eventually you'll get a haircut. I don't want the madness of alcohol, and don't want to spend time with an active alcoholic, however much I love and understand her. It's just too dangerous for me.

A word about my counsellor.

Without Susie I'm not going to say I wouldn't have made it. But with her support and dedication she has brought a quality into my life, my recovery, that would not have existed without her. She believed in me and showed she believed in me when I couldn't. She challenged my belief systems. She helped me see my denial, when I hid things from myself. Her expertise meant she didn't cruelly rip my masks off before I was ready. I have never felt shamed by her. In our four-year relationship she has helped me grow towards my goal. The woman I was always meant to be. Our work is far from finished and I still see her once a week. Am I dependent on her? If she walked away, would I fall down? No. Dependent on her to learn, yes, I am. I needed to see the evidence in my life to recognize I was changing. She has shown me and reminded me, in times when I've lost sight of where I've come from, and where I am today.

I will always be grateful to Susie for guiding me.

Not only have I learned how to get the best out of relationships with men, I have also torn down the walls between my family and me, and built bridges. While writing this book I went home to my mother's to collect the photographs I needed. I wasn't looking forward to going up in the attic to sift through all the childhood memories. I didn't want to be reminded of how painful it was growing up. My mother and I were sitting on the landing, surrounded by photos. I came across a little white envelope that said:

POLLY'S HAIR – ONE YEAR OLD

I took the delicate lock of pure blonde hair and sniffed at it. It still smelt of talc and baby, and I felt a huge wave of sadness wash over me, and I began to cry. My mother went to hug me but I drew back, sobbing 'Don't touch me!' Every time my mother has tried to comfort me or hold me when I've been upset, I've pushed her away. I realized then that there had been a time when I was once innocent, knew only love and trust, a time when I was free of fears. I felt all this from holding the hair that belonged to me before all the harm had been done. My mother held her arms out.

'Please, Polly, please, let me hold you.'

Finally, for the first time in years, I accepted my mother's comforting arms. I allowed her to love and hold me, I felt all the hurt and harm, the betrayal and mistrust, melt away, and slowly I felt forgiveness towards her, and myself. I had found the way back to my mother's love. We sat, cried and hugged for a long, long time.

Today my mother and I have a loving relationship. We don't feel we need to seek approval from each other; when we talk on the phone it's supportive; we no longer feel we have to rescue each other; we no longer blame each other, we just leave each other be. I have come to understand and adore her. Today she has taken a writing course for the media, Spanish lessons, she studies Iyengar yoga, goes to the gym three times a week, swims and works out, and has never looked better. Her eyes twinkle when she speaks and her enthusiasm for life is catching. Gone are the dark days of depression and feeling low. My mother has had to tackle a number of illnesses before she was able to lose her depression and I take my hat off to her for changing her diet and dragging herself from doctor to nutritionist. Today I feel freer in this mother–daughter relationship than I ever thought possible. Thank you for being there, Mummy, and thank you for growing and reaching into the unknown. There was a time when our paths were too wide to reach each other and to understand. Not today. Today we have cut our own track, yet travel side by side on a spiritual path.

It's obvious that the relationship between myself and my stepfather was destructive and negative. But over the years, I have come to realize that circumstances can bring out the best or worst in people; I know I saw the worst side of this man. But there are always two sides to every story. While it would be wrong to say we are close, I am at peace, knowing that he is leading a full and happier life today. I could not ask for more.

My younger sister and I have carefully and delicately learned to communicate. Neither of us wanted to blast open the other's heart, so it's been a long and sometimes tiring process. Our relationship means so much to me now precisely because we've worked so hard at it, and I value it tremendously. Today I am consistent and trustworthy and the pay off is that my little sister, although now grown up, comes to me to ask advice, or to share her news, or just to say hello. It may seem normal to you but for me it is the best gift in the world. My older sister and I now have a friendship, and although we're not terribly close, I love and respect her and will always be there if she needs me, and I know she'd be there for me too.

The older of my brothers will soon be leaving for Australia and I feel strangely sad, yet at the same time terribly excited for him. I know he will blossom in the outdoor life Australia has to offer. I am proud of him for following his dreams and admire the fact that he's gone from boy to man and found his feet. He is the most gentle male I have ever met, and my only regret is that I have not had more time to spend with him. I feel he could have taught me a lot about gentleness, something I need to cultivate and not be afraid of. Good luck, my darling brother. May you find freedom and happiness – I'm so very proud of you.

My youngest brother has worked hard for peace of mind, searching for it while his contemporaries were busy growing up. Our friendship has always been precarious: love and war and a battle of wills. We're close and I adore him but because of this, I have often been guilty of thinking I know what's best for him. I have tried to rescue him, tried to help until he has run from me, screaming for space. Since then a few years have passed and I tread more carefully. The baby of the family is no baby, he's a man, and it took me a long time to accept that. Today when I think of him, which is often, a smile covers my face.

My family are safe and well and my job is to love and accept them as they are. I am proud to do it.

Epilogue – Psst, Pass It On

I am writing this in Capri in a beautiful villa, with a partner whom I love and care deeply for: who is my friend. It didn't come easily, much ground work was needed. This brings me to the topic of co-dependency. I have tried to define this term previously in the book. Even as I write I am still continuing to learn, to understand, and I believe today that co-dependency stems from immaturity, and that immaturity stems from not being nurtured in childhood: not being shown we are valuable, bright, intelligent, wanted, needed, approved of, encouraged and loved.

Today it has become more and more difficult. Thirty per cent of the population live alone. We are becoming more and more isolated. Too many children in classrooms, not enough time on a one-to-one basis with adults, less and less guidance. The penalty is an immature society in which we are just supposed to exist. Who has real quality time to reflect on where our lives are going today? Are we encouraged to do so? Those who do are ridiculed. A clear example of this is the protests against live animal exports, where New Age travellers, vegetarians and conservative matriarchs all banded together to highlight the plight of calves and lambs. Why do people ridicule that sort of gathering? What are we so afraid of?

The power of advertising is phenomenal. Cosmetic companies drive us on through our fear. The end result is that we're paranoid about getting old, and these companies grow rich on our fears. Too simple? I think not. Having been in the modelling industry, at the top, for over a decade, I've witnessed it with my own eyes and heard it with my own ears.

Don't misunderstand me, there's nothing wrong with buying face creams, clothes, going to the gym, dieting, health plans, purchasing a new car or wardrobe. BUT, and it's a *big* but: if you find yourself falling into the seductive trap of advertising over and over again, thinking that these purchases will some-how make you more beautiful, more desirable, more exciting, that these purchases will fix your feelings – then read on and come to your own conclusions!

Look at how women are portrayed on the catwalk. Over eighty per cent of top international designers are gay men. Women that glide on the catwalks are looking more and more androgynous. Are the designers living out their fantasies through the models and the images they build? A growing number of models have had plastic surgery. Breasts are bigger, hips grow smaller to compensate. Two ribs are removed to create smaller waists. '*No*, not possible,' I hear you say. I was shocked too when I began to look around me.

Why is it that we reject the natural shape of a woman? Why is it that more and more women are being led to look like men? Interesting, don't you think? The irony of this is that, within our environment, hormones released into our water supply, and other factors, are reducing male fertility. Are men going to become more feminine? Are we going to end up as an androgy-nous society?

How far gone are we? What do we want to look like? If we don't know, then they've done a good job on us with their power of advertising. We're no longer just fashion victims; we're flesh and blood victims too, because if we don't look like the models, we don't feel we look right. The tragic thing is that we believe it.

Now comes an interesting development. Women in the work-ing environment follow the impossible quest to look right. It was Naomi Wolf's book, *The Beauty Myth*, that made me aware of the statistics in the career of beauty. The average work-ing woman, who is single and lives alone, will spend up to a third of her wages on image control; the higher she moves up the career ladder, the more she feels she has to spend on her image to keep her in that position. A woman today can be, or fears she can be, fired for looking too dowdy, too sexy, or too ordinary. Unlike men and their suits, we do not have a uniform. Some women who have brought cases to the courts over sexual harassment in the office have lost their cases because their clothes were too provocative, or they walked with a swing to their hips. Naomi Wolf tells of the case of Mechelle Vinson, who filed a sex discrimination case in 1986 against her employer, on the grounds that she had been subjected to sexual harassment. She was young and 'beautiful' and dressed herself carefully for work. The district court ruled that her so-called 'provocative' dress counted against her. But as her lawyer put it, realistically, 'Mechelle Vinson wore *clothes*.' The fact that she looked good, and had paid attention to her image was used as evidence in a court of law that she welcomed harassment from her employer.

Women have also been fired and replaced with prettier women, because the presence of pretty women is important to the company's image! Naomi Wolf uses the example of Hugh Hefner's Bunny Girls. At a Playboy Club there was a list of 'employment standards' for waitresses to fit the Bunny Image. One woman who worked there, Margarita St Cross, took her dismissal to the board of appeal. She argued that while she did not fit the club's criteria of 'a flawless beauty, or an exceptionally beautiful girl', she had gone through the 'physiological transition from that youthful fresh, pretty look to the womanly look, mature'. It was also pointed out that her male counterparts who did the same kind of work were not subjected to appraisals of any kind. However, Margarita lost the case, as her male employer's judgement was given greater weight than her own. Women in image-related jobs have to satisfy the male idea of beauty, which is not necessarily their own.

I'm not against beauty aids or fashion. If they make people feel better, that's fine. What I'm saying is that women should be aware that they have been manipulated to try and achieve a certain look, and, in particular, everlasting youth. *This is another type of addiction.* At the end of the day – like most addictions – it is meaningless and empty. We are consumer addicts and slaves.

I am writing this from first-hand experience. I, too, have fallen victim to the surgeon's knife. In the summer of 1995, due to over a decade of monthly sunbed sessions that activated a cancerous mole, which would otherwise have remained dormant and benign, I had to have surgery to remove it. I, too, have drawers full of make-up bought with the promise that each item would change my life. I, too, fell victim to anorexia in my teens, and bulimia in my twenties.

I have learnt, through many a painful and sometimes lonely lesson, that people, places, property, power, prestige and looking good do not fix how I feel about myself. A woman's fear of ageing is very real. But women need to be aware that they have been manipulated to try to achieve a certain look promoting everlasting youth. It is up to us as females to recognize that: at least then we have a choice, either to buy further into the myth, or to step back and change it.

Our busts begin to sag and we desperately look for corrective firming creams, only to find magazines filled with ads of young girls applying cream to pert young bosoms that haven't breast-fed, that don't have stretch marks and so on. The bust cream will never remould a bosom back to the youthful breast it advertises. Let's face it, most of us over the age of twenty-five notice our buttocks are not as firm as they were, or that cellulite has appeared. Again we look at cream adverts featuring tight, young little bottoms; it's ludicrous, yet how many times do we find ourselves buying that cream? The minute we find ourselves outside what is acceptable, taking into account the conditioning we are brought up with as women, it affects self-esteem. 'Youth is beauty, beauty is youth.' What about us?

Recently, in *Vogue* November 1995, a contributor was quoted as saying: 'Paula Hamilton was sexy five years ago.' Five years ago I was *only* twenty-nine years old. Today my male and female friends say they have never seen me looking better. I ask if they are referring to my face or my body and the reply is always – both. They say I look more comfortable with myself, and I hang onto this; that's what all this work is about. I have to work hard at accepting my age, accepting that my fine lines will turn to wrinkles. It isn't easy when my whole existence has been based on my looks and my body. You're not alone and I openly admit this; since writing this book I realize with honesty just how much my own existence has bought into the whole myth of beauty. I'm not saying I can give you any answers, there isn't a magical recipe, but I feel that by being honest with myself, I may encourage others to do the same.

This hard sell on external youth is damaging our society. We are becoming obsessed and preoccupied by beauty, way out of proportion to the main priorities of life, such as peace of mind. We're putting it before everything else. It's very scary and very real and keeps women from valuing themselves based on who they are, not how they look, or how they should look according to the media. 'If you look good, sound good, smell good, you'll be loved and accepted.'

When grunge fashion came in, I believe it was a statement, a statement that tried to say: 'Don't look at the outside, look at me, the person.' Frankly, I feel it backfired badly and we all looked like lost, hopeless, depressed cases. Still, it was a good attempt, even if the fashion industry saw a fast buck and abused it.

We only have to look around to see how we treat our old people; we discard them, push them out of the way, sometimes out of sight. Our lives move too fast to take them into consideration. To look after our own who become old is time-consuming and sometimes complicated. Our fast lives do not permit caring when it takes time from us, and it is not encouraged either. In fact, it is strongly discouraged. More and more old people end their last precious years alone, isolated and feeling a burden to society.

Fewer and fewer families have a third generation on hand to

listen to and learn from. Yet they have so much to say, so much to teach us and so much to give. I look at women who are over fifty and I see the ones who have lived their beauty and accept their inner selves: they are magnificent. I see the ones that haven't and they wear their faces like the façade of a decaying building. How sad that we have no time to listen, no time to learn and no time to receive. How much we lose out by living alone, or away from family. We spend more and more time trying to create images of ourselves for strangers, rather than just being ourselves with the people we really love, our families.

Modern life has become more and more shallow and we concentrate so intensely on the packaging. Women, particularly, suffer severely from the guilt of being working mothers, and the loss of time spent with their children because of social pressures and the need to work. On any woman who is expected to be a mother, expected to work, to run a home and, on top of it, look like a million dollars, that type of pressure evokes an enormous amount of stress.

I know how easy it is to have a drink at the end of the day and feel the liquor hit my stomach, slowly untying the knots, helping me relax until the day feels less like a nightmare. This action, slowly over time, becomes a habit. Slowly I begin to think at about four o'clock – God, I can't wait to put my feet up and have a drink. It becomes a reward system. Hadn't I worked hard, therefore didn't I deserve it? Then the idea hit me – why wait until I get home? I could nip across the road with a friend and have a quickie on the way home. I rewarded myself when I achieved success.

The pressures of life won't turn us all into alcoholics or sufferers from some form of addiction. What I'm saying is that the pressures of life to look good, sound good and focus our attention on the outside packaging, take us further and further away from being in touch with ourselves. Therefore, ignoring our needs and being deaf to them, pushing ourselves beyond reasonable limits, feeling we aren't achieving enough and incurring penalty points, are all going to make us lose a little of ourselves somewhere along the way. This comes out as a serious problem, such as addiction, in only some people, but it does affect us all to some extent.

Alcoholism is cunning, baffling and powerful. We've placed men on the moon with our technology; yet, the fact that this disease has been a recognized illness since 1950, and is the third biggest killer of human life on this planet, slips by us. The three main killers are alcoholism, coronary artery disease and cancer. And alcoholism has the least money spent on research about this very real disease that is rapidly becoming an epidemic. There are over four million recovering addicts on this planet, which is the equivalent of the population of Israel. And alcoholics are getting younger and younger.

Why isn't yoga taught at schools, or avenues of spirituality, and why is it that these activities are brushed off as fads? Today by the pool I spoke to a woman whose nephew in the States, California, has just quit teaching. He said ninety per cent of his class arrived in the morning either drunk or high and with attitude problems. The age of his pupils was seven. True, yet the States have more education than any other on addictions, on alcohol. Intelligence doesn't work alone. You need to take this education on board and then apply it to every aspect of your life. It's a tall order to look, reflect and change, and unless we're brave or stupid enough to write about it, pushing it into the foreground, we'll all run along like a bunch of blinkered lemmings with plugs in our ears.

The scariest move, career-wise, came with doing the film *Mad Dogs and Englishmen* and committing myself to acting. For months after the film was finished I spent my time preparing my showreel and finding a film agent who understood what I was aiming to achieve. During that process I began to write this book, the toughest project so far. More time consuming, more painful and more lonely than I ever imagined, I often doubted my abilities, not only to write it, but to actually finish it.

It was only recently, a few days before this book went to the publishers (like that moment in an exam when you know your time is up), that I had those awful thoughts: 'Oh my God, what have I done? Who do I think I am? A book? I must be mad. It's just further ammunition for the press to have a field day.' I sat in an AA room filled once again with 'Doubting Thomas' and that bucket-load of fear.

Then it hit me. I've written a book, something I could never have done unless sober and sane. I've starred in two films, with future work already booked. I have my own pages in England's number one bestselling catalogue. I've helped design my own collection and it's selling. I have friends who care. I'm brave enough to keep looking at this thing called life and not run away. I work hard in relationships. Stop! Is this not enough? If not, make it enough, recognize it, accept it and embrace it.

Today I'm doing well and am grateful for what I have in my life. Life is difficult but not impossible. When I'm not having a good time, it's generally because I'm finding someone or something not acceptable. To move out of that pain, I need to accept whatever it is I'm struggling with and give myself time to decide whether I can live with it or not. If I need to take action, I will, however painful or scary. I have faith that, as long as I stay sober, a day at a time, I am able and at last equipped to deal with life on life's terms.

Little by little my mind has become sharp, aware. It questions and reflects. It stretches outside the comfort zone. I, who used to run from feelings and emotions, now welcome them; when I find myself in emotional pain and feel stuck, I instinctively know I'm resisting change. The moment I let go and go with the flow, stop fighting, stop fussing and complaining, the moment I accept a situation as it is, I feel balanced again, calm enough to sit back and look objectively at what's going on. I can now see light at the end of the tunnel, and through experience, I know it is not an express train coming at me.

From October 1991 to October 1993, I stayed celibate through choice. It was one of the loneliest journeys I've gone on. I really wanted to know myself and couldn't as long as I was focusing on another person and keeping busy seeking to please, seeking approval. I lived alone in a beautiful house that was everything to me. People said it portrayed me well – independent and unique. I looked at it and wondered what they saw. I was blind to the beauty I had created and was only aware of the flaws and cracks, and the bits that 'weren't quite right'. Today I see its originality, its uniqueness. I spend time, when alone, drawing, writing, growing a garden, going to meetings, forcing myself to grow and stretch myself into the person I believe I was always meant to be.

The loneliness is excruciating at times. But it also propels me towards looking for my self-worth inside, makes me aware of how and when I people-please, which can only end up with me harbouring resentment. Doing things for others when we don't want to, or when it is inconvenient, or when it hurts us, is a great recipe for resentment. Slowly all my behaviour was scrutinized and observed, and sometimes I was plain disgusted with myself, but then even that changed to slight annoyance, when I behaved in a way which was outside my new value system. I had to detach myself and look at why and how this behaviour was raising itself again. When I look around me, I realize how extremely lucky I am that I'm an alcoholic, because if I wasn't, I wouldn't have been forced to face up to all these issues.

Through personal experience and being in an environment where I see vulnerable people learning to slowly peel back the layers of their old self and discover that what lies beneath that protective layer is a kind stranger and truthful being, I see the extraordinary process of spirituality at work.

The key is willingness, a willingness to work through the emotions. Let's face it, I've said it before. There's nothing more distasteful to a person than the pathway that leads back to self.

There was a storm here in Capri last night and I am sitting on the balcony writing this, looking out over the olive orchards and scattered villas that lead the eye down to the sea, and the damp humid mist hanging over it.

My partner and I had gone over to Sorrento for the day and

hired a car. The views were magnificent. We had a succulent lunch in a tiny fishing village and long lazy walks through cobbled streets. On the drive back, going round the bend too near the middle of the road, I nearly caused an accident and came to a skidding halt. I looked up and waited for the explosion of abuse I'm so used to from driving in London. Instead, the other driver, a young man, looked at me, smiled and shrugged. What a lovely surprise. What a sweet moment. What a lesson for me. Both smiling, we rearranged ourselves and carried on with our respective journeys with a song in our hearts. The lesson went deep. I really can't be bothered any more to get angry and indignant, to fight back. It is a waste of energy. I'm no longer afraid that if I relax for a moment I will be taken advantage of, ridiculed, used. I trust myself.

None of these things has come easily. There's no such thing as a free lunch. It's taken blood, sweat and tears and even though I've dug my heels in, not wanting to go forward, I have done so, despite myself.

This is a never-ending journey of self-discovery which one never finishes. There are no exams to pass, no certificates given, no starting or stopping point. Resting places, yes, but with the knowledge that the journey is for ever onwards.

I had to write this book. My journey is one I had to share.

We've had our fill of fiction; like gluttons we've gorged ourselves. I see people searching through newspapers and greedily reading about others' lives. It makes us feel temporarily better when we see that someone is worse off than us, more guilty than us, more greedy than us, more unsure than us. We all have a dark side lurking.

I went to the deepest corners of mine. Just because I didn't murder, steal, kidnap, doesn't make me any better than those that do. It just means I didn't go down that far. Just because I didn't sleep on the streets, just because I didn't prostitute myself, doesn't make me any better than those that have.

I see people hungry to understand, searching, looking for

knowledge that will help. I hope my story will give you the faith and encouragement to face your adversities.

Journeying with me as you have by reading this book, you may travel on, but this is my station; this is where I leave you. Your destiny is your own. Each of us has to cut our own path, but none of us has to do it alone.

I wish you luck.